THE ENGLISH FOLKSINGER

159 modern and traditional folksongs
collected and edited by

SAM RICHARDS
and TISH STUBBS

COLLINS
Glasgow and London

First published 1979
Published by William Collins Sons and Company Limited
© Sam Richards and Tish Stubbs 1979
ISBN 0 00 411067 6 (paperback)
ISBN 0 00 411068 4 (hardback)
Printed in Great Britain

CONTENTS

ACKNOWLEDGEMENTS

A book of this nature necessarily relies on the co-operation of a large number of people. In such a vast field, any anthology must be a selection reflecting the editors' tastes and, of necessity, other more practical restrictions. However, a sizable number of collections was consulted as well as library collections of broadside ballads.

To those individuals who allowed us free access to their valuable tapes and manuscripts we extend our thanks. Others have generously responded to our requests to use single items from their collections. The Library staffs and directors of the following institutions and organizations helped by providing material for study and answering queries: The Vaughan Williams Memorial Library, Cecil Sharp House (The English Folk Dance and Song Society); the BBC Sound Archive; the Devon County Librarian, Mr Charlesworth; the Harris Library, Preston; the Mitchell Library, Glasgow; Manchester City Library; The British Museum; The Institute of Dialect and Folk Life Studies, Leeds University; Tony Engle and Topic Records; and a special thanks to Edmund Frow of the Working Class Movement Library, Manchester, for introducing us to a fascinating source of material.

All the contemporary songwriters represented in this book are duly acknowledged in the notes to each song, as are the traditional singers from whom the older songs were originally noted or recorded. We should like to mention here, however, that superb Norfolk traditional singer Walter Pardon who gave us an unforgettable afternoon with his apparently endless stream of excellent versions of excellent songs. To him, and to all the other singers and songwriters in this book we extend our thanks.

The editors and publishers are grateful to the following singers, publishers and owners of copyright who have given permission for songs to be printed in this book:

Ron Angel for The Chemical Worker's Song and Steelmen
Ascherberg, Hopwood and Crew Ltd for The Soldier on the Battlefield and We Be from
  Cornish Dialect and Folksongs
John Brunner for Who's Who
Jim Carroll and Pat MacKenzie for Rounding Cape Horn
Tony Deane for the words of Harvest Song
Bert Draycott for They're Closing Down the Pit I've Always Worked In, The Forty Pound
  Car and Just an Old Fashioned Push Bike
Ron Elliott for Freddie Mathews
John Faulkner for The Knife in the Window
A. E. Green for A Collier Lad, The Old Woman in Yorkshire, The Tailor's Breeches,
  Timothy Briggs the Barber, Botany Bay and Bugs are Bigger than Fleas
Mrs M. Hamer for The Lace Makers' Song, Trotting Song, The Game of Football, Brian
  O'Flynn, Stevington May Carol and Ladies Won't You Marry
Roy Harris for All Through the Ale
Frank Hinchliffe for The Pear Tree
Alan Lavercombe for Canteen Tea
Dave Lowry for Come My Lads
Ewan McColl and Peggy Seeger for The Bermondsey Boys, Diddling Song, The Penny
  Wager, Forty Miles, Drinking, Th'Owd Chap Came O'er T'Bank, 2 Popeye rhymes,
  B I Buy, Strike for Better Wages
Ian Scott Massie for The Dole Boys, The Banks of Tyne, Nice Young Maidens, Do Ye
  Know My Father
Colin Meadows for Tea Leaf Song
Bill Meek for The Lumper's Life
Dave Mountford for The Big Hewer and the Little Marra
Peter Nalder for The Borstal Boy
Walter Pardon for Broomfield Hill, Van Diemen's Land, The Deserter, Cock-A-Doodle-Do
Ian and Sue Parr for Guy Fawkes Song
Bob Patten for Shepton Beauchamp Wassail and John Wesley
John Pole for Nothing Between Us Now, Mr Fox, See It Come Down, Punch and Judy
Sam Richards and Tish Stubbs for 1 Popeye rhyme, Jingle Bells, Batman and Robin, As I
  Was Out a-Walking, Seventeen Come Sunday, Exmoor Ram, The Old Herring's Head,
  Very Good Song, The Prentice Boy, Elwood Mead, Time To Be Moving On, King Kong,
  The Leg o' the Mallard, Farmer in Leicester, Evening Love Song, Down Marsh Lane,
  Molly Riley, The Trico Strike, Still He Slumbered, The Lofthouse Colliery Disaster
Martin Scragg for Jackie's Building Site
Rod and Danny Stradling for Cod Banging, The Game of All Fours, Australia
Ken Stubbs for I Mounted My Neddy, the tune of Harvest Song, Hopping Down in Kent,
  and The Old Miser
Professor R. Thompson for Bold Archer
Dennis Turner for Factory Doll
Mrs Ralph Vaughan Williams for The Robbers
D. Wheeler for Bless This House
Miles Wootton for Early One Evening

A number of songs have been taken from the Journal of the Folk Song Society. Details are given in the Notes to each section, with the abbreviation JFSS.

EDITORS' PREFACE

From Land's End to the Borders, England sings. The sons and daughters of old Cornwall's tin miners and fishermen bellow out their block harmonies on Saturday nights, and five hundred miles away in the Northeast a lively songwriting tradition flourishes.

England's folksongs are witness to the variety of its people. From sailors and seafarers we inherit a vast collection of shanties and songs of adventure; there are the boozy, bawdy old songs of the sheep farmers of the West Country moors; the softer tones of the farming and fishing folk of East Anglia; balladeers such as Frank Hinchliffe of Yorkshire or Walter Pardon of Nofolk – quiet, impassive singers with impressive repertoires; and today's industrial songwriters – Ron Angel of Cleveland, Bert Draycott or Dave Mountford of the Northeast, with their sardonic realistic views of life in those parts – descendants of the 19th-century songmakers of pit, factory and mill. Then there are the gypsies on the road, the labourers on the move and the farm people on the land – they have all contributed to a rich repertoire of songs, helped to spread it around, changed it, preserved it and, alas, in more recent times often forgotten it.

What was the value of folksong to these people? And what is its value in today's world of high technology? In *The Horn Book*, Gershon Legman, the specialist in erotic folklore, has said, 'Folklore is that which serves a certain function: the function of social or individual expression, appreciation, communication or control of particularly feared or valued aspects of the natural or civilised life being lived. Whatever serves this function is folklore.' In *Folksongs of North America*, Alan Lomax says, 'The first function of music, especially of folk music, is to produce a feeling of security for the listener by voicing the particular quality of a land and the life of its people . . . Folk song calls the native back to his roots and prepares him emotionally to dance, worship, work, fight, or make love in ways normal to his place.'

Legman's view that folklore fulfils deep-seated needs is particularly relevant because, while folksong in its older forms and contexts has waned, the needs of human beings remain unchanged despite a new world, new technology and new culture. The principal subjects of folksong, such as fantasy, magic, adventure, love, sex and polemic, are subjects which are heavily exploited by our present-day culture, particularly in the media and in advertising, to produce sensation or sell objects, whereas folksong is less subject to passing trends and the distorting influence of the market.

In a world which turns us into consumers not only of objects but of the arts, folksongs are a most ecological form. Their former role as the principal form of expression has been usurped by glossy substitutes with no real relevance, which can bring frustration and impotence for they are based on a social system which must propagate the insane cycle of consumption and waste to survive and therefore preaches the gospel of the growth economy and rigid division of work. Strangely enough, even the most conservative economists are now becoming convinced that this is the opposite path to that of survival.

Folksongs express something more human, and react very directly against alienation – Ron Angel's magnificent 'Chemical Workers'

Song', for instance. People at work need to feel integrated, important and useful, and hundreds of songs express the swaggering pride of working communities. The Cornish tin miners sang, 'The miner with his picks and gads he'll never miss a blaw', the Littlehampton Collier Lads, 'We are the boys to rough it through, we never do complain', and when the factory lass in her clogs is confronted by the gaffer in his fancy togs she defiantly tells him, 'I'm as good as thee, although I'm only a factory doll'. A line from the first song in our anthology puts the case as well as it can be put, 'There's not a trade in old England like we poor labouring men'.

Despite this enormous pride in the value of labour, English folk-singers rarely reveal themselves as totally committed to hard work from any moralistic point of view. The strictures of religious repression may sometimes crop up in our folk carols and May songs, but the old bawdy energy of a previous age often shines through the sterner exterior. In comparison with North America where, as Lomax has said, 'a sense of sin is at the marrow of folklore', the English repertoire offers an astonishingly large number of incitements to drink, a great deal of bawdy and erotic detail, a passion for lovemaking in the open air, and a love of dancing, gambling and plain-fun comedy.

A strong sense of folk justice runs through from the wild outlawry of the Robin Hood ballads, to the highwaymen, the poachers, and the transportation songs of the 19th-century. It runs on into the 20th-century with many industrial songs of, for instance, mining disasters. It is a justice based on what can clearly be seen as fair and customary rather than on any written law. Robin Hood robbed the rich to give to the poor so the legend has it. This was not a crime; according to the un-written law of the folk it was a noble and heroic act of vengeance. A few hundred years later the broadside balladeers were still singing about the same rough justice only this time about the highwaymen, the notorious knights of the high toby (literally, 'high road') many of whom, daring Dick Turpin included, were mere thugs who robbed from rich and poor alike. In his book *Bandits*, the historian E. J. Hobsbawm has noted, '. . . such is the need for heroes and champions, that if there are no real ones, unsuitable candidates are pressed into service. In real life most Robin Hoods were far from noble.'

Songs of adventure, polemic and protest all testify to an attitude of mind that would live life to its fullest, accept its joys, resign to its sorrows and, ultimately, not worry overmuch about the end of it all. This profoundly irreligious view can be seen in a vast class of going-out-with-a-bang songs, ranging from the ceremonial 'Young Sailor Cut Down In His Prime' to the humorous 'Dying Airman' or the pickle-my-bones-in-alcohol spirit of 'The Rakish Young Fellow'. On a more serious note 'The Unquiet Grave' deals with the same subject in ballad form. Its message? The dead cannot rest if the living mourn excessively. Is there not an old, pagan idea glimmering through here – an idea which explains an attitude that is characteristic of English folk song?

The performance of these songs in England eventually went into decline. It may be the price an ascendant, colonizing nation has to pay for its progress. The oppressed, exploited, and yet proud peoples of the world often seem to cling to their folklore longer, though often in ossi-fied form. The Irish, a prime example, regard their folksong with an almost fanatical passion wherever they may travel or gather.

To be sure, English working people have needed the security of their folk culture, and industrial and dialect songs by the score rolled off the broadside presses of the 19th-century, not to mention the efforts of regional bards, but the decline of the song tradition was inevitable. This does not mean that songs are no longer known, recoverable or even being written. It does indicate a gradual process of forgetting, but there are still singers all over the country who remember and perform the songs. By a decline we refer simply to the fading of a dominant form of expression; folksong firstly lost its contexts, was replaced by other forms of popular songs, but still survives either in pubs or, more usually, as a memory stirred by people with tape recorders. And yet it is curious how much we can learn from this quiet tradition, and how much it has re-surfaced in recent times due to the conscious efforts of those involved in the folk 'revival'. It is interesting too that song writing inspired by a knowledge of folk tradition has been healthily developing for the last two decades or more. We make no distinction in this book between the old and the new, as we see them as essentially part of the same process, the same creative need.

Finally, a few ideas for singers. Lifting songs off the printed page is a vastly different process to learning them by hearing them. We offer a few of our own tricks in the hope that they are helpful and that singers might also discover their own.

1. Listen critically to traditional singers from many countries. There are plenty of commercial recordings available.

2. Speak songs first, out loud. Note the speech rhythms of the words.

3. Decide what the intention of each song is. Our headings might help. What is it all about? What does it have to say? How? If an old song, why is it worth singing now?

4. Decide whether you want to sing it free or in time, fast or slow, loud or soft, decorated or plain. In between. Why?

5. Learn it gradually. Unaccompanied. Take time.

6. All this time there should not have been a musical instrument in sight other than, perhaps, to pick out the melody. Accompaniments are the last thing to think about. If you think an accompaniment will help, put in a simple one. Put it in for a musical or textual reason, not just because you want to play your guitar. Folksingers all over the country have been discovering that the guitar is not the only, or even the best instrument to use. Concertinas, dulcimers, banjos, melodeons, harmoniums, tin whistles, mouthorgans, autoharps, even spoons are now used. Maybe try drones first. Build it up slowly. If, however, you are starting with a guitar, we have added chords to a selection of the most suitable tunes.

7. Sing it somewhere. Look for signs of how people react to it. Be prepared to start again.

We hope you find good songs in this book, and plenty of interesting places to sing them. Sincerely we say with Woody Guthrie: 'Just as long as folks are on their way in, folk songs will be on their way in.'

CELEBRATION

At first glance it may seem that some of the songs in this section belong elsewhere. 'The Lace Makers' Song', 'We Poor Labouring Men' and 'Harvest Song', for example, could appear in our group of songs about work. Many of them mention work, some in detail, and contain insights into attitudes to work.

There is an important difference of emphasis, though; one which is particularly relevant to any interpreter. Songs about work deal either with the labour process itself, or with the singer's attitude to it; the songs in this section show the singers celebrating their own lives and identities, many of them by reference to work, but the work is not the primary subject of the song; the worker – the singer – is.

This kind of self or group celebration is not exclusively sung against a work background, however. The sailor in 'The Rakish Young Fellow' celebrates himself with few references to his life at sea, more to his rakish ways. Likewise, the gay deceiver of 'I Mounted My Neddy' gives no indication of what he does for a living, but leaves us in no doubt about his opinion of himself amongst the London ladies.

In this section, therefore, it is the singer who is the focal point of the song, not the setting.

WE POOR LABOURING MEN

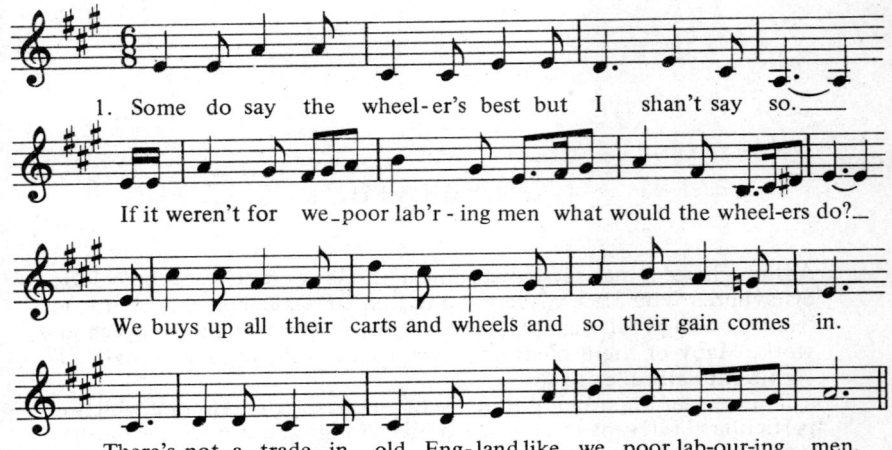

1. Some do say the wheel-er's best but I shan't say so.___
If it weren't for we poor lab'r-ing men what would the wheel-ers do?___
We buys up all their carts and wheels and so their gain comes in.
There's not a trade in old Eng-land like we poor lab-our-ing men.

2   Some do say the butcher's best but I shan't say so.
If it weren't for we poor labouring men what would the butchers do?
We buys up all their odds and ends and so their gain comes in.
There's not a trade in old England like we poor labouring men.

3   Some do say the blacksmith's best but I shan't say so.
If it weren't for we poor labouring men what would the blacksmiths do?
We wears out all their cutters and shares and so their gain comes in.
There's not a trade in old England like we poor labouring men.

4   Some do say the tailor's best but I shan't say so.
If it weren't for we poor labouring men what would the tailors do?
We wears out all their breeches and gaiters and so their gain comes in.
There's not a trade in old England like we poor labouring men.

5   Some do say the shoemaker's best but I shan't say so.
If it weren't for we poor labouring men what would the shoemakers do?
We wears out all their boots and shoes and so their gain comes in.
There's not a trade in old England like we poor labouring men.

6   Some do say the baker's best but I shan't say so.
If it weren't for we poor labouring men what would the bakers do?
We buys up all their old stale bread and so their gain comes in.
There's not a trade in old England like we poor labouring men.

7   Some do say the brewer's best but I shan't say so.
If it weren't for we poor labouring men what would the brewers do?
We buys up all their fourpenny beer and so their gain comes in.
There's not a trade in old England like we poor labouring men.

LACE MAKERS' SONG

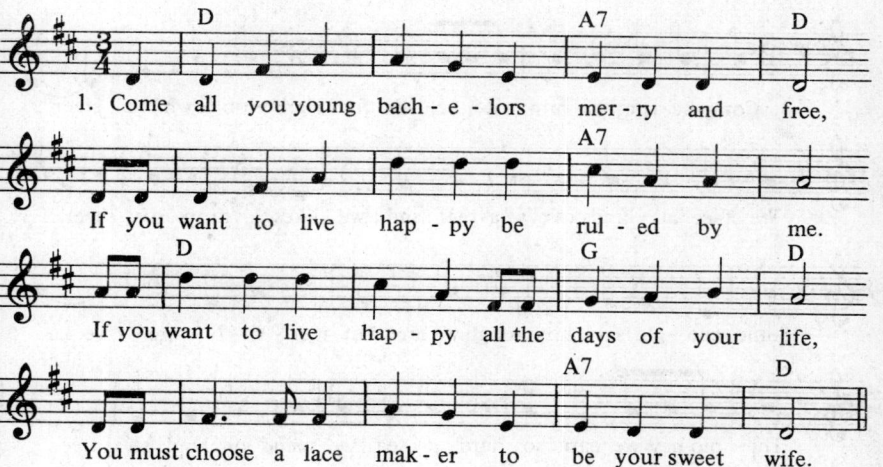

1. Come all you young bach-e-lors mer-ry and free,
If you want to live hap-py be rul-ed by me.
If you want to live hap-py all the days of your life,
You must choose a lace mak-er to be your sweet wife.

2   Lace makers rise early in the morning betimes
     And do their odd jobs before the sun shines,
     Then they sit down to their pillows complete,
     I love to see lace makers work it so neat.

3   The great servant girl she runs down the hall
     Great holes in her stockings, no shoes on at all,
     Great holes in her stockings, scarce a rag to her back,
     So take the lace maker, it is all that you lack.

4   We all get together on a sun shiny day,
     Our pillows they shine like the blossom in May,
     Our fingers are lissom, our bobbins are small,
     And now I have told you the truth of it all.

LITTLEHAMPTON COLLIER LADS

1. Come ha-rum sca-rum col-li-er lads for 'Hamp-ton town we steer,__
We face all kinds of wea-ther and we likes a drop of beer.__
Some peo-ple say how rough we are but mer-ri-ly are we,__
The mo-ney we earn so hard at sea we spend on land so free.

Ch. *Watch us,   twig   us with a   pop-u-lar jou-bi-jou,__*
We'll give her some sheet to make her rip, We're the lads to pull her through.
You ought to see us run-ning with our square sail all   a-full__
From the. pas-sage of New-cas-tle   to   the town of Whit-sta-ble.__

2   Our old skipper's a roosteroo he likes a drop of ale,
The second division has been in prison and seen the inside of a jail,
The third he is a bushranger, he comes on deck with a smile
And as for the cook you can tell by his look that he comes from an African isle.

3   When our coal is all on board for 'Hampton town we steer,
And nothing else is in our heads but old George Oliver's beer.
We face all stormy weather and we batter through every gale
When the outer light is out of sight it's then we set our sail.

4 People say we're a noisy lot when we come home from sea,
We call for liquor merrily and cheerily are we,
But when our money all is gone to sea we'll go again,
We are the boys to rough it though we never do complain.

THE BERMONDSEY BOYS

1. We are some of the Ber - mon - dsey boys,
We are some of the boys.
We know our man - ners, we spend our tan - ners,
We are res - pec - ted where e - ver we go.
We go walk - ing down the Old Kent Road,
All the wind - ows o - pen wide.
Can't you hear those bob - bies shout: blow those blood-y wood-bines out?
We are some of the boys.

THE DYING AIRMAN

1. A— hand-some young air-man lay dy-ing: *lay dy-ing*
And as on the aer'-drome he lay: *he lay,*
To the me-cha-nics who round him came sigh-ing: *came sigh-ing,*
These last dy-ing words he did say: *did say.*
Take the cy-lin-der out of my kid-neys: *of his kid-neys,*
The con-nect-ing rod out of my brain: *of his brain:*
The— cam box from un-der my back-bone: *his back-bone*
And as-sem-ble the en-gine a-gain: *a-gain.*

2   Two valve springs you'll find in my stomach: *his stomach,*
Three spark plugs are safe in my lung: *his lung,*
The prop is in splinters inside me: *inside him,*
To my fingers the joystick has clung: *has clung,*
Take the propellor boss out of my liver: *his liver,*
Take the aileron out of my thigh: *his thigh,*
From the seat of my pants take the piston: *the piston,*
Then see if the old crate will fly: *will fly.*

THE SOLDIER ON THE BATTLEFIELD

1. The sol-dier on the bat-tle-field may fight and run a-way,

Oh the sol-dier on the bat-tle-field may fight and run a-way,

But the min-ers in the pow-der smoke do work both night and day—

Ch. So a-min-ing we will go, will go, will go,

So a-min-ing we will go.————

2   The sailor sinketh in the deep with many an aching heart,
Oh the sailor sinketh in the deep with many an aching heart,
But the more the miner sinks, my boys, the more he fills his quart.

3   The farmer with his buckskins on has boots tied up with straw,
Oh the farmer with his buckskins on has boots tied up with straw,
But the miner with his picks and gads he'll never miss a blaw.

THE FACTORY DOLL

1. O' t'o-ther morn at six o'-clock
In come the gaf-fer with his lit-tle black book,
Said: All you win-ders, you reel-ers too,
You mun' mind your bad ends or that'll not do.
Ch. *To me rum-pty bumpty too-ral-ay, D'you e-ver see a girl like me?*
They used to call me Pret-ty Poll, But now I am a fact-ory doll.

2   As I were going to Wigan Fair
I see'd the gaffer on his grey mare,
For his grey mare and his grey hat
Was worse than my old factory brat.

3   I were gooin' to church o' Sunday morn
And see'd the gaffer with his fancy togs,
And he looked at me and I looked at him,
And he said: thee'rt only a factory doll.

4   I looked at him in 'is fancy togs
And I looked at me in me factory clogs,
And I said to him: I'm as good as thee,
Although I'm only a factory doll.

I MOUNTED MY NEDDY

1. I mounted my Neddy and away I did ride,
I rode off to London to seek for a bride.
It's lasses there were plenty but money they had none
So I told them all I'd marry,
I told them all I'd marry but I never told 'em when.

2   I courted a pretty girl, I loved her as my life.
I always did promise her I'd make her my wife.
The kisses that I gave to her was one hundred and ten,
For I told her I would marry,
I told her I would marry but I never told her when.

3   I courted a widow with a purse full of gold,
I courted her as long as her money did behold,
Until she proved deceitful and walked with other men,
So I told her I would marry,
I told her I would marry but I never told her when.

4   I mounted my Neddy and away I did ride,
I rode back from London without e'er a bride,
But if they should run after me they catch me if they can,
For I told them all I'd marry,
I told them all I'd marry but I never told 'em when.

HARVEST SONG

1. Here's luck to the jol-ly wood-cut-ter that stays at home at his ease,

He takes to work and he's light of hand and he leaves off when he please.

He takes the withe and he winds it, he lays it on the ground

And round the fag-got he binds it, drink round brave boys drink round.

Ch. *Drink round, brave boys, drink round un - til it does come to me,*

For the long-er we sit here and drink the mer-ri-er we shall be,

So put your hat on ___ and keep your head warm,

A lit - tle more beer won't do us no harm.

2   Here's a health unto the shepherd who tends his flocks by day
And with his dogs to aid him he spends his life so gay,
At night into the ale house to take his fill he goes
With thoughts of sheep behind him, the beer it freely flows.

3   Here's a health unto the ploughman who toils beneath the sun,
He takes his ploughshare on his back and he sings for everyone,
He treads the meadows daily whatever the weather may be
And takes his quart pot gaily, a hearty drinker he.

4   Here's a health unto the blacksmith bold who swings his hammer fine,
He has such strength to hand, my boys, I wish as much were mine. .
His anvil rings the country round — a pleasant sound to hear,
Until the maltster calls him with a brimming cup of beer.

5   Here's a health unto our master, the founder of the feast.
We wish him well with all our hearts that in Heaven his soul may rest,
That all his works may prosper whatever he takes in hand,
For we are all his servants and all at his command.

6   And now we've drunk our master's health why should our mistress go free?
Why shouldn't she go up to Heaven and rest as well as he?
You'll never find her equal where ever you chance to roam,
So fill your cups and drink, my boys, it is our harvest home.

THE DOLE BOYS

1. We are two jol - ly scroung-ers be - long to the sons of rest,—

We din-net in - tend to look for work and at that we'll do our best,—

And as we tra - vel round the world we'll not take a-no-ther man's job. —

We'd rath-er scrounge a pint of beer or a lend of a coup-le of bob. —

And our un - ion is the old-est e - ver since the world be - gan, —

We pay nowt in, we get nowt out but we'll stick to it to a man.—

FROM SWEET DUNDEE

1. From sweet Dun-dee where we set sail
All with a sweet and a plea-sant gale
With our ring-tails set all a-baft our miz-zen peak
For to see my jol-ly tars how she's scud-ding o'er the deep.
Ch. To my he-ri-ro To my he-ri-ro,
To my he-ri-ro rite fal de ral de day.

2   Now by and by there came along a squall,
Haul down your ring-tails, our captain loudly bawls,
Clew up your top-gallant sails and take them in.
Let two hands lay forward and your jib run down.

3   It's now our captain he goes below
And he calls for his cabin boy Little Joe,
Saying: Bring me one stiff glass of grog,
For it's far better weather down below than above.

4   Then our chief mate he goes down below
And he sups his grog just just so,
But he never cries for Jack or Joe.
He does all the bullying and he goes down below.

THE RAKISH YOUNG FELLOW

1. I once was a rak-ish young fel-low— I ne-ver took care of my life.— I sailed— the o-cean all o-ver— And found in each port a fresh wife.— But now— the wars are all o-ver— And I land-ed safe on the shore.— It's God bless me now and for-e-ver,— If I go to sea an-y more.—

Ch. *I've sailed— through storm - y wea - ther, ____ I've trav - elled through hot and through cold ____ I ventured my life on the o-cean, I ventured for hon-our and gold.—*

2   I'll send for my friends and relations.
I'll send for them every one.
And all for to make them quite welcome
I'll send for a cask of good rum.
I'll send for a cask of good rum, boys,
And two or three barrels of beer,
It's done for to make them quite welcome
To meet me at Derry Down Fair.

3   Now when I am dead and am buried
And past all the troubles of life,
There shall be no more sobbing and sighing
But do a good turn for my wife.
There shall be no more sobbing and sighing
But one single favour I crave,
Wrap me up in my tarpaulin jacket
And fiddle and dance on my grave.

4   Six jolly fellows shall carry me
And let them be terribly drunk.
And as they are going along with me
O let them fall down with my trunk.
There shall be so much laughing and joking,
Like so many young men going mad,
They shall take a glass over my coffin
Saying: Here goes a true-hearted lad.

NOTES

We Poor Labouring Men (p. 10) Sung by an unnamed singer, East Meon, near Petersfield, Hampshire. Collected by George Butterworth, *c.* 1908.

The only other version of this song that has so far come to light was recorded by Peggy Seeger and Ewan MacColl in the 1960s from Caroline Hughes, an aged gypsy queen living in Dorset. Butterworth's version, from neighbouring Hampshire, has many more verses, although it lacks the concluding verse:

> 'Let every true-born Englishman lift up a flowing glass
> And drink a toast to the labouring man, likewise his bonnie lass,
> And when these cruel times are gone, good days will come again.
> There's never a trade in old England like we poor labouring men.'

> *Travellers' Songs from England and Scotland*
> Seeger and MacColl, Routledge & Kegan Paul, 1977

The Lace Makers' Song (p. 11) Sung by Mrs Robinson, Wootten, Bedfordshire. Collected by Fred Hamer, 1960s.

Lace making existed as a cottage industry, and later a factory one, in most English counties at one time, although, traditionally, it was centred in counties such as Bedfordshire, Northamptonshire, Derbyshire and Buckinghamshire. This song seems to be unique; we know of no other version, although there is a Pitts broadside in the same meter in praise of 'The Flashy Lace-Makers', which suggests the importance of lace in these counties.

Littlehampton Collier Lads (p. 12) Sung by an unnamed singer, Sussex. Collected by R. J. Sharp, sometime between 1930 and 1945.

These collier lads used to man the coal barges from Newcastle round the east and south coasts to Littlehampton in Sussex. George Oliver of verse 3 was the landlord of The Rose and Crown, a pub which once stood in Littlehampton. R. J. Sharp was fiddle player with the Boxgrove Tipteers (mummers) in Sussex. He dabbled in collecting songs, making notes in margins of books and on scrap pieces of music paper. This song was tucked away in the back of a copy of Broadwood's *Songs and Carols,* and is clearly related to 'The Dogger Bank', an East Anglian fishing version current in the folk revival.

The Bermondsey Boys (p. 13) Sung by Mr W. Sherriff, Brixton, London. Collected by Ewan MacColl, 1961.

The singer recalled a local parson in Bermondsey who championed the poor, provided dinners, Saturday cinema, and regular outings for children, as well as standing for MP. As many as 20 special trams were laid on to carry the extra passengers: 'We all used to climb aboard. . . . and we used to sing this. Raise the roof of the tram practically. . . ' The tune which is 'Donkey Row Lads', another self-assertive song, was also used for political parodies in London and became the anthem of striking garment workers from Rego and Polikoff's factory in 1928:

> 'We are the Rego strikers, we are no dirty shirkers.
> We know our manners, behind our Union banners,
> We want justice wherever we go.
> When we went to Edmonton they thought they had us whacked,
> But we know we're in the right and we're sure to win the fight.
> We are the Rego girls!'

The Dying Airman (p. 14) From *Tommy's Tunes* by F. T. Nettleingham 2nd Lt RFC, Erskine MacDonald Ltd, London 1917.

The motif of a ceremonial funeral occurs frequently in folksong in England most notably in the evergreen 'the young sailor/soldier/trooper/girl cut down in his/her prime'. Here we have a 20th-century re-interpretation of the idea from the Royal Flying Corps of the 1914-18 war.

23

The Soldier on the Battlefield (p. 15)   Sung by Jim Thomas, Camborne, Cornwall. Collected by Ralph Dunstan, 1920s. Published in *Cornish Dialect and Folk Songs,* Ascherberg, Hopwood & Crew Ltd, London 1932.

This song is typical of the handful of Cornish folksongs that have come down to us from the 19th century. The strong choral tradition of Cornwall still flourishes. It was developed by zealous Wesleyans who filled the many chapels and sang together in harmony. Although tin mining was one of Cornwall's oldest industries, it is strange how few industrial pieces from Cornwall there are. We attribute it to lack of collectors at the right time and not to lack of creativity on the part of the folk.

The Factory Doll (p. 16)   Sung by Mrs Kathleen Topping, Ashton-in-Makerfield, Lancashire. Collected by Denis Turner, 1965.

A Preston broadside, published by Harkness in the 19th century, has the chorus:

> 'Ki fum, ti fum, fun and glee
> You'll seldom see a gal like me.
> The folks all call me charming Sal.
> I'm a regular flare-up factory girl.'

The close similarity between this chorus and the one in Mrs Topping's song is provocative, but none of the seven verses show any resemblance to the rest of her song. Given that the singer actually named the 'gaffer' in verse 1, she could be preserving a local remake of a song already known.

I Mounted My Neddy (p. 17)   Sung by George Townshend, Lewes, Sussex. Collected by Ken Stubbs, 1962.

Harvest Song (p. 18)   Tune, verse and chorus sung by Pop Maynard, Copthorne, Surrey-Sussex border. Collected by Ken Stubbs, 1961. All other verses from unnamed singer, Bristol, collected by Tony Deane, 1965. Tune almost the same.

In agricultural communities the harvest is an occasion for celebration. Even today church harvest festivals persist but these are worlds away from the ritual, wild merry-making that accompanied older harvest homes and suppers. English harvest songs tend to be concerned with praising the master and mistress and celebrating the work and workers. This song was widespread throughout the south of England. In 1893 in *English County Songs,* Lucy Broadwood gives only the master and mistress verses.

The Dole Boys (p. 19)   Sung by Bert Draycott, Fishburn, Cleveland. Collected by Ian Scott Massie, 1976, Beamish Museum Music Collection.

From Sweet Dundee (p. 20)   Sung by Frederick White, Southampton. Collected by George Gardiner and J. F. Guyer, 1906.

This is a pleasant version of the song known in the current folk revival for some years as 'Boston Harbour'. In their songs, seamen often mitigate the rigours of life at sea by heaping abuse on lazy, drunken, or strict captains and mates. According to Whall, who had the 'Boston Harbour' version, the song was very popular during the 1860s and 1870s, though, he adds, 'I fear it has gone the way of all songs with choruses, and is replaced by music-hall inanities'.

The Rakish Young Fellow (p. 21)   Sung by William Nott, Meshaw, North Devon. Collected by Cecil Sharp, 1904.

William Nott's version of this song closely follows the printed text which was widely circulated in the 19th century on broadsides, turning up a few times in various parts of North America. Nott's tune is clearly related to one perhaps most commonly encountered as 'Caroline and her Young Sailor Bold'.

SONGS ABOUT WORK

Our selection has a predominance of industrial and contemporary songs but also some rural songs, sea songs, and songs of emigration (caused by lack of work), all of which afford a picture of working life from the inside.

Songs which describe or directly reflect attitudes to work gather in strength and numbers the nearer we get to the present day. Perhaps the medieval peasant did sing about ploughing, sowing, reaping and mowing, but little has come down to us. Rural communities have produced a handful of later classic pieces such as 'The Painful Plough' and 'All Jolly Fellows that Follow the Plough' and one or two rarer pieces, often partly celebratory, but that is about all. Important though these songs are, compared to the repertoires of both industrial towns and seafarers they represent a small body.

Part of the explanation may lie in the fact that rural workers live in communities in which each person's function is firmly understood and is general to the whole community or group, while the industrial worker is part of a sub-group, identified by the type of labour rather than the industry. Industrial work songs reflect this group identity very closely; indeed, it is one of their strengths. But the hallmarks of the typical and best songs about work — whether industrial or rural — are the use of 'in' terminology, little real narrative and a high awareness of social position.

THE MONTHS OF THE YEAR

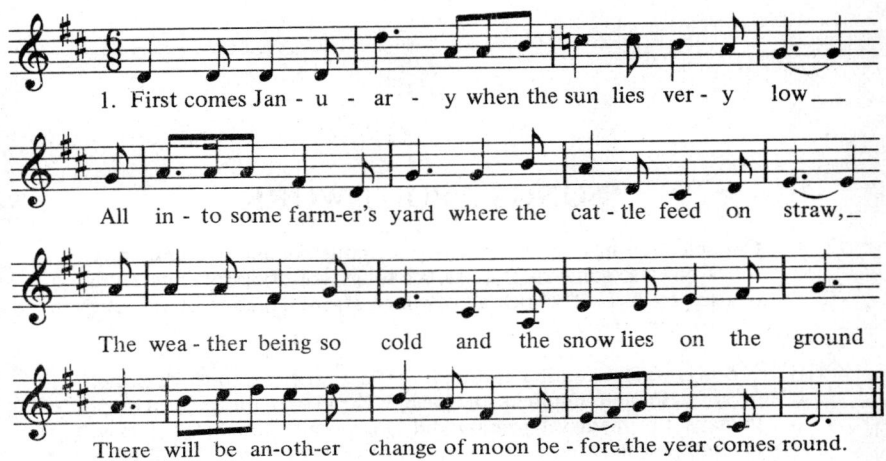

1. First comes January when the sun lies very low ___
All in-to some farmer's yard where the cattle feed on straw, ___
The weather being so cold and the snow lies on the ground
There will be an-oth-er change of moon be-fore the year comes round.

2 Next is February so early in the spring,
  The farmer's ploughs are ploughing — it's such a glorious thing,
  The little lambs are playing, by their dams they skip and dance
  And I hope all things may prosper that we may leave to chance.

3 March being a noted month above all in the year
  In preparing for the harvest and in brewing of strong beer,
  It's long before the time when we'll see the harvest come
  And drink the ale we're brewing and dance at harvest home.

4 April is the next month so early in the morn,
  The farmer's rather industrious a-sowing of his corn,
  The horses they come after a-smoothing of the land
  And I hope all things may prosper whatever he takes in hand.

5 In May I go a-walking to hear the small birds sing,
  Their notes were so delightful being humble to their king,
  It cheers my heart to hear them as I walk upon my way
  And each one they have warbling notes as they sit upon yonder spray.

6 So early in the morning awakes the summer sun,
  The month of June is come now and winter's cold is done,
  The cuckoo is a fine bird, she whistles as she flies,
  And as she whistles cuckoo the bluer come the skies.

7   Six months I have named now, the seventh is July,
Come lads and lasses to the fields your valour for to try,
The farmer says: Me hearty boys be all of one good mind
And then we will expose the hay all to the sun and wind.

8   August brings the harvest, the reapers now advance,
With meat and liquor plentiful the work won't stand much chance,
The farmer says: Well done me boys this day shall be your friend,
Come let us drink and make good work and so the harvest ends.

9   By the middle of September the rakes are laid aside,
The horses wear the breeching rich dressing to provide,
To do all things in season I think it just and right,
The summer season's ended and frost begins at night.

10   October leads the winter, the nights are cold and long,
By day we're felling timber and we spend the night in song,
All in the chimney corner we cider drink and all,
We'll kiss the pretty maidens and tell a merry tale.

11   The fifth day of November they call it Gunpowder Plot,
They'll keep it down in London, 'twill never be forgot,
The trees are stripped of all their leaves, the elm alone is green,
The frost will bite them sharply and not a flower is seen.

12   Oh then comes dark December the last month of the year,
The holly, yew, and laurel they fil our hearts with cheer,
We'll sing our Christmas carols as we go from door to door
And at the same time wondering what next year has in store.

THE BIG HEWER AND THE LITTLE MARRA

1. Why there was this grit big coal he-wer,
Said he had coal dust in his veins.
He had grit big arms and a grit broad back
But he ne-ver had ne brains, ne brains,
But he ne-ver had ne brains.

2   He could lift grit big girders
      And set arches by his sel',
    But his other marras always used to say
      In time the strain will tell, will tell,
      In time the strain will tell.

3   Now he had a skinny little marra
      Who was only five foot nowt.
    When he met his skinny little marra coming outbye
      At him he would bawl and shout, he would,
      At him he would bawl and shout.

4   He would curse his skinny little marra,
      On his head he would always heap scorn.
    He'd say: How come today I've filled twelve
      And you you've only filled one, you idle sod,
      And you you've only filled one.

5   The skinny little marra niver said nowt,
      Took everything the big hewer had to say.
    'Cause he knew on Thursday when he got the note
      They'd both have the very same pay, it's true,
      They'd both have the very same pay.

6 The big hewer kept on hewing,
  Riving and filling every day.
 But at last he went and strained his heart
  And he deed and passed away, he did,
  And he deed and passed away.

7 The skinny little marra went to see him,
  He looked lovely in the front room laid out.
 He looked down and said: Today I've filled one
  And you lad, you've filled nowt, 'cause you're dead,
 And you lad, you've filled nowt.

8 So all you young lads who's listening,
  Just do as little as you can,
 'Cause if you're a lazy young fella,
  You'll make a strong old man, it's true,
  You'll make a strong old man.

COD BANGING

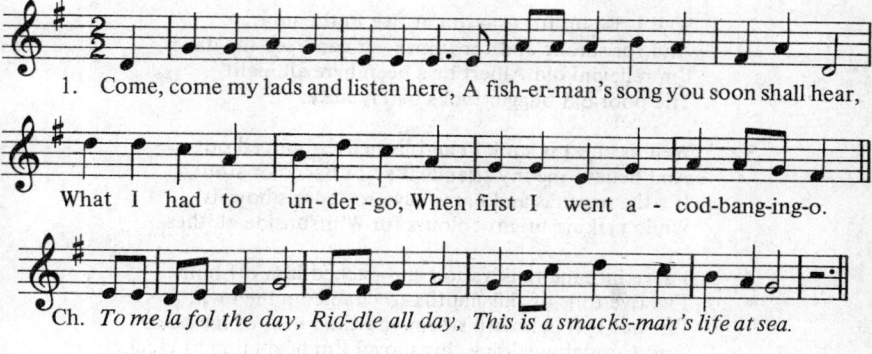

1. Come, come my lads and listen here, A fish-er-man's song you soon shall hear,

What I had to un-der-go, When first I went a - cod-bang-ing-o.

Ch. *To me la fol the day, Rid-dle all day, This is a smacks-man's life at sea.*

2 How well I remember on the fourteenth of May
 A big barque ship she came our way,
 She came our way and did let fly
 And the tops'l halyards a-flew sky high.

3 And now we draw near Harwich pier,
 The young and old they both draw near
 To see us get our fish on deck
 And crack their skulls with a little short stick.

4 And now my song is nearly done
 And I hope I've not offended one,
 I don't think I've got it complete
 'Cause I've only been in the trade about a week.

29

THE CLAYTON ANALINE SONG

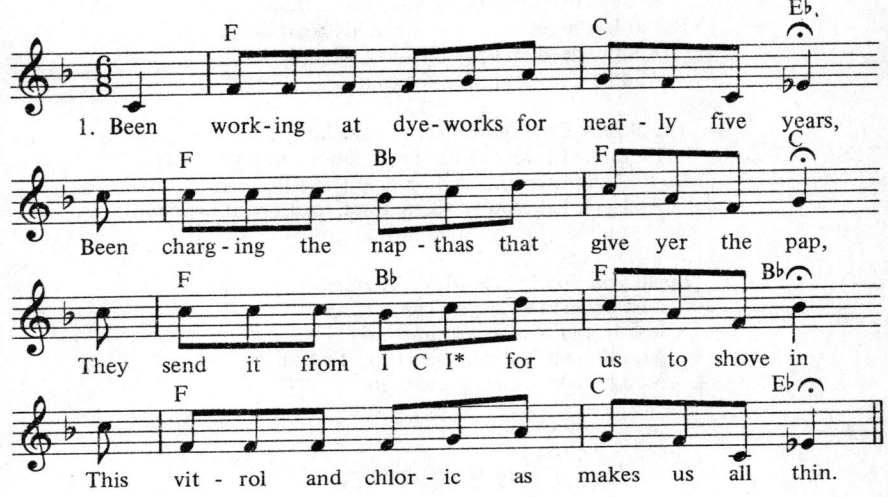

1. Been work-ing at dye-works for near-ly five years,
Been charg-ing the nap-thas that give yer the pap,
They send it from I C I* for us to shove in
This vit-rol and chlor-ic as makes us all thin.

2   Well I rise up for Clayton at five in the morn
And for smoke and for fumes yer can't see the dawn,
I'm relievin' old Albert he's been here all night,
The poor old bugger looks barely alive.

3   Well 'is chest is sunk in and 'is belly's popped out
And believe me my friends it's not bacco or stout,
It's the napthas and paras have rotted his bowels
While making bright colours for Whitsunside clothes.

4   I gave him me milk ration and packed him off home,
I've five tons of this naptha to charge on me own,
I'm wet through with steam and the sweat of me back
And through wielding this shovel I'm beginning to crack.

5   Well I'm damned if I'll work in this hole any more
For me belly feels tight and me chest is right sore,
I think of old Albert his face white and drawn,
He'll be back here tonight and just praying for dawn.

* pronounced 'Ikey'

THE SHEFFIELD GRINDERS' SONG

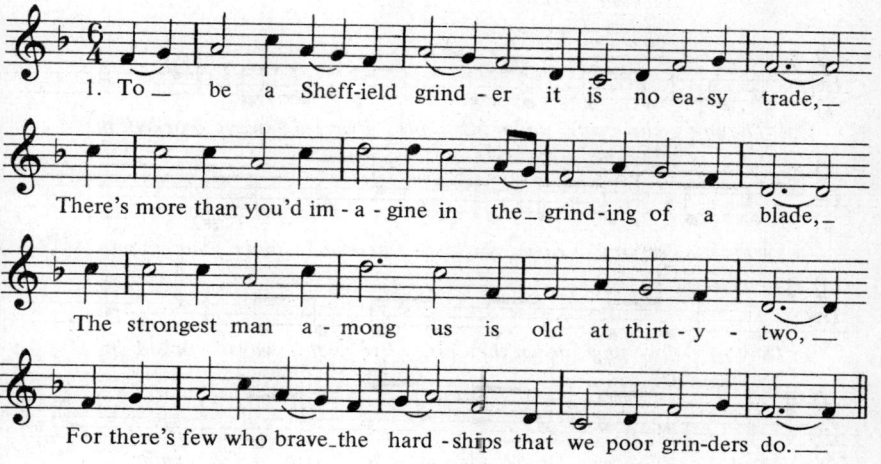

1. To — be a Sheff-ield grind - er it is no ea-sy trade, —
There's more than you'd im - a - gine in the — grind-ing of a blade, —
The strongest man a - mong us is old at thirt - y - two, —
For there's few who brave — the hard - ships that we poor grin-ders do. —

2   When the country goes to war then our masters quickly cry
     Orders countermanded — our goods we all lay by,
     Your prices we must settle and you'll be stinted too,
     There's few who brave such hardships as we poor grinders do.

3   And every working day we are breathing dust and steel
     And a broken stone can give to us a wound that will not heal,
     There's many an honest grinder who's ground down by such a blow,
     For there's few who brave such hardships as we poor grinders do.

4   There's many a poor grinder who's thus been snatched away
     Without a moment's warning to meet the Judgement Day,
     Before his judge he must appear his final doom to know,
     There's few who brave such hardships as we poor grinders do.

5   There's many a poor grinder whose family is large
     With all his best endeavours cannot his debts discharge,
     When his children cry for bread, how pitiful to view,
     There's few can brave such hardships as we poor grinders do.

6   And now I will conclude and end these few and humble lines
     With success to all grinders who suffer in hard times.
     I wish them better fortune and all their families too.
     There are few who brave such hardships as we poor grinders do.

THEY'RE CLOSING DOWN THE PIT I'VE ALWAYS WORKED IN

Ch. They're clo-sing down the pit I've al-ways worked in
And they're say-ing go else-where and make your pile,
They're clo-sing down the pit I've al-ways worked in
And ev-ery-bod-y's go-ing with a smile.

1. I star-ted on Brock-well two's but it's not the place you'd choose,
The coal was can-ny but the ram-ble was four foot high,
And the face was on the sid-dle with a big fault in the mid-dle
And a blood-y big stone came down and broke my thigh.

2   Now another awful place was that Brockwell fourth east face,
It was water and ramble and gas and trouble and strife.
But the worst bit of it all was that rotten exit stall
Where the cutter shortened Ishy Jowett's life.

3   Then I cut up the top coal and I'll say: Upon my soul
What a place to work, the coal was one foot eight,
Belly flopping all the way and the owerman wouldn't pay
And you hardly dared to stop to get your bait.

4   Well I'm in the Busty now, another stinking cow
     One foot ten of coal, I cannot find no more,
     And it's clarts from end to end enough to drive you round the bend
     But we're leaving it, it's there for evermore.

HOPPING DOWN IN KENT

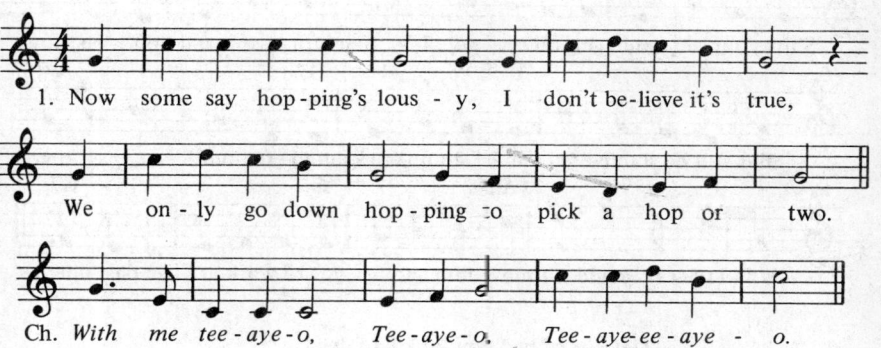

1. Now some say hop-ping's lous - y, I don't be-lieve it's true,

We on - ly go down hop-ping to pick a hop or two.

Ch. With me tee - aye - o, Tee - aye - o, Tee - aye - ee - aye - o.

2   Now when I went a-hopping, hopping down in Kent
     I saw old Mrs Riley a-sweeping out her tent.

3   Now every Monday morning just at six-o-clock
     You'll hear the old hoppers calling: Get up and boil your pot.

4   Now Sunday is our washing day, don't we wash it clean.
     We boil it in our hopping pots and hang it on the green.

5   Now do you want any money? Yes sir if you please
     To buy a hock of bacon, a pound of mouldy cheese.

6   Now here comes our old measurer with his long nose and chin,
     With his ten gallon basket, and don't he pop 'em in!

7   Now when our old pole-puller he does come around
     He says: Come on you dirty ol' hop-pickers, pick 'em up all off the ground.

8   Now hopping is all over, all the money spent
     And don't I wish I never went a-hopping down in Kent.

STILL HE SLUMBERED

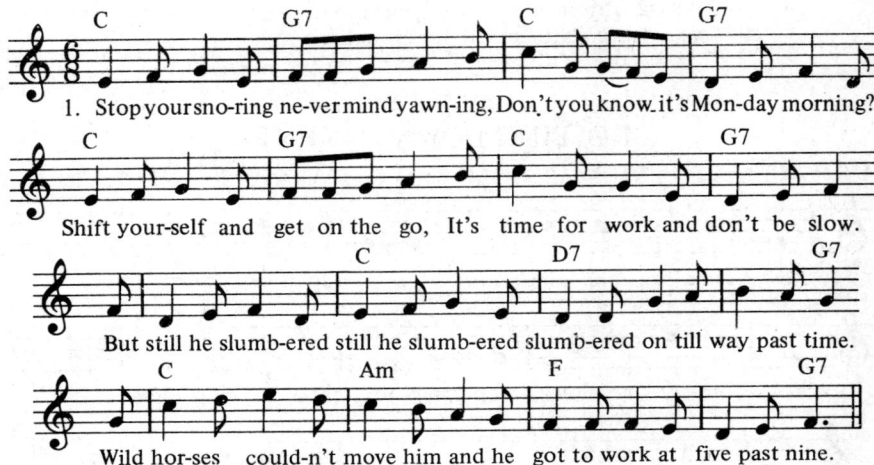

1. Stop your sno-ring ne-ver mind yawn-ing, Don't you know it's Mon-day morning?

Shift your-self and get on the go, It's time for work and don't be slow.

But still he slumb-ered still he slumb-ered slumb-ered on till way past time.

Wild hor-ses could-n't move him and he got to work at five past nine.

2 Get out of bed you look half dead,
It's Tuesday morning you sleepyhead.
You're gonna be late again today,
Your breakfast's nearly shrivelled away.
  But still he slumbered still he slumbered
  Slumbered on till way past time.
  Come hell or high water he wouldn't budge
  And he got to work at half past nine.

3 Come on get moving stop your snoozing,
Think of all the pay you're losing.
Wednesday morning's nearly done;
It's time that you were up and gone.
  But still he slumbered still he slumbered
  Slumbered on till God knows when.
  Thunder couldn't move him
  And he got to work at twenty to ten.

4 Get out of the sack and don't be slack,
It's Thursday morning off your back.
The factory bell went long ago,
Get up and off and down the road.
  But still he slumbered still he slumbered
  Slumbered on just like a crock.
  The H-bomb couldn't move him
  And he got to work at ten o'clock.

5   Come on you tyke they're all on strike,
It's Friday morning, on your bike.
The boss is acting tough, the swine
You'd better get down to the picket line.
       And he never slumbered never slumbered
       Made sure that he wasn't late.
       He was up that day and a mile away
       And he got to work at twenty to eight.

OUR ESSEX CAMP

1. Down in our Es-sex camp, __ That's where we get the cramp

Through slee-ping in the damp, __ We're not all-owed a lamp.

All we get there each day, Is left right left right all the way,

Ser-geants call-ing __ lance-jacks* baw-ling: Get out on pa-rade.

2. We go to bed at night, __ You ought to see the sight,

The ear-wigs on the floors, __ All night are form-ing fours.

If we're in bed in the morn-ing, You will hear the ser-geant yawn-ing: __

Show a leg there __ show a leg there, __ Way down in our Es-sex camp.

* lance-corporals

35

ROUNDING CAPE HORN

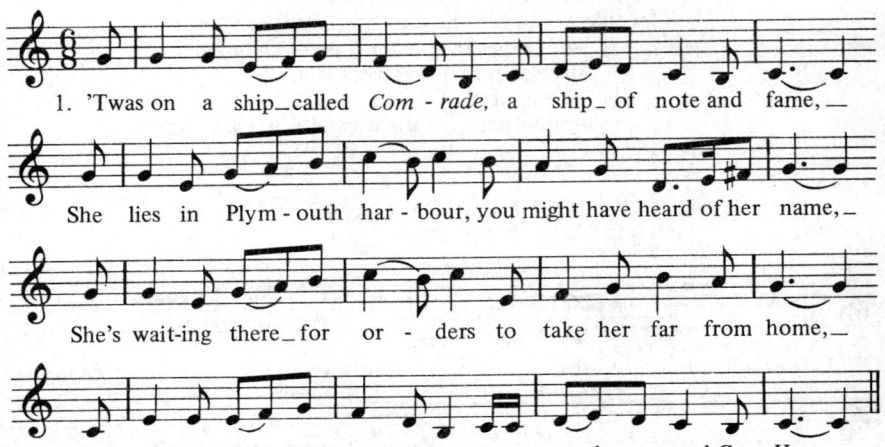

1. 'Twas on a ship called *Com-rade,* a ship of note and fame,—
She lies in Plym-outh har-bour, you might have heard of her name,—
She's wait-ing there for or - ders to take her far from home,—
When or-ders came on board of her to pro- ceed a-round Cape Horn. —

2   And now we're round the Horn my boys, fine weather and fine days,
We sighted Valliparaiso and anchored in the bay.
The Spanish girls came up to us, I solemnly declare
They're far before your English girls with their heads of golden hair.

3   They love a British sailor because he is true blue
And when your money it is all spent some more they'll give to you.
They're far before your English girls who on you will impose
And when your money is all spent they'll pawn and sell your clothes.

4   Now farewell Valliparaiso, farewell for just a while,
Farewell to yonder green mountains, farewell to yonder green isle.
And when our ship it do pay off we'll sing this grand old song,
God bless those little Spanish girls around the north Cape Horn.

DITTON BAY

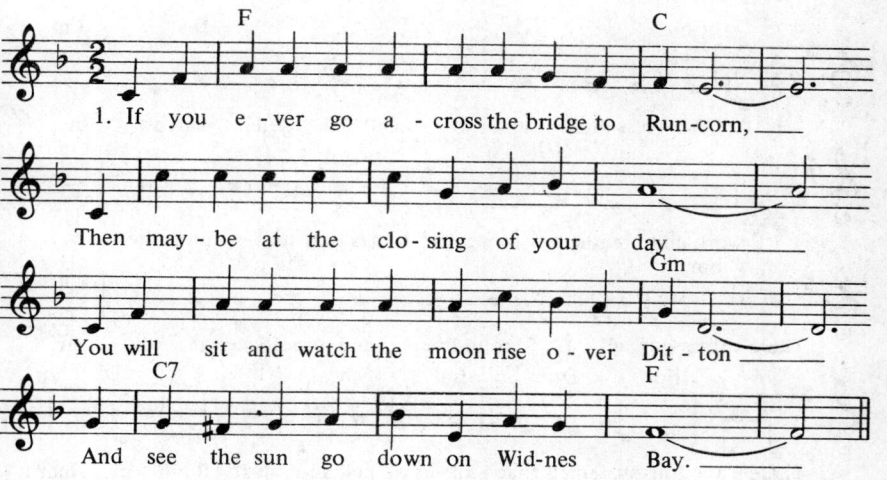

1. If you e-ver go a-cross the bridge to Run-corn, _____
Then may-be at the clo-sing of your day _____
You will sit and watch the moon rise o-ver Dit-ton _____
And see the sun go down on Wid-nes Bay. _____

2 Just to hear again the rattle of the brake vans,
The shunters in the goods yard shackling up,
And to sit beside the stovepipes in the cabin
And hear the sure-foot shunters have their say.

3 For the breezes blowing o'er the tracks from Widnes
Are perfumed by ICI's as they blow,
And the lengthmen in the cutting digging ballast
Speak a language that the RE does not know.

4 For the RE came and tried to teach us their way,
They scorned us just for being what we are,
But they might as well go chasing after runaways
Or try to build a decent buffet car.

5 And if there is going to be a lot of traffic
And somehow I am sure there's going to be,
I will ask my chief to let me work my rest day
In that dear land not far from the old Mersey.

CHEMICAL WORKERS' SONG

1. A pro-cess man am I and I'll tell you no lie,
I work and breathe a-mong the fumes that trail a-cross the sky,
There's thun-der all a-round me and poi-son in the air,
There's a lou-sy smell that smacks of hell and dust all in me hair.
Ch. And it's go boys — go, They'll time your e-very breath,
And ev-ery day you're in this place,
You're two days near-er death, But you go. _____

2   I've worked amongst the spinners, I've breathed in the oily smoke,
I've shovelled up the gypsum that nigh on makes you choke,
I've stood knee deep in cyanide, gone sick with a caustic burn,
Been working rough and seen enough to make your stomach turn.

3   There's overtime and bonus opportunities galore,
Young lads like the money and they all come back for more,
But soon you're knocking on and look older than you should
For every bob made on this job you pay with flesh and blood.

WHEN THAT I WAS WEARY

1. Give ear un-to a maid that late-ly was be-trayed
And sent in-to Vir - gin - ny - O.
In brief I shall de-clare what I have suf - fered there,
When that I was wea - ry wea - ry wea - ry wea - ry O.

2 It's since that first I came unto this land of fame
Which is called Virginny O,
The axe and the hoe have wrought my overthrow
When that I was weary weary weary weary O.

3 Five years and more served I all under Master Guy
In the land of Virginny O,
Which made me for to know sorrow grief and woe
When that I was weary weary weary weary O.

4 Oh when my dame says go, it's then I must do so
In the land of Virginny O.
When she sits at meat then I have none to eat
When that I am weary weary weary weary O.

5 Instead of beds of ease to lie down when I please
In the land of Virginny O,
Upon a bed of straw I lie down full of woe
When that I am weary weary weary weary O.

6 Oh I have played my part both at plough and cart
In the land of Virginny O.
Billets from the wood upon my back they load
When that I am weary weary weary weary O.

7 And when the mill doth stand I'm ready at command
In the land of Virginny O.
The mortar for to make which makes my heart to ache
When that I am weary weary weary weary O.

8   And when the child doth cry I must sing bye-a-bye
In the land of Virginny O.
No rest that I can have while I am here a slave
When that I am weary weary weary weary O.

9   But if it be my chance homeward to advance
In the land of Virginny O,
If that I once more should land on England's shore
I'll no more be weary weary weary O.

THE LUMPER'S LIFE

1. The fish is wait-ing in the hold, the night's u-pon the town,
Folk with sense are in their beds, but the lump-ers they go down,
Down Pneu-mon-ia Jet-ty where the wind cuts like a knife,
I wish to Christ I'd nev-er start-ed on the lump-er's life.

Ch. And it's all the night and half the day,
Sweat-ing for your lump-er's pay,
Fill the box-es, lump 'em down,
lump-ing's hard in Grims-by Town.

2   We're called the 'Midnight Millionaires' by folk who never know
       How yer hands go stiff encased in ice when the temperature's below,
       The wind cuts through yer guts, me lads, and yer face is stiff and blue
       And you wish the trawler-owners were down there instead of you.

3   Me Dad he was a lumper, a dockman all his life,
       Me mother told me sister: Never be a lumper's wife,
       You wash his fishy overalls and darn his stiff old socks
       And every night you sleep alone while he goes down the docks.

4   If ever I win the pools, me lads, me lumping days are through,
       I'll cash me cheque from Littlewoods and I know just what I'll do,
       I'll treat me mates and say goodbye and leave the lumping life
       And then I'll go to bed at nights and get to know me wife.

5   I'll burn me dirty clogs and throw me lumping card away,
       Shove me leggins in the shed and leave 'em there to stay,
       I'll tell the lousy setter-on to stuff his midnight call
       And turn me back for ever on the bloody cold North Wall.

JACKY'S BUILDING SITE

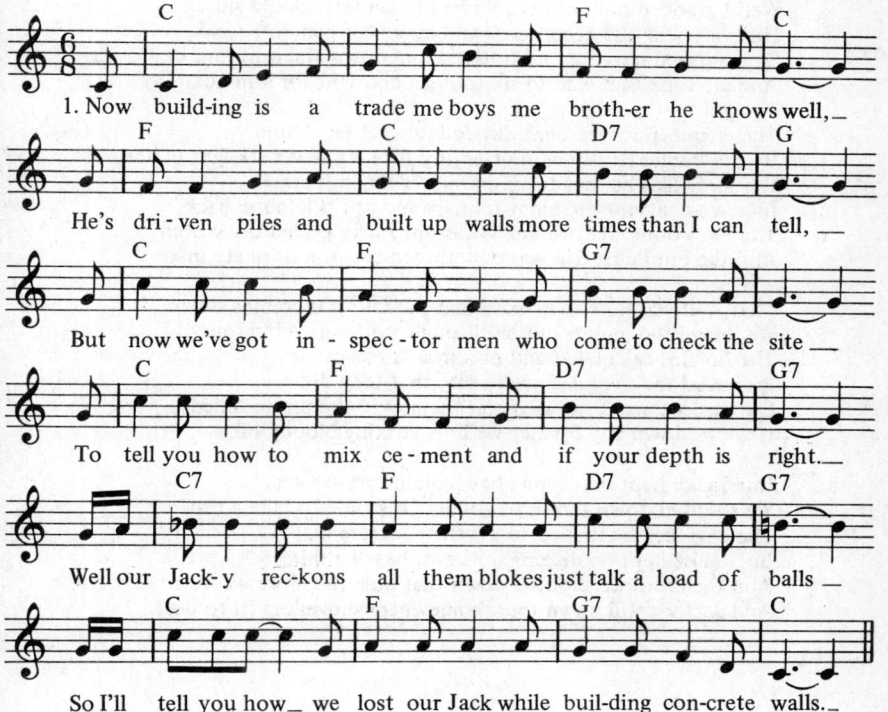

1. Now building is a trade me boys me brother he knows well,___

He's dri-ven piles and built up walls more times than I can tell, ___

But now we've got in - spec-tor men who come to check the site ___

To tell you how to mix ce-ment and if your depth is right.___

Well our Jack-y rec-kons all them blokes just talk a load of balls ___

So I'll tell you how___ we lost our Jack while buil-ding con-crete walls.___

2   We started excavations in the May of seventy six
With just two ton of concrete and a stack of facing bricks,
We're standing in the trenches and we're knee deep in the clay
Waiting for the council men to give us the OK.
And the rain is coming down and our Jacky says: Damn me
If he don't come soon by this afternoon there'll be sod all here to see.

3   We're standing in this sea of mud about to blow a fuse,
When down he come to inspect the site in his patent pigskin shoes.
We're ready for the concrete sir we're ready for hard core,
I'm sorry lads, he says, but go down two foot more.
Our Jacky went through shades of pink to scarlet through to blue,
Thank God he never did to him the things he said he'd do.

4   We took that wall to four foot six and got the concrete in,
We started building up the walls — she's looking very trim,
Then arrives an engineer: I'm sorry lads them bricks
Are not sufficient strength, he says, go down to six foot six.
Well our Jacky picks a shovel up and screams: I'll kill the twit
And he lands the engineer a blow which puts him in the pit.

5   Before the engineer had time to get his senses trim
Our Jacky backed the JCB and started to fill in.
Well I grabbed hold of his collar and panic-struck did shriek
His body will just decompose and make the concrete weak.
So we fished him out and brushed him down and sent him on his way
And we took that wall to six foot six and sent for him next day.

6   The engineer arrived next day followed close behind
By the Public Health who promptly found a sewer straight in line.
I'm sorry lads he says to us, me sewer mustn't crack,
Increase the depth to eight foot six and put the fabric back.
The next thing that we knew was our Jacky pulled the switch
And the Public Health was underneath two ton of ready mix.

7   That wall was now so massive and the rain was coming down,
We joined the miners' union through working underground,
The boffins calculated and prodded lumps of clay,
Produced their regulations to see what they did say.
Our Jacky cursed and swore at them as in the pit he toiled
If we go down any further we'll be striking bloody oil.

8   Our Jacky kept on digging like a maniac possessed,
We shouted down that hole to him: It's time to take a rest,
The engineer is satisfied to get the concrete in,
But Jacky kept on digging, he never heard a thing.
And the more we shouted down that hole the more we heard him cuss
And Jacky's still down there somewhere shovelling fit to bust.

TO THE SHEEPSHEARING WE WILL GO

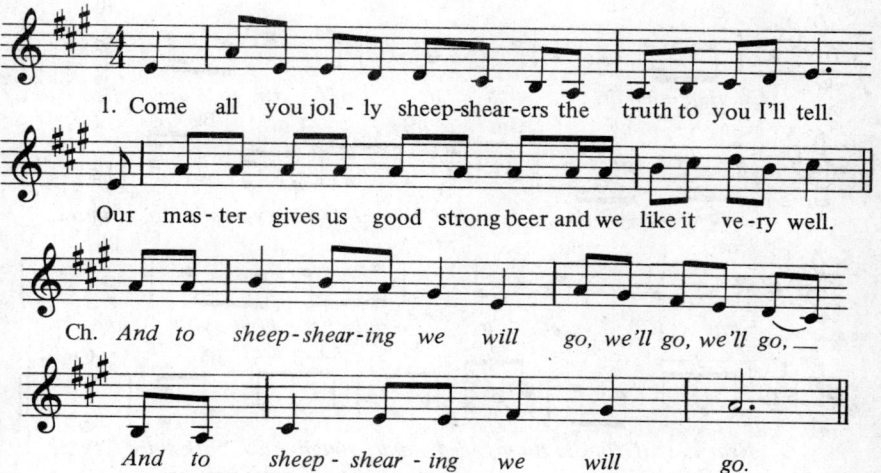

1. Come all you jol-ly sheep-shear-ers the truth to you I'll tell.
Our mas-ter gives us good strong beer and we like it ve-ry well.
Ch. *And to sheep-shear-ing we will go, we'll go, we'll go,—*
And to sheep-shear-ing we will go.

2   We get up in the morning we grind up our shears
        Then away unto some farmhouse to breakfast we do steer.

3   Then after our breakfast out into the barn we go
        Like jolly brave fellows we stand all in two rows.

4   We shear on till eleven, till eleven by the clock
        And then says our captain, it's time for us to stop.

5   The dinner on the cloth, O then our mistress she replies
        I've not forgot your lamb beer, you should have it bye and bye.

6   Then after dinner's over out into the barn we go,
        And now, says our captain, we must go a quicker blow.

7   As for old skin-and-bone, he's neither good nor harm
        For he'll turn out as many sheep as any man in the barn.

8   As for little Steven he is as good as any,
        He'll turn his back agin' the coop and ask for a pale belly.

9   As for little Abraham he's just about a man,
        He'll turn his back agin' the coop and cry out for a ram.

10   As for the old sheep-washers they are deceitful devils,
        They often spoil our shears by cutting dirt and gravel.

11   And now to conclude and to finish up my song
        We'll have another glass all round and then we won't go home.

STEELMEN

Ch. Ham-mer it, weld it, roll it to and fro.
Cleve-land steel is of the best I'd have yers all to know.
Forge it, cast it, mould it how you like,
Neat as a Geor-die hin-ny bird_ and tough as a York-shire tyke.

1. There's men that work be-low the ground where day-light_ nev-er comes
And some grow food u-pon the land and on-ly_ get the crumbs.
There's men stand in the as-sem-bly line and wish the time-'d fly.
But gim-me the lad to roll the slab and bounce the sparks up high.

2   The cold Northeaster from the Gare'll freeze your very soul.
     Then it's the open hearth for me or where the ingots roll
     Where thunder shakes the walls about and trembles all the floor
     And sparks jump out the soaking pits and sweat runs down galore.

3   Take iron by the waggonload and burn it till it's white.
     Then blast it through with jets of gas until your mixture's right.
     Then shovel in your lumps of lime and set the sky aglow.
     Add some spit and lots of sweat and make your steel to flow.

44

CALLERFORNEY

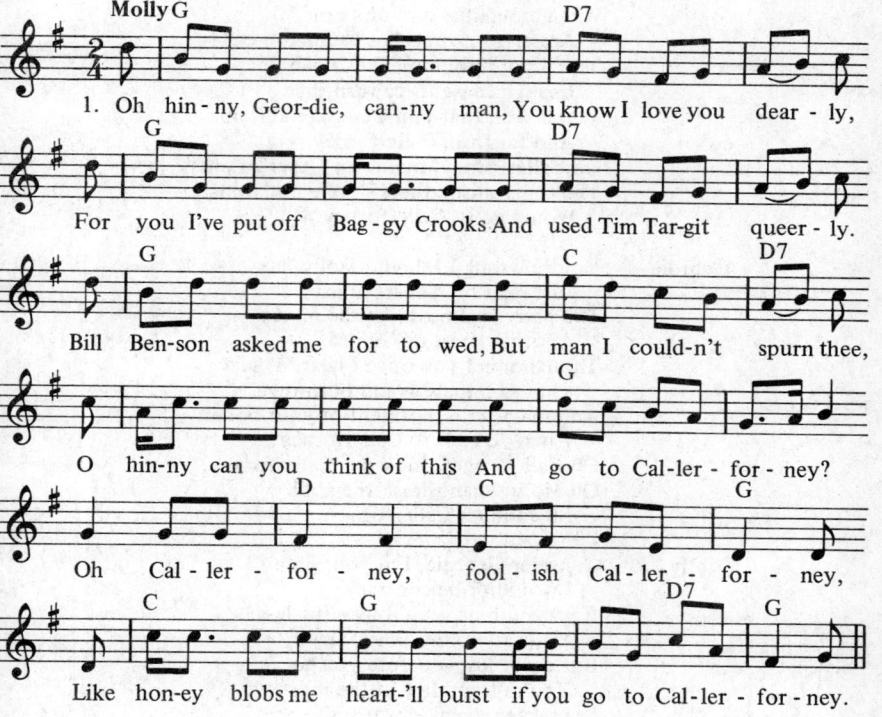

1. Oh hin-ny, Geor-die, can-ny man, You know I love you dear-ly,
For you I've put off Bag-gy Crooks And used Tim Tar-git queer-ly.
Bill Ben-son asked me for to wed, But man I could-n't spurn thee,
O hin-ny can you think of this And go to Cal-ler-for-ney?
Oh Cal-ler-for-ney, fool-ish Cal-ler-for-ney,
Like hon-ey blobs me heart-'ll burst if you go to Cal-ler-for-ney.

2 **Geordie** Now Molly hold your whinin' gob
     My mind's made up for certain,
My picks and spades is in my chest
     Come morning I'll be startin'.
I'll soon be bobbin' on the sea
     And flying round Cape Horney,
I know the seam to hew for gold
     When I gets to Callerforney.
Oh Callerforney, bonny Callerforney,
There's gold beneath your very feet
     Out there in Callerforney.

3   **Molly**

You'll rue the day my collier lad
    When in the waves you're sprawlin',
When crocodiles and unicorns
    Are at your breeches haulin'.
You'll not have luck like Jonah, man
    In a whale's guts to turn thee,
You'll wish that you were safe at home
    And far from Callerforney.
Oh Callerforney, shame on Callerforney,
The folks all say there's none but fools
    Would go to Callerforney.

4   **Geordie**

You're wrong I tell you Molly lass
    Just read the papers hinny,
The place is almost like the mint
    Another coast of Guinea.
Though mind you once I heard it said
    That cannibals would burn thee,
And make gold ointment of your bones
    When you get to Callerforney.
Oh Callerforney, look out Callerforney,
Oh Molly I can thrash them all,
    I'll conquer Callerforney.

5   **Molly**

Consider Geordie, I'm your wife
    I wouldn't be contrary,
If go you must you'll take the lass
    You call your bonny Mary.
But well I know before you go
    You're trembling at the journey,
Sea serpents may up-turn the boat
    Then where's your Callerforney?
Oh Callerforney, enticing Callerforney,
I wish that folks was not so poor
    To want thee Callerforney.

6   **Geordie**

Cheer up my duck, you'll come with me,
    I never heeds the danger,
Poor collier lads works hard for nowt
    And still to death's no stranger.
Like Whittington I hear the bells
    That say: Come on your journey,
So goodbye to the pit
    I'll hew for gold in Callerforney.
Oh Callerforney, we're coming Callerforney,
Farewell to splint, choke, damp, and blast,
    Hurrah for Callerforney.

NOTES

The Months of the Year (p. 26)   Sung by Harry Westaway, Belstone, Devon, and J. Potter, Postbridge, Devon. Collected by Sabine Baring-Gould, 1888.

Says Baring-Gould, 'Still a popular song among the labouring class', which is not surprising as this is a gem of agricultural observation. Our version has Potter's tune and (mainly) Westaway's words, the match being made by Paul Wilson of Exeter. This song is sometimes referred to as 'The Seasons', although most singers know it as 'The Months of the Year', which is less confusing as there are a couple of songs dealing specifically with the four seasons rather than the twelve months.

The Big Hewer and the Little Marra (p. 28)   By Dave Mountford, Seaham, Durham. Written in 1972.

'Big Hewer' tales abound in Britain's coalfields, although he is known by a different name in each area. This superhuman figure belongs to the days of hand hewing, but the legend has survived in spite of mechanization. Perhaps miners' attitudes to him have changed, though, as a miner from Seaham illustrates in this wry song.

Cod Banging (p. 29)   Sung by Bob Hart, Snape, Suffolk. Collected by Rod and Danny Stradling, late 1960s.

Bob Hart, an excellent East Anglian singer with a vigorous sense of rhythm, learnt this song around 1912. It is rare, only odd fragments being otherwise known, and confined to the fishing communities of Norfolk and Suffolk. The singer had worked briefly on both sailing smack trawlers and on steamers.

The Clayton Analine Song (p. 30)   By Pete Smith. Written in the 1960s.

This song describes a grim reality which is becoming a major cause for concern. Fears about the safety of chemicals are reported as the biggest single cause of enquiries to the AUEW's safety department. The 'pap' in the song, or papilloma of the bladder, is a cancer caused by working with certain organic chemicals often used in the rubber and dyeworks industries. In 1967 a ban was imposed on the manufacture and use of beta-naphthylamine, although serious health complaints can continue for up to 40 years after contact.

The Sheffield Grinders' Song (p. 31)   From a broadside contributed by Ewan MacColl.

From the early 19th century, this broadside ballad gives a harsh but realistic impression of the work of the grinders of the Sheffield cutlery industry. It was a proud trade which reached a point of impoverishment in the early 19th century. The cutlers were well organized, highly traditional and conscious of their own position. It was said that every cutler had a copy of *The Rights of Man*. A passage in E. P. Thompson's *Making of the English Working Classes* tells us that Dr Holland, physician to Sheffield Royal Infirmary, 'wrote a detailed treatise on disease and accident among Sheffield grinders', accurately reflecting verses 3 and 4 of this song.

They're Closing Down the Pit I've Always Worked In (p. 32)   By Bert Draycott, Fishburn, Cleveland. Written in 1970.

Bert Draycott started work as a coal miner when he was 23 and stayed until he was 43 when the colliery closed. He is now a deputy at Horden colliery.

Hopping Down in Kent (p. 33)   Sung by Louey Saunders/Fuller, Lingfield, Surrey. Collected by Ken Stubbs, 1967.

Before hop picking was mechanized, the Kent hopfields provided traditional seasonal work for many gypsies. As far as we know this song has only been collected from gypsies, and only within recent years. All the singers have been women.

Still He Slumbered (p. 34)   By Sam Richards, Totnes, Devon. Written in 1973.

Our Essex Camp (p. 35)   From *Tommy's Tunes* by F. T. Nettleingham 2nd Lt, RFC. Published by Erskine MacDonald Ltd, London 1917.

A First World War parody. The tune is from the popular song 'Back Home in Tennessee'.

Rounding Cape Horn (p. 36) Sung by John Goffin, Winterton, Norfolk. Collected by Jim Carroll and Pat Mackenzie, 1976.

Cape Horn is one of the most hazardous areas of any sea voyage. Some versions actually describe the conditions rounding the Horn, but in this one, pride in the ship and the delights at the end of the journey take precedence.

Ditton Bay (p. 37) Source unknown, but written in 1950s.

'Galway Bay' is a much parodied song. 'Ditton Bay' was written in the 1950s and the implied equation between Ditton Bay and the original Galway Bay is ironic, Ditton being heavily industrial and Galway idyllic. There is a traditional local rivalry between Runcorn people and Widnesians which accounts for the sly comment in the first line. Runcorn people are known as 'woolybacks' to those in Widnes, and they vie with each other in reputation for being tight-fisted. The main subject of the song is railway activity.

Chemical Workers' Song (p. 38) By Ron Angel, Middlesborough, Cleveland. Written in 1964.

When That I Was Weary (p. 39) Broadside ballad in the Douce Collection. Also in Pepys, Crawford, and Roxburgh. Tune fitted by Sam Richards.

The Roxburgh copy tells us that this ballad was printed c. 1690. The Virginia Company was formed in 1606, and the government offered incentives for traders and colonizers to go there. One way of providing labourers for the colony was simply to kidnap and sell into slavery any victims that could be conveniently seized, and petty criminals were given transportation sentences as well. This system had ceased by the end of the century, although white slavery (euphemistically referred to as 'indentured servitude' in old history books) continued for some time. The broadside copies have 16 verses. We have found that slightly long for modern audiences.

The Lumpers' Life (p. 40) By Bill Meek with Martin Haxby and John Connelly, Grimsby, Lincolnshire. Written in 1965.

Bill Meek's note to the song says: 'My father was a lumper for 40 years. His constant wish was to win the pools and leave the docks. He never did. The docks killed him in the end and this song was written shortly after his death. A lumper is a dock-worker who unloads fish from the trawlers. "Pneumonia Jetty" is a name given to the North Wall, the main landing area for trawlers. A "setter on" allocates work to the lumpers. The song lay in a drawer for months until Martin Haxby provided it with a new tune and John Connelly added a chorus to give the song its present format.'

Jacky's Building Site (p. 41) By Martin Scragg, Torquay, Devon. Written in 1977.

The writer works as an architectural designer and tells us this song was based on personal experience!

To the Sheepshearing We Will Go (p. 43) Sung by J. C. Falconer, details unknown. Collected by George Gardiner, c. 1910.

Shearing time is the sheep farmer's harvest and used to be accompanied by drinking, feasting, singing and dancing, something of which still survives in places such as Exmoor or the Yorkshire moors.

Steelmen (p. 44) By Ron Angel, Middlesborough, Cleveland. Written in 1970.

This magnificent song, full of the rhythms and sounds of a steelworks, comes from prolific Ron Angel who wrote it after a visit to a works on Teesside.

Callerforney (p. 45) From *Allan's Tyneside Songs*, 1891. Originally published Newcastle-on-Tyne, 1891; republished Graham, Newcastle-on-Tyne 1972.

A song from the latter part of the Californian gold rush, it was originally printed in Tyneside dialect. This version is the one we sing. Some of the dialect has been reduced without any loss to the song. Like any good verse, it does not rely on regional spellings for its effect.

MOTION SONGS

Motion songs are wedded to a physical, normally repetitive activity which determines the rhythm of the song, leaving the melody relatively free. To listen to a motion song without the motion is like looking at a fossil: the activity itself is missing and the imprint only is present.

Into this category come work songs, dance songs, marching songs, play and game songs — and the sea shanty, being perhaps the best known. In practice, any song at all can be pressed into service by mere alteration or accentuation of its rhythm. We have collected many pieces used as work songs in Devon stone quarries, and our examples could, no doubt, be matched by many song collectors.

Our small selection consists of songs which, if they did not originate as such, have achieved their present form as co-ordinators of physical activity.

TROTTING SONG

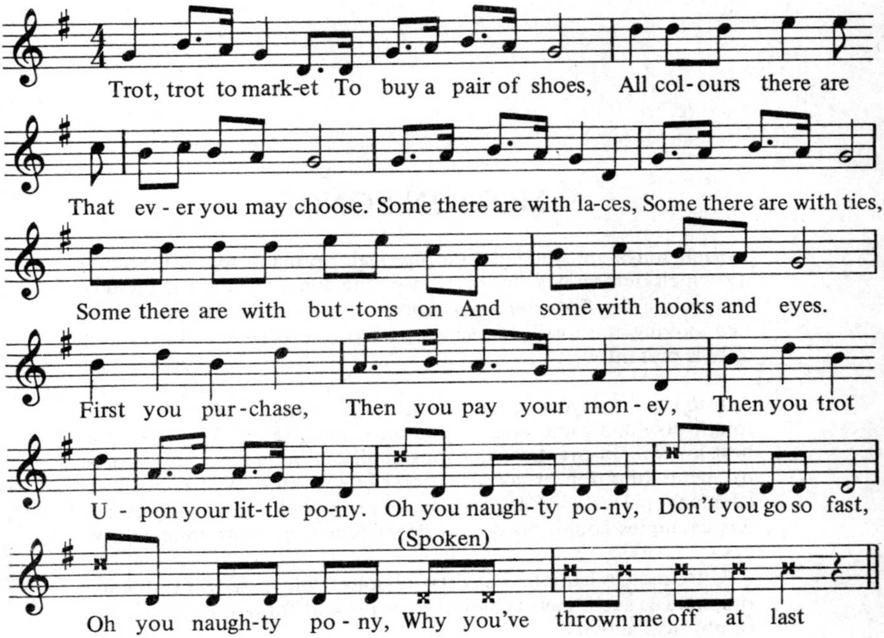

Trot, trot to mark-et To buy a pair of shoes, All col-ours there are

That ev-er you may choose. Some there are with la-ces, Some there are with ties,

Some there are with but-tons on And some with hooks and eyes.

First you pur-chase, Then you pay your mon-ey, Then you trot

U - pon your lit-tle po-ny. Oh you naugh-ty po-ny, Don't you go so fast,

(Spoken)

Oh you naugh-ty po - ny, Why you've thrown me off at last

'WARE OUT MOTHER

'Ware out mo-ther there's a nav - vy in the cel - lar

And two more look-ing through the win-dow out - side.

Do you go a-long you naugh-ty fil-thy hus-sy Else I'll put a stick a-cross your back.

'Ware out mo - ther there's a nav - vy in the cel - lar

And two more look-ing through the win - dow out - side.

A HANDY SHIP

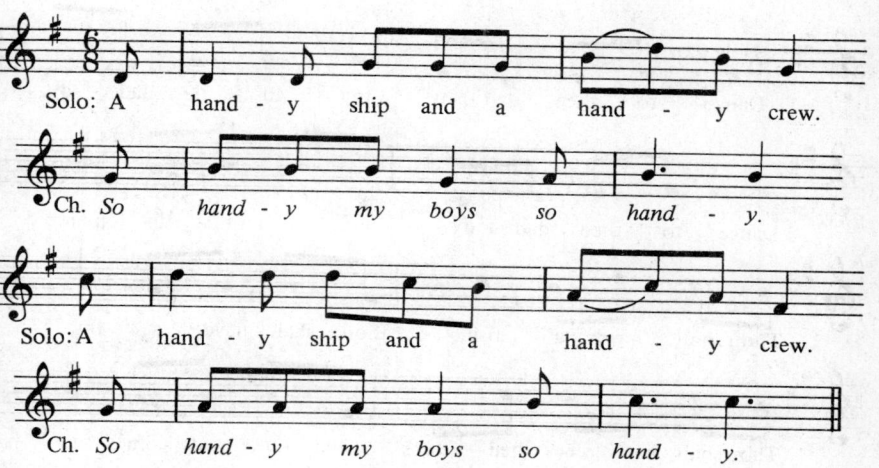

Solo: A hand-y ship and a hand-y crew.
Ch. So hand-y my boys so hand-y.
Solo: A hand-y ship and a hand-y crew.
Ch. So hand-y my boys so hand-y.

2   A handy mate to pull us through.
      A handy mate to pull us through.

3   The mate will tell us when to belay.
      I think that's just what he's going to say.

4   So up aloft on this yard we must go.
      So up aloft on the yard we must go.

      (additional verses)

5   A handy bosun an' handy sails.
      A handy rig an' handy sails.

6   A handy cook an' steward too
      Who spoil the grub they give the crew.

7   Oh shake her up an' away we'll go.
      Be handy there wid a handy-o.

8   My fancyman's a dandy-o
      He loves the girls who are handy-o.

DANCE TO THEE DADDY

1. Dance to thee dad-dy my lit-tle lad-dy,
Dance to thee dad-dy my___ lit-tle man.
Thou shalt have a fish, thou shalt have a fin,
Thou shalt have a had-dock when the boat comes in.
Thou shalt have a cod-lin boiled ___ in a pan,
Dance to thee dad-dy my___ lit-tle man.

2   Dance to thee daddy my bonnie laddie,
Dance to thee daddy my bonnie lamb.
When thou art a feller fitter to be married
Thou shalt have a penny for to buy a lass.
Thou shalt have a penny, thou shalt have a penny,
Dance to thee daddy my little lamb.

WE BE

We___ be work-ing on the board ___ all ___ a-slav-ing on the cord

Ch. We___ be here, we be we be, yes we be, we be, we be. ___

We be pressing out a seam while the young 'uns sneaks the cream.

We be wrasslin' in the yard while the farmer's working hard.

We be cackin' with the geese while the public we do fleece.

We be singing with the silk like a milkmaid with the milk.

We be covering up the feathers while we'm wearin' out our leathers.

We be traipsin' on the roads while we'm wetter'n any toads.

We be soggin' cross the downs while the gentry's with the hounds.

We be workin' night and day through the merry month of May.

We be alt'rin' of our tune 'fore the sunny end of June.

We be ever so good on Sundays but we'm never so good on Mondays.

We be middlin' through the week but o' Saturdays mustn' speak.

We be warm as any blanket while we double thread an' twank et (it).

We be wish't and thurl for sure when the trade be gettin' poor.

We be ready the boss to sack when the tiddly's at our back.

We be whistlin' while 'tis light but we 'ums it when 'tis night.

We be walking arm in arm when the beer be like the barm.

We be puttin' on the piskies what we ought to on the whiskies.

We be nearin' Sticker's Plat where we soon will whip the cat.

We can see the place in sight so we'll wish thee all goodnight.

LEFT LEFT

(Back to beginning, ad infinitum)

ROLL (THE) COTTON DOWN

Solo: O 'tis ten long years since I left my home. Ch. *Roll cotton down,*

Solo: O__ ten wea-ry years since I left my home. Ch. *Roll cotton down,*

Solo: And we'll roll her up and we'll roll her down. Ch. *Roll cotton down,*

Solo: And we'll roll her up and we'll roll her down. Ch. *Roll cotton down.*

(Chorus and last two solo lines to be repeated in each verse.)

2   So I shipped aboard of a Yankee clipper.
      Now first time I sailed with a blue-nosed skipper.

3   O the mate was drunk and the skipper not sober
      And he drunk more rum till he keeled right over.

4   Now when you go to sea try a blue-nosed schooner.
      You'll pay off in hell either later or sooner.

DIDDLING SONG

1. O it's me and me bro - ther took a pick and a sho - vel

And a - we were all the lot - o,

To the hole in the wall and the hole in the wall

With the hob - nail boots your fath - er wore.

2. Dl a lod - dle dee - dle all the dee - dle all the dee - dle all the

Did - dle all the did - dle um a did - dle all a dear dol the

Lie - dle the doo, lie - dle the dear dol the

Lie - dle the dee - dle de de da dee dum.

3. Dl the lod - dle dee - dle um a dee - dle all the dee - dle um a

Did - dle all the dee - dle all the did - dle all the dear dum a

Did - dle all dum a did - dle all the dee - dle dum a

Well - a done - a girl - a when you shows good time.

4. Skip it a - way you pret - ty boys, skip it a - way your time now.

Skip it a - way you pret - ty boys skip it a - way your time now.

Skip it a - way you pret - ty boys skip it a - way your time now.

This time now you shows good time.

5. Dl the lod - dle dee - dle all the dee - dle all the dee dum

Dl the lod - dle dee - dle all the dee - dle all the dear dol a

Lid - dle all the did - dle all the dee - dle all the dear dol

Well done girl when you shows good time.

NOTES

Trotting Song (p. 50) Sung by Mrs B. Rye, Weston, Somerset. Collected by Fred Hamer, 1968.

Mrs Rye learned this song in Lancashire as a child. It is a dandling song, the child being bounced on its parent's knees in time to the melody. On the last line, where notes are indicated with a cross, the child is bounced higher and higher until the final word 'last', when the singer's knees are opened and the child falls through, to be quickly caught of course.

'Ware Out Mother (p. 50) Sung by Mrs Russell, Upwey, Dorset. Collected by H. E. D. Hammond, 1907. JFSS vol. 8, p. 217.

Just this one verse was collected. We surmise on the evidence of countless songs collected since, especially from gypsies, that this was a piece of 'tuning' for dancing, probably step dancing. It may have been followed by verses of mouth music.

A Handy Ship (p. 51) Sung by John Perring, Dartmouth, Devon. Collected by H. E. Piggot, 1912. JFSS vol. 5, p. 311.

John Perring told the collector: 'Of course I can't think of words to sing now. I am out of practice. Besides it is so different singing in a room. If I were on board with all the fellows round me I should know their names and all about them and I was a good hand at making up little rhymes which would fit in. I should think of the next verse while they were singing the chorus.' We have added a few usual verses from Stan Hugill's *Shanties from the Seven Seas.*

Dance to Thee Daddy (p. 52) Sung by Sister Emma, Clewer, Berkshire. Collected by Cecil Sharp, 1909.

Any song can provide the rhythm for bouncing a child on the knee, but, traditionally, 'Dance to Your Daddy' is associated specifically with dandling. It is better known in a longer Northumbrian version. We have made some minor alterations in verse 2. The singer evidently had the sex of the infant confused, as she sang to her bonnie laddie 'when thou art a woman fitter to be married.'

We Be (p. 52) Contributed by Mr W. W. Piper, St Austell, Cornwall. Collected by Ralph Dunstan in 1920s. Published in *Cornish Dialect and Folk Songs*, 1932, Ascherberg, Hopwood & Crew Ltd, London, reprinted 1972, Lodenek Press, Padstow, Cornwall.

Considering the rarity of English work songs, it is strange that 'We Be' has not attracted more attention. This song belonged to Cornish outworking tailors who visited farms and cottages to 'make up' clothes on the spot. According to Dunstan, 'These "Whip-the-cats" frequently travelled in company, generally on foot and enlivened their often long journeys by singing and whistling. In the workroom too they were noted for their singing and whistling of songs and hymns. To "sing like a tailor" was a mark of vocal superiority.' It was porbably a marching and working song. Clearly the verses were often improvised, and may have been endless if the trudge were a lengthy one.

Left, Left (p. 53) Current in the army in the 1914-18 war. From *Tommy's Tunes* by F. T. Nettleingham, 2nd Lt, RFC. Published by Erskine MacDonald Ltd, London 1917.

A marching song. Try marching to it!

Roll (the) Cotton Down (p. 54) Sung by Tim Walsh, retired sailor, Devonport, Devon. Collected by Cyril Tawney, and in BBC archives.

The BBC archive recording of Tim Walsh reveals a shanty singer of great stature. The performance is slow and deliberate with heavy efforts: the effect is majestic. It is originally a negro shanty although Stan Hugill cites white American, British and German versions. (*Shanties from the Seven Seas*, RKP 1961)

Diddling Song (p. 55) Sung by Caroline Hughes, a gypsy, Dorset. Collected by Ewan MacColl and Peggy Seeger 1963.

Caroline Hughes, a magnificent gypsy singer who died in 1971, sang this piece for step dancing. We reproduced Seeger and MacColl's precise notation of the music as it gives some idea of the fluidity involved even within a very strict rhythm. We hope singers will be able to make up their own 'tuning' on this basis.

SONGS OF DIVERSION

Songs of diversion include short rhymes, convivial pieces, songs in praise of drink and songs which are just fun to sing, especially when, as in 'The Game of Football', it is a feat to remember all the words. A ragbag of songs, they are disparate in origin and nearly all from recent collections.

Some have a long history. 'The Shepton Beauchamp Wassail Song', for instance, is a beautiful example of a class of songs associated with ancient ceremonies once essential to the life of the community and tied up with pre-Christian belief. The lives of one-time sacred songs such as this follow a predictable pattern. Once the old magic loses its power the ceremony and its songs live on for centuries as a kind of local sport — taken no less seriously for that, but plainly a lot tamer than their pagan ancestors.

Sometimes the songs pass into children's lore as seasonal begging pieces; sometimes the customs simply die out; and sometimes the songs live on as semi-nonsense, which has happened to many cumulative pieces. And yet something of the power of the original emerges in a good, rhythmic performance of, say, 'The Leg of the Mallard' and 'The Old Herring's Head', both no doubt forfeit songs at one time, when a forfeit had to be paid if not sung correctly!

THE GAME OF FOOTBALL

Last week for di-ver-sion, bad luck to it all, I thought I would wit-ness a game of foot-ball.

So off I went, the game to see
Along with McGurk and McGook and McGhee.
As far as I heard sure the game was set up
To play for a sort of a kind of a cup.
The clubs that were playing I hardly could name
They were What'y'may-call 'em and some other team.
To get there in time I'd to walk very smart
I arrived as the game was commencing to start.
McMann, he skeedaddled away with the ball
And nobody could take it from him at all,
Till he tumbled over some feller's foot
And for nearly ten minutes he stood on his nut.
A feller behind me shouted: Put the ball through
And he gave me a kick with his tackerty shoe.
I turned around and I gave him a whack,
I shifted his nose round the neck of his back,
Saying: Take that, you spalpeen, for I'll let you see
You're not going to make an old football of me.
Said he: What is that for? Says I: It's for you.
Said he: Take it back — and I did take it too,
For he gave me a clout, boys, he near knocked me sick,
He couldn't have hit me as hard with a brick.
But bad as I was I got nothing at all
Compared to the boys who were kicking the ball.
One feller was groaning and panting for breath
While another begged someone to put him to death.
The goalkeeper, he was a terrible wreck,
He broke both his arms, his legs and his neck.
A half dozen doctors arrived, out of puff
With bales of skin plaster and that sort of stuff.
To see the way they plastered them all
You would think they were trying to paper a wall.
There's some of them lying in hospital yet,
While others are looking for crutches to let.
But take my advice boys and take it from me
It's the last football match ever I go to see.

(Last two lines only are sung to the following tune—)

But take my ad-vice, boys, and take it from me, It's the last foot-ball match ev-er I go to see.

COME MY LADS

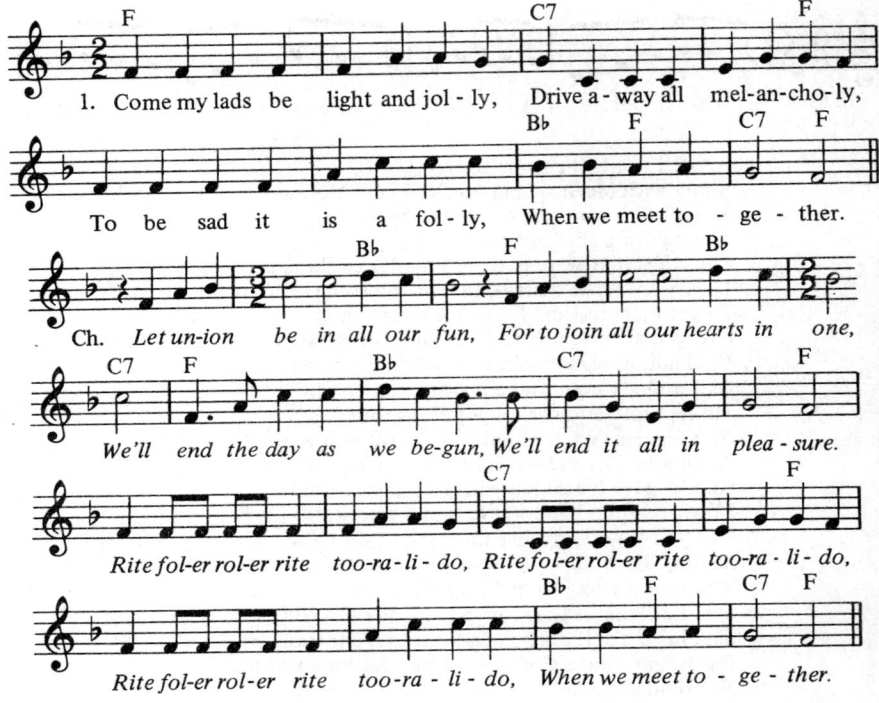

1. Come my lads be light and jol-ly, Drive a-way all mel-an-cho-ly, To be sad it is a fol-ly, When we meet to-ge-ther.

Ch. Let un-ion be in all our fun, For to join all our hearts in one, We'll end the day as we be-gun, We'll end it all in plea-sure.

Rite fol-er rol-er rite too-ra-li-do, Rite fol-er rol-er rite too-ra-li-do, Rite fol-er rol-er rite too-ra-li-do, When we meet to-ge-ther.

2 Solomon tells us in his glory,
   Tells us quite a different story,
   Tells us to be good and holy,
   When we meet together.

3 Use the bottle as it passes,
   Do not fail to fill your glasses,
   Water drinkers are dull asses,
   When they're met together.

BRIAN O'FLYNN

1. O Bri-an O'-Flynn had no trous-ers to wear,
So he bought him a sheep-skin and made him a pair
With the skin-ny side out and the fur-ry side in,
Why, sure it-'ll do, says Bri-an O'-Flynn.

Ch. It-'ll do, do, do, do, Says Bri-an O'-Flynn it-'ll do.___

2   O Brian O'Flynn had no shirt to his back
So he went to his neighbours to borrow a sack.
He puckered the meal bags under his chin.
They'll take it for ruffles, says Brian O'Flynn.

3   O Brian O'Flynn had no coat to put on
So he borrowed a goat skin to make him a one.
He planted the horns right under his chin.
They'll answer for pistols, says Brian O'Flynn.

4   O Brian O'Flynn had no watch for to wear
So he bought him a turnip and scooped it out fair
And he put him a cricket right under the skin.
They'll think it's a-ticking, says Brian O'Flynn.

5   O Brian O'Flynn and his wife and wife's mother,
They all went to sleep in the same bed together,
The bed it was small and the clothes they were thin.
Lie close to the wall, says Brian O'Flynn.

6   Brian O'Flynn and his wife and wife's mother
Were all going over the bridge together.
The bridge it broke down and they all tumbled in.
We'll find ground at the bottom, says Brian O'Flynn.

THE FORTY POUND CAR

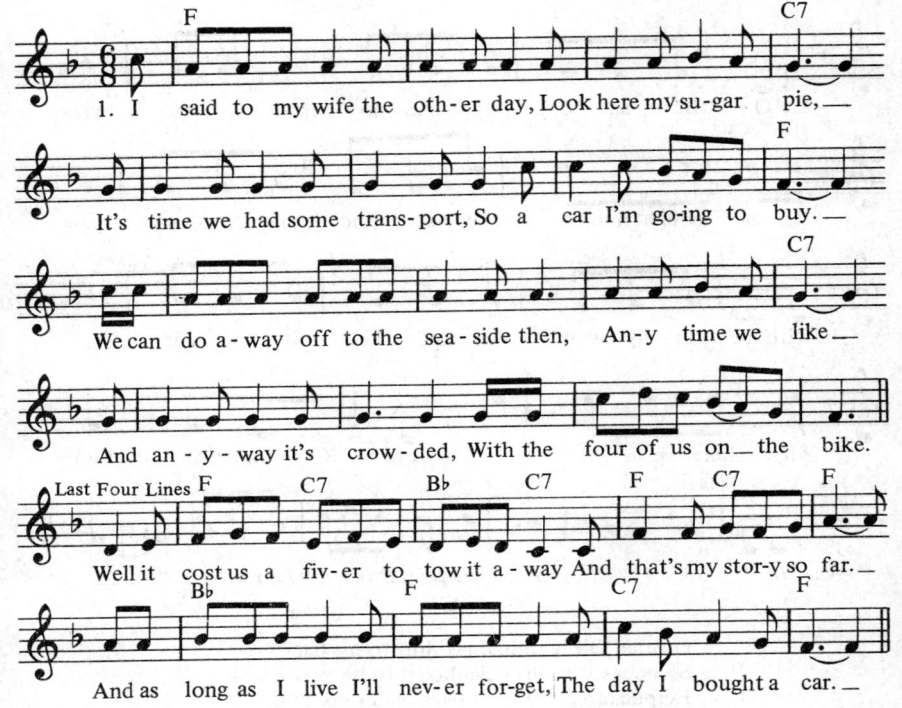

1. I said to my wife the oth-er day, Look here my su-gar pie, —
It's time we had some trans-port, So a car I'm go-ing to buy. —
We can do a-way off to the sea-side then, An-y time we like —
And an-y-way it's crow-ded, With the four of us on — the bike.
Well it cost us a fiv-er to — tow it a-way And that's my stor-y so far. —
And as long as I live I'll nev-er for-get, The day I bought a car. —

2   So I gets my money and off ah gans
Straight down to Darlington town.
I'm shouting: Fetch your motors out
'Cause I've got money down.
A fella comes up says: I've got a car,
It will suit you down to the ground,
It's taxed and tested the rest of the week,
It will cost you forty pounds.

3   Why I blew the horn
And I clashed the doors,
I waggled the starting wheel.
Kicked the tyres and revved the engine,
Ah says: Mate you've got a deal.
Pays me money, jumps straight in,
The proudest day of my life.
And I drove my forty pound car back home
To show off to the wife.

4   Why she comes out and glowered at it,
I'll not ride in that thing.
The two front doors are hanging off
And the back 'uns tied up with string.
Ah said: Shut your face, get yourself in
And tell us how it feels.
She says: It's like a corned beef tin
That's been fixed up with wheels.

5   Then my marra comes up all poppely-eyed
And he stands and he looks and he laughs.
He says: I can see the marks on the front
Where the fella's sawn off the shafts.
And who was the previous owner? he says,
To me that car looks queer.
I looked in the book and then ah sees
Some body called Bodicea.

6   But we puts up some bait and all jumped in
As happy as can be.
With three grit bangs and a cloud of smoke
We sets away for the sea.
We flew away past Hope House
And up past the Bird In The Hand.
And apart from the bangs and the clouds of smoke
The car was gannin' grand.

7   But the Mother-In-Law fell out of the back
As we went past Wyniard Road.
And the polis gave us a ticket
For an insecure load.
And another for having no mudguards on
And another for giving him lip.
He says: Do yourself a favour mate,
Bool it over the tip.

8   Then the car wouldn't start and try as I may
I just couldn't get it to gan.
And the missus says: Why Berty
Go and get the AA man.
He took a look and he shook his head,
He says it's had its day.
You'd better go and get Norman Hitch
To come and tow it away.

9   So I goes to the phone and I gives him a ring
It's Sedgefield 189.
He says: Don't go away, stay where you are
I'll be there any time.
I said: What'll you give us to tow it away?
He looked with a bit of a smile.
Me pay you? It's you pay me,
Fifty bob a mile.

10   Well it cost us a fiver to tow it away
And that's my story so far.
And as long as ah live I'll never forget
The day I bought a car.

SHEPTON BEAUCHAMP WASSAIL SONG— 1

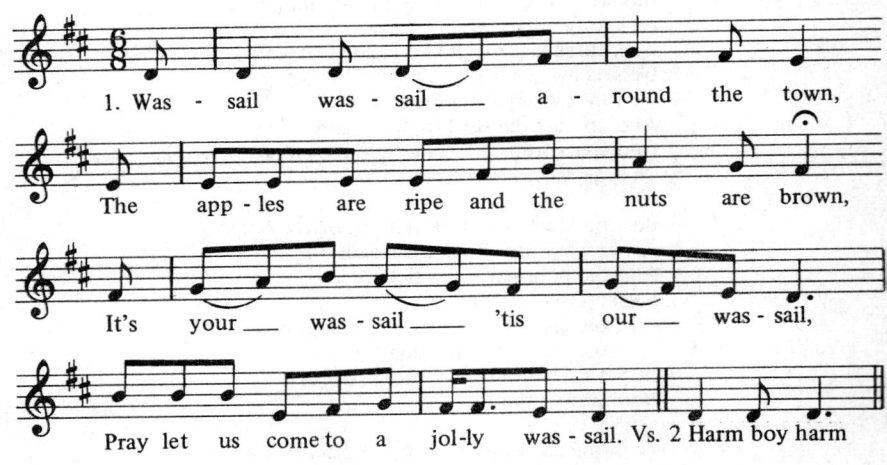

1. Was - sail was - sail ___ a - round the town,
The app - les are ripe and the nuts are brown,
It's your ___ was - sail ___ 'tis our ___ was - sail,
Pray let us come to a jol-ly was - sail. Vs. 2 Harm boy harm

2   There was an old man he had an old cow,
How to keep it he didn't know how,
He built up a barn to keep himself warm
And a cup of good liquor will do him no harm.
Harm boy harm.

3   Apple tree apple tree bear and bough,
This year and next year and all the year round,
It's apples and capfulls and three corned apples,
Pray let us come to our jolly wassail.

SHEPTON BEAUCHAMP WASSAIL SONG— 2

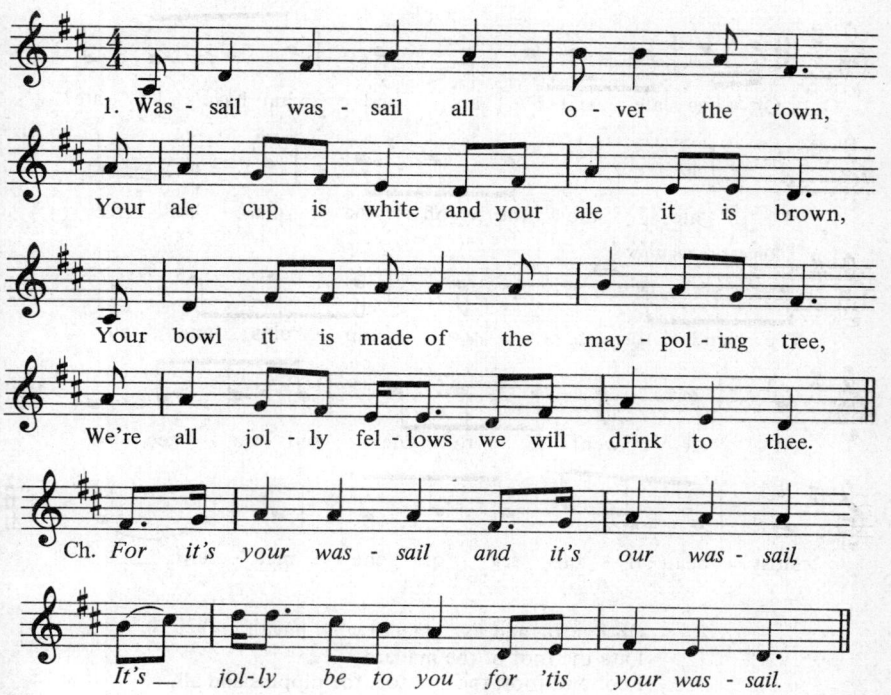

1. Was - sail was - sail all o - ver the town,

Your ale cup is white and your ale it is brown,

Your bowl it is made of the may - pol - ing tree,

We're all jol - ly fel - lows we will drink to thee.

Ch. *For it's your was - sail and it's our was - sail,*

It's __ jol-ly be to you for 'tis your was - sail.

2 And to the mare and to her right eye
 God send our Misses an old Christmas pie,
 An old Christmas pie as ever I did see,
 A wassailing bowl we will drink to thee.

3 And to the apell and to her long tail
 God pray that our Master he never will fail.
 A cup of good beer I pray draw near
 And a jolly wassail we all will be here.

4 Come butler come bring us a bowl of the best,
 Then I hope that your soul in heaven will rest.
 But if you do bring us a bowl of the small,
 Then down goes the butler the bowl and all.

 (To second half of tune)

 Misses and master sitting by the fire
 While we poor travellers go travelling the mire.

65

THE LEG OF THE MALLARD

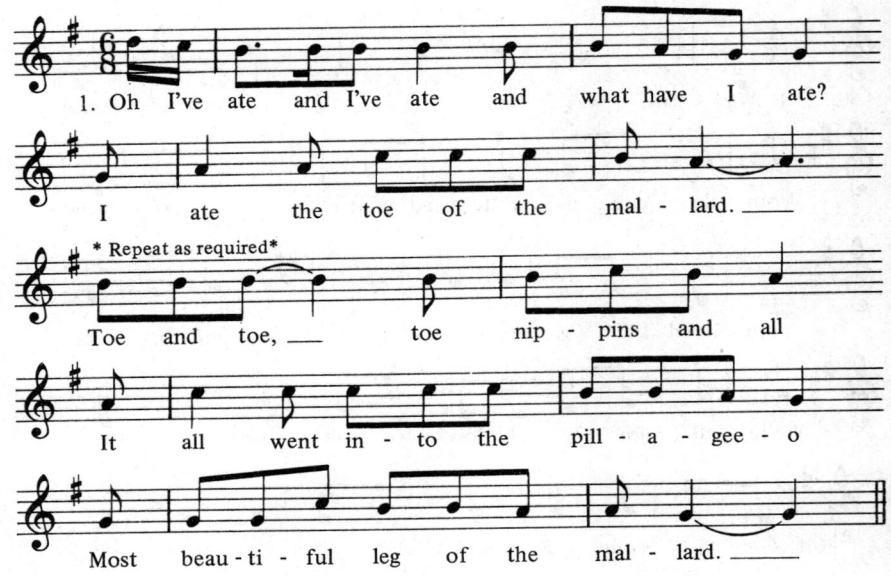

2   Oh I've ate and I've ate and what have I ate?
I ate the foot of the mallard.
Foot and foot, toe and toe, toe nippins and all,
It all went into the pillagee-o,
Most beautiful leg of the mallard.

(Cumulative formula remains throughout.)

3   Leg of the mallard

4   Thigh of the mallard

5   Side of the mallard

6   Back of the mallard

7   Wing of the mallard

8   Breast of the mallard

9   Neck of the mallard

10   Head of the mallard

11   Bill of the mallard

THE EXMOOR RAM

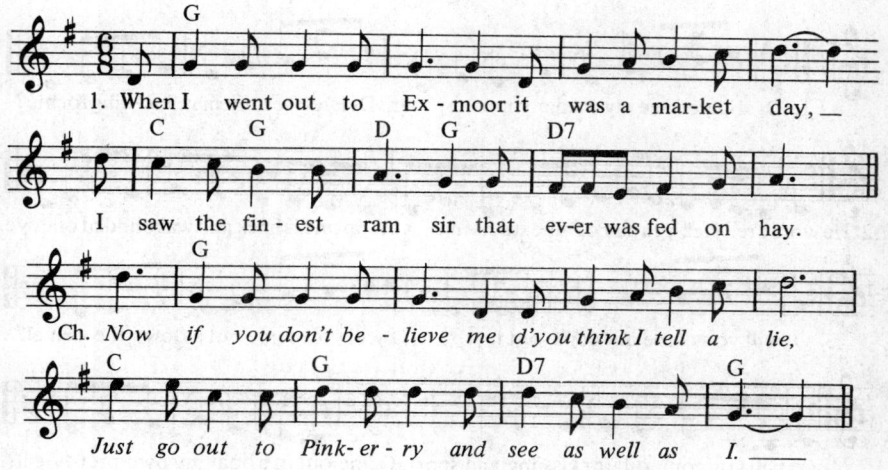

1. When I went out to Ex-moor it was a mar-ket day, —
I saw the fin-est ram sir that ev-er was fed on hay.
Ch. *Now if you don't be-lieve me d'you think I tell a lie,*
Just go out to Pink-er-ry and see as well as I. —

2 Now this ram it had two horns that went up to the moon.
 Two men went up in January and never came down till June.

3 Now this ram it had four feet, four feet you understand
 And every time it put them down it covered an acre of land.

4 Now this ram it had two eyes, they were so large and round
 That all the girls in Barnstaple kicked them round the town.

5 Now this ram it had such wool, it was so very thick
 For the eagles built their nests in it for I heard the young ones squeak.

6 Now this ram it had a tail, it reached four miles and an ell
 And we sent it over to New York to pull the parish bell.

7 The butcher who killed that ram he was up to his neck in blood
 And four and twenty butcher boys was washed away in the flood.

8 Now the man who owned that ram, he was so very rich
 And the boy that sang the song was a lying son of a bitch.

9 Now when my dear old ram died I took it to St Paul's
 And it took two·men and an elephant to carry one of his. . . .

(The last verse is what is known to folklorists as a "suspended chain" —
i.e. a word is avoided by going straight into the chorus.)

DID YOU SEE MY MAN?

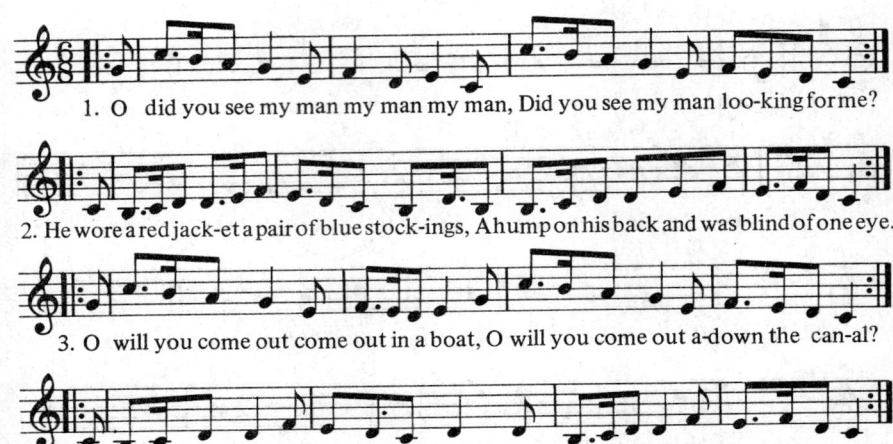

1. O did you see my man my man my man, Did you see my man loo-king for me?

2. He wore a red jack-et a pair of blue stock-ings, A hump on his back and was blind of one eye.

3. O will you come out come out in a boat, O will you come out a-down the can-al?

4. O will you come out for kiss-ing and sport, Come out in a boat my own pret-ty gal?

STEVINGTON MAY CAROL

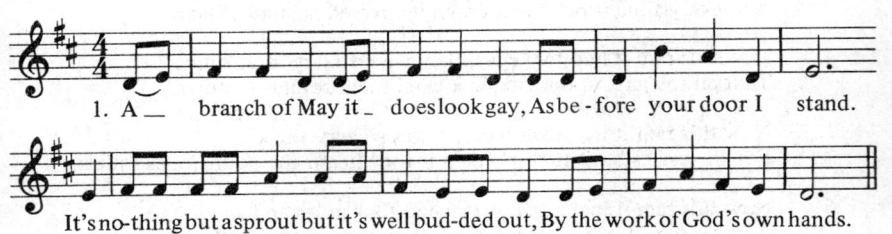

1. A — branch of May it — does look gay, As be-fore your door I stand.

It's no-thing but a sprout but it's well bud-ded out, By the work of God's own hands.

2   I have a bag within my hand,
    'Tis drawn with a silken string.
    And all I ask is a little silver
    To line it well within.

3   Give me a cup of your cook's cream,
    A bowl of your brown beer,
    And if I live to tarry round the town
    I'll call on you next year.

4   The clock struck one, I must be gone
    Bid you all good day.
    God bless you all both great and small,
    We wish you a happy May.

(From Miss Marion Field. Her mother added another verse, said to be the first verse—)

I've been a-rambling all night long,
The best part of the day.
Now we have returned back again
We've brought you a branch of May.

BLESS THIS HOUSE

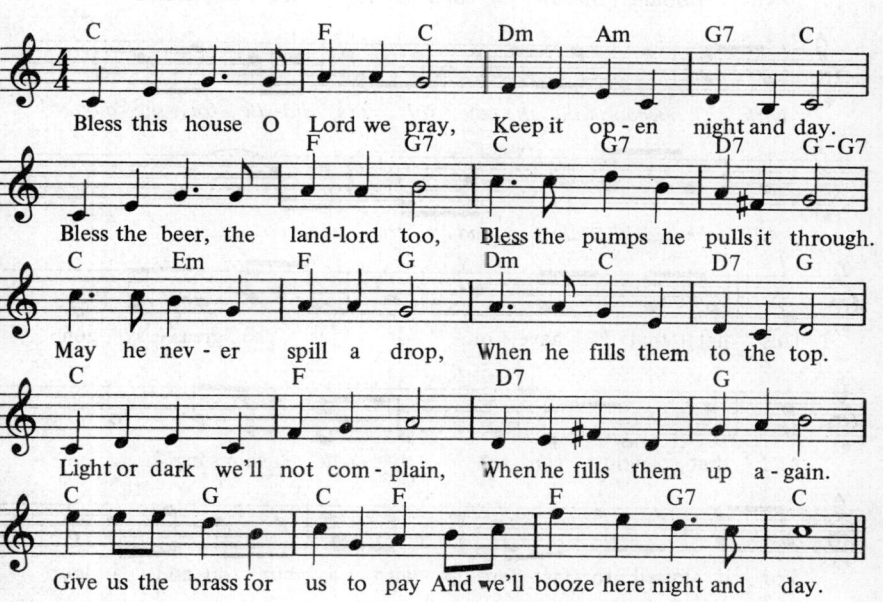

Bless this house O Lord we pray, Keep it op-en night and day.
Bless the beer, the land-lord too, Bless the pumps he pulls it through.
May he nev-er spill a drop, When he fills them to the top.
Light or dark we'll not com-plain, When he fills them up a-gain.
Give us the brass for us to pay And we'll booze here night and day.

ALL THROUGH THE ALE

Ch. All through the ale, the con-foun-ded ale,
All through the ale and to-bac-co.
With a whack fol the day fol the did-dle fol the day,
All through the ale and to-bac-co.
1. This hat that I have on, it is so grea-sy gone
And that you can tell by its shin-ing.
For it used to fas-ten up with a but-ton and a loop
But now it's all wore out to the lin-ing. Ch. And it's ...

2   This coat that I have on, it is so far run down,
     It's out at the sleeves and the elbow.
     It's needing of repair like a soldier in despair
     That's been seven years in the battle.

3   The breeches I put on, they are so poor run down,
     My legs you can plainly see them.
     Pockets I have two but it's long since they were new.
     I never have a farthing to put in them.

4 Stockings I have two, long since they were new,
The boots they are open to all weathers.
I have pulled them off and on till the undersole is gone
And shockingly destroyed the upper leathers.

5 As for me rags, I don't give a jag,
I'm not afraid that anyone will rob me.
And when I am dead you can put it on me grave,
I left the old world as it found me.

VERY GOOD SONG

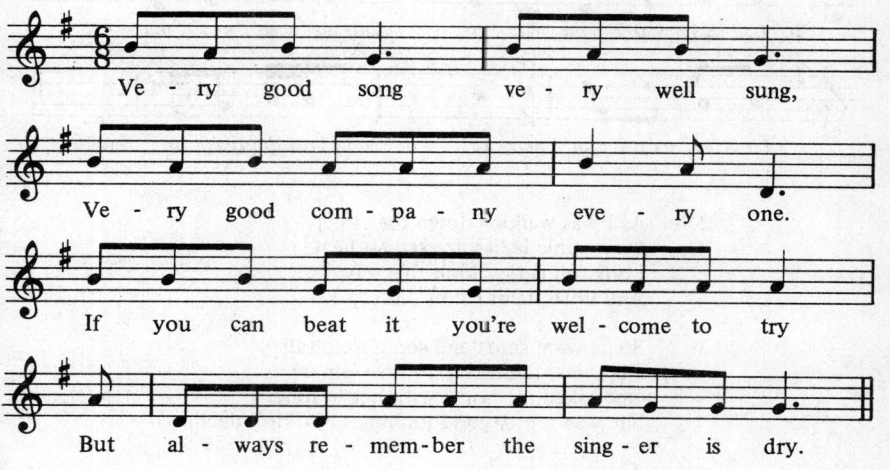

Ve - ry good song ve - ry well sung,

Ve - ry good com - pa - ny eve - ry one.

If you can beat it you're wel - come to try

But al - ways re - mem - ber the sing - er is dry.

LADIES WON'T YOU MARRY?

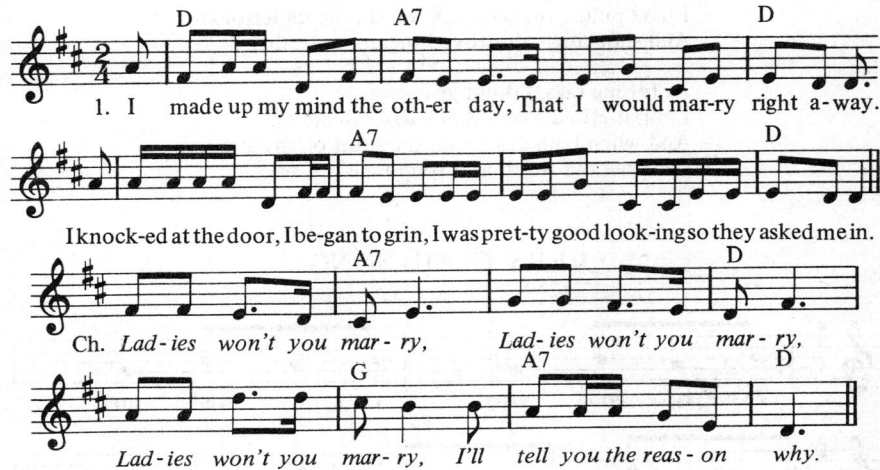

1. I made up my mind the oth-er day, That I would mar-ry right a-way.
I knock-ed at the door, I be-gan to grin, I was pret-ty good look-ing so they asked me in.
Ch. Lad-ies won't you mar-ry, Lad-ies won't you mar-ry,
Lad-ies won't you mar-ry, I'll tell you the reas-on why.

2   As I was walking down the street
I saw some ladies dressed so neat.
Look, oh ladies, look this way
And unto them I thus did say.

3   Some were short and some were tall
God bless their hearts I love 'em all.
One asked me home with her to dine.
She was pretty good looking so I didn't decline.

(Spoken)

Ladies and gentlemen. Of course I could not refuse her invitation as I felt very hungry. But talk about a dinner! By God, that was a twister! And no two ways about it, mother!

Now I'll tell you what we had for dinner. We had cocoa, nuts and onion sauce, boiled beef and oranges, turkey and rhubarb tart, birds and pickles, goose and geese, meat and mutton, sprats and fish, roast pork and watercress, cod-liver-oil and cheese.

Then came the dessert. They had shrimps, apples, whelks, nuts, pears, and pipes of 'bacca.

Now I'll tell you who was invited to this dinner. There was Rosie Anna, Clarie Anna, Sally Weaver, Betsy Squeaver, Humpty-Back Sue, Screw-Mouth Poll, they were the ladies.

There was Dandy Jim, Jealous Bill, Poppysquash, Uncle Jess, and Old Sam Johnson. He was master of the quality.

Lor, I shall never forget that day. When they all arranged themselves round the room, and they pitched out in a dance—

O Ladies won't you marry,
Ladies won't you marry,
Ladies won't you marry,
I'll tell you the reason why.

Because they don't like babies,
Because they don't like babies,
Because they don't like babies,
And that's the reason why.

ODE TO THE RAF

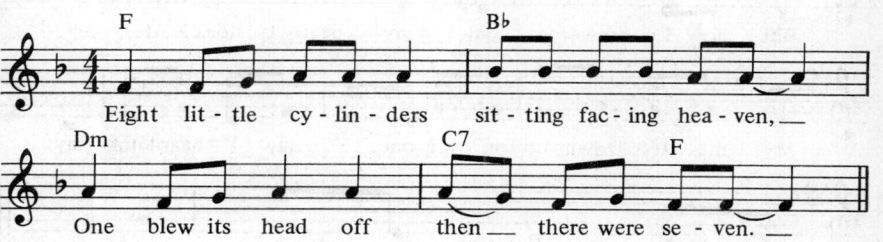

Eight lit - tle cy - lin - ders sit - ting fac - ing hea - ven, ___
One blew its head off then ___ there were se - ven. ___

Seven little cylinders used to playing tricks,
One warped its inlet valve, then there were six.
Six little cylinders working all alive,
One got a sooted plug, then there were five.
Five little cylinders working all the more,
One overworked itself, then there were four.
Four little cylinders flying o'er the sea,
One shed a piston ring, then there were three.
Three little cylinders wondering what to do,
One over-oiled itself, then there were two.
Two little cylinders very nearly done,
One broke a valve stem, then there was one.
One little cylinder trying to pull round seven,
At length gave its efforts up and ascended into heaven.

POOR OLD HORSE

1. My cloth-ing was of the lin-sey wool-sey fine,
My tail it grew at length my— coat did like-wise shine,
But now I'm grow-ing old my beau-ty does_ de-cay,
My mas-ter frowns up-on me one_ day I heard him say:
Poor old horse poor old horse.

2 Once I was kept in the stable snug and warm
To keep my tender limbs from any cold or harm.
But now in open fields I am forced for to go
In all sorts of weather let it be hail rain freeze or snow.
Poor old horse poor old horse.

3 Once I was fed on the very best corn and hay
That ever grew in yon fields or in yon meadow gay.
But now there's no such doing can I find at all,
I'm glad to pick the green sprouts that grow behind yon wall.
Poor old horse poor old horse.

4 You are old you are cold you are deaf dull dumb and slow,
You are not fit for anything or in my team to draw,
You have eaten all my hay you have spoiled all my straw,
So hang him whip him stick him to the huntsman let him go.
Poor old horse poor old horse.

5 My hide unto the tanners then I would freely give,
My body to the hound dog I would rather die than live,
Likewise my poor old bones they have carried you many a mile
Over hedges ditches brooks and bridges likewise gates and stiles.
Poor old horse poor old horse.

THE OLD HERRING'S HEAD

1. Now what shall we do with old her-ring's head?
Make 'em in loaves and sell 'em for bread.
* (Repeat as required)
For 'tis her - ring's head and loaves of bread,
And all such things as that.
For of all the fish that live in the sea
The her - ring is the fish for me.
Ch. Ri - fol-lol lad - de - dee Ri - fol-lol la - de - dee
Ri - fol - lol lad - de - dee - o.

2   Now what shall we do with old herring's eyes?
Make 'em in puddings and sell 'em for pies.
For 'tis herring's eyes, and puddings and pies,
Herring's head, and loaves of bread,
And all such things as that.
For of all the fish that live in the sea
The herring is the fish for me.

(Cumulative formula remains throughout.)

3   Now what shall we do with old herring's fins?
Make 'em in needles and sell 'em for pins.

4   Now what shall we do with old herring's back?
Make 'em in boys and call 'em Jack.

5   Now what shall we do with old herring's belly?
Make 'em in girls and call 'em Nelly.

6   Now what shall we do with old herring's tail?
Make 'em in ships and set 'em a-sail.

NOTES

The Game of Football (p. 59) Sung by Mary Duffy, Stockton-on-Tees, Cleveland. Collected by Fred Hamer, 1968.

Mary Duffy's father, from whom she learnt most of her songs, came from Glasgow and her Irish ancestry may explain one or two Irish words here. We do not know this song from elsewhere but it sings particularly well, with a relaxed light effort and well-defined rhythm (as the singer sang it, in fact).

Come my Lads (p. 60) Sung by Mrs F. Lowry, South Brent, Devon. Collected by Dave Lowry, 1969.

This song was twice noted by Baring-Gould in the 1880s, and also appears in *Folk Songs of the Upper Thames* where Alfred Williams disparages it as 'a second-rate drinking song'. It's a typical convivial piece — a little high-flown, with a Biblical reference thrown in, and influenced by hymn and glee singing. The point of the song, though, is that it is good to join in. The collector heard it from his grandmother, a native of Ivybridge, near Plymouth.

Brian O'Flynn (p. 61) Sung by Mrs Todd, Chesterfield, Derby. Collected by Fred Hamer, 1960s.

The theme of this song can be traced back to the middle of the 16th century. It originated as a satire on the roughness of the Scots, but changed during the centuries Many versions have been found in Britain and North America — 'Tom Bolin', 'Harry Trewin', 'Tom o' the Lynn' — and scraps have even appeared in nursery rhyme collections. The hero's imperturbable optimism and inventiveness still have immense appeal.

The Forty Pound Car (p. 62) By Bert Draycott, Fishburn, Cleveland. Written in 1974.

Bert Draycott, a coal miner, won the folksong writing competition at Newcastle Festival in 1975 with this song. He says: 'I wrote it after working for a secondhand car dealer for a year's part-time when pay wasn't so good. I got to know a few sharky dealers. . . . ' The tune is more or less 'Wor Nanny's a Maizor', the Tommy Armstrong classic, and Bert Draycott's words follow closely in the Armstrong tradition.

Shepton Beauchamp Wassail Song Parts 1 and 2 (p. 64-5) Sung by Eddie Cornelius, Shepton Beauchamp, Somerset. Collected by Bob Patten, 1977.

The singer sang both parts, which he called the verses, as one song, pitching accurately throughout. The Shepton Beauchamp Wassail died out in 1948. The singer, 84 when recorded, remembered it as a visiting wassail taken around by four singers and a melodeon on old Christmas Eve (January 5th). Bob Patten contributes the following comments: 'Part 1 is a degenerate version of a typical visiting song used in South Somerset. . . . Part 2 has worried me ever since I recorded it. The words and the tempo don't belong to the south Somerset visiting wassail tradition. I think the answer to the tempo problem lies in the fact that it was accompanied by a melodeon — it's just the right sort of tune for a squeezebox. Considering that it was sung out of doors in mid-winter and the amount of booze consumed it is likely to end up as it did. This may also explain the unusual syncopation in line 1 of Part 2 (p. 65). 'Beauchamp', by the way, is pronounced 'Beecham'.

The Leg of the Mallard (p. 66) Sung by Henry Mitchemore, Broadhempston, Devon. Collected by Sam Richards and Tish Stubbs, 1972.

This bit of ancient magic, now a forfeit song, has been particularly popular in the West Country, although it has been found further afield. It was mangled by Baring-Gould in the 1880s. He said of it: 'A country dance tune, so called because of some silly words that go to it relative to the gobbling up of a mallard', yet in our opinion his version was scarcely an improvement! The dismembering of a magical animal, often a bird, is a well-known ritual, applied also in English songs to the wren, the herring, and the old Derby ram. Nowadays cumulative songs are often sung for sheer virtuosity, speed being important, although the measured, deliberate performances usually recorded from traditional singers hold more of the old mystery.

The Exmoor Ram (p. 67) Sung by 'Nobby' Clarke, Swimbridge, Devon. Collected by Sam Richards and Paul Wilson, 1976.

This version of 'The Derby Ram' is localized to North Devon. Pinkery Pond, at one time, had the reputation of being bottomless, as well as having other mysterious connotations. Maybe local singers appreciated the idea that Pinkery was hardly the place at which to affirm the truth.

Did You See My Man? (p. 68) Printed in *A Garland of Country Song*. Collected and arranged by Sabine Baring-Gould and H. Fleetwood Sheppard, Methuen & Co., London, 1895.

A song of diversion for children, Baring-Gould says that he learnt it from his nursemaid. It works well as a dandling song.

Stevington May Carol (p. 68) Sung by Marion Field, Stevington, Bedfordshire. Collected by Fred Hamer, 1965.

May 1st has been a time for celebration from the most ancient times to the present. This song is a typical visiting song. The carollers would display their May garland, sing their song and be rewarded with food, drink, or money at all the houses in the town.

Bless This House (p. 69) Written and sung by Walter Wheeler, a coal miner, Methley, Yorkshire. Collected by A. E. Green, 1966. In the archives of the Institute of Dialect and Folk Life Studies, Leeds University.

It was inevitable that someone would transfer the blessing in the well-known original of this parody to that ubiquitous institution, the British pub.

All Through the Ale (p. 70) Sung by Mrs Smedley, Matlock, Derbyshire. Collected by Roy Harris, 1965.

This song shows how many moods can be wrung out of one simple idea. There are slow, wistful versions, boozy versions, melancholy and bawdy ones. We have encountered it as an excuse for a male striptease, once in Essex, once in Devon. Mrs Smedley's Derbyshire version is a gem. The nearest we have seen to it is one verse found in Wiltshire by Alfred Williams, published without a tune in *Folk Songs of the Upper Thames*, 1923.

Very Good Song (p. 71) Sung by Jack Hunt, Ivybridge, Devon. Collected by Sam Richards, Tish Stubbs and Paul Wilson, 1974.

In 1859 William Chappell briefly referred to this verse as being sung to the first part of 'Lilliburlero', so it must be of some vintage. Jack Hunt used it when singing to indicate it was time for a rest.

Ladies Won't You Marry? (p. 72) Sung and spoken by Harry Green, Tiltey, Essex. Collected by Fred Hamer, 1967.

93 year-old Harry Green delivered this aimiable piece of nonsense with energy worthy of a much younger man. This song may be derived from broadside poets who were fond of strings of nonsense. We can't help thinking, though, that we heard something similar in the school playground.

Ode to the RAF (p. 73) From *Tommy's Tunes* by F. T. Nettleingham 2nd Lt, RFC, Erskine MacDonald Ltd, London 1917.

This clever piece from the First World War introduced a well-tried traditional formula into the 20th century.

Poor Old Horse (p. 74) Sung by Mr Barber, Westmorland Festival. Collected by Frank Kidson, exact date not given. Printed in JFSS vol. 2, p. 260-1.

Broadside ballad, ritual song, and nursery song, this peice was associated with a Christmas visiting custom in which the skull of a horse, painted red and black, was carried from house to house. A form of mumming play was enacted and this song was sung. It has, however, often been collected to be sung without any ritual. Like Tom Pearce's old grey mare, it seems to have connections with ancient horse-head cults. Kidson's tune is particularly good.

The Old Herring's Head (p. 75) Sung by Bill 'Pop' Hingston, Dittisham, Devon. Collected by Sam Richards and Tish Stubbs, April 1978.

OUTWITTING SONGS

Just a few songs in this section, but they do represent a definite group in the traditional repertoire. Tales of outwitting abound in folk narrative. Indeed it's an ancient theme, found in countless stories of gods trying to outmagic each other. These songs are more life-size, although magic does appear in 'The Broomfield Hill', but for the rest it's a battle of earthly wits.

It is important to note the backgrounds against which these contests take place. In the outwitting narrative a comment is made on a more general situation. The young women who win out against highwaymen, rakes or randy gentlemen cut their assailants down to size by leaving them looking ridiculous. Likewise, the almost penniless hero of 'The Penny Wager' leaves the listener chuckling about his victory over the high-class gentlemen he encounters over a game of dice; the wife receives her just deserts in 'The Old Woman in Yorkshire'. Some of these songs could have been included elsewhere, but here it is the jest, not the background, that is important.

As ever, the folksong is on the side of the underdog. We know of no outwitting narratives, spoken or sung, in which the poor chap, the young woman, henpecked spouse, or harassed labourer comes off worst.

THE PEAR TREE

1. Now me and two oth-er boys went on a spree.

On our way we met a pear tree.

Up this pear tree I did climb

For to get some pears I felt in - clined.

Ch. *To me ay me oh, me am - mer like a dais - y,*

Why fol de did - dle to me why fol de day.

2 When up this pear tree I'd got landed
The other two lads from me they'd squandered.
It was not the pears that pleased me,
But a man and a woman came under the tree.

3 Now with sweet kisses he embraced her,
Swore for many a mile he'd chased her,
Pulled off his coat to save her gown,
And he gently sits this fair maid down.

4 Now I shook this pear tree just like thunder.
The man and the woman ran away in wonder.
It was not the pears that pleased me,
But a damn good coat left under this tree.

5 Now off to town I ran like fire,
The owner of the coat being my desire.
The owner of the coat were never found out,
So I got a damn good coat for nowt.

6 Come all ye lads where ever you may be,
Never go a-courting under a pear tree.
Never pull your coat off to save her gown,
For the pears they will come tumbling down.

THE BROOMFIELD HILL

1. It's of a young squi-re who rode out one day
By chance his la-dy love did meet.
'Twas down in the lane that led to Broom-field Hill
With these words his la-dy love did greet.

2   A wager, a wager with you pretty maid,
      My one hundred pounds to your ten,
    That a maid you shall go into yonder green broom
      But a maid you shall never return.

3   A wager, a wager with you kind sir,
      Your one hundred pounds to my ten,
    That a maid I shall go into yonder green broom
      And a maid I shall boldly return.

4   And when she arrived down in yonder green broom
      She found her love fast asleep,
    Dressed in fine silken hose with a new suit of clothes
      And a bunch of green broom at his feet.

5   Then nine times did she go to the soles of his feet,
       Nine times to the crown of his head,
    And nine times she kissed his cherry red lips,
       As he lay on his green mossy bed.

6   Then she took a gold ring from off her hand
       And placed it on his right thumb.
    And that was to let her true love to know
       That his lady had been there and gone.

7   Then nine times did she go to the crown of his head,
       Nine times to the soles of his feet,
    And nine times she kissed his cherry red lips,
       As he lay on the ground fast asleep.

8   And when he awoke from out of his sleep
       'Twas then that he counted the cost,
    For he knew that his true love had been there and gone
       And he thought of the wager he had lost.

9   He called three times for his horse and his man
       The horse that he bought so dear,
    Saying: Why didn't you wake me out of my sleep
       When my lady my true love was here?

10   O master I called unto you three times
       And three times I blew on my horn,
    But I could not wake you from out of your sleep
       Till your lady your true love had gone.

11   Farewell and adieu to her loved one in gloom.
       Farewell to the birds on Broomfield Hill.
    A maid she did go into yonder green broom
       And a maid she remains for ever still.

YOUNG MAIDENHEAD

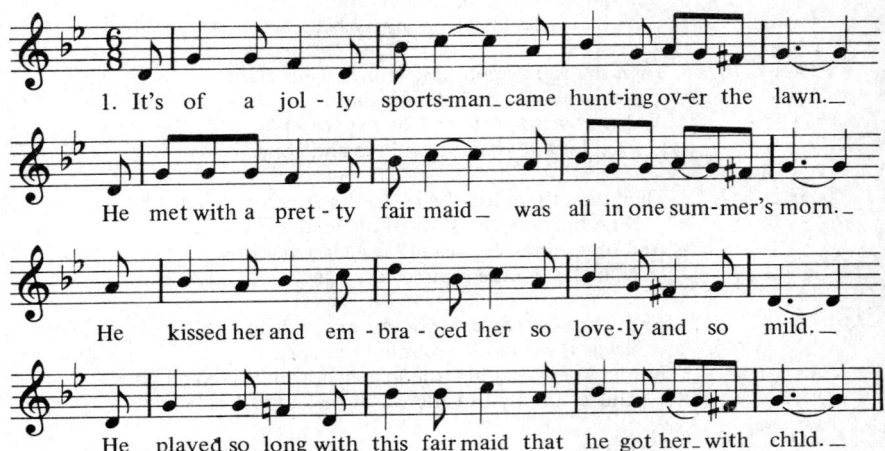

1. It's of a jol-ly sports-man came hunt-ing ov-er the lawn.
He met with a pret-ty fair maid was all in one sum-mer's morn.
He kissed her and em-bra-ced her so love-ly and so mild.
He played so long with this fair maid that he got her with child.

2 When nine months were over this girl was put to bed
And with a handsome child which she christened Maidenhead.
Her mother loudly scolded her and in a passion fell
And sent her up to London her Maidenhead to sell.

3 Then she bought horse and hamper and likewise cherries red
And in one of those hampers she placed her Maidenhead.
And like a buxom daughter so handsome she did ride
Till she met with another sportsman down by the greenwood side.

4 This sportsman fell in love with her and said: My pretty maid
Here's forty guineas I'll give to you for this and your maidenhead
And what you have in your hampers I'll have when I comes to town.
That's a bargain sir, replied the girl, come pay the money down.

5 When he came unto the inn he called for wine galore,
He called for a witness all for to view his store.
He called for a witness to view his cherries red.
Here's forty guineas I gave this girl for this and her maidenhead.

6 He searched the other hamper and then he found the child.
Oh then he stamped and swore just like a man that was wild.
He swore it was a cheat and the bargain should not stand.
You might kiss my foot, replied the girl, the money is in my hand.

7 Oh when you bought my maidenhead you bought it off me fair.
The child was christened Maidenhead and you have got it there.
But if to some justice you do go a laughing stock you'll be,
So I pray take up your Maidenhead and dance it on your knee.

8   Oh now I am outwitted all by a beauty bright
      For I did mean the other thing, to lie with you all night.
      If this is buying maidenheads oh I never will buy any more
      For I have bought a maidenhead and now I repent full sore.

THE OLD WOMAN IN YORKSHIRE

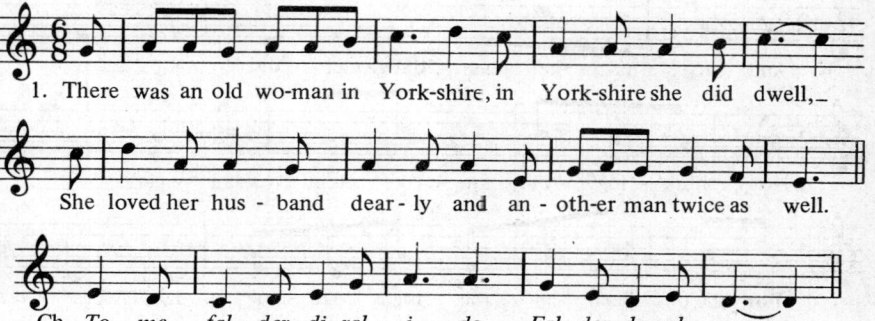

1. There was an old wo-man in York-shire, in York-shire she did dwell,—
She loved her hus-band dear-ly and an-oth-er man twice as well.
Ch. To me fal-der-di-ral-i-do, Fal-der-do-ral-a.——

2   She went unto the doctor to see what she could find,
      To know what was the very best thing to make her husband blind.

3   You get a stone of marrowbones and make him eat them all
      And after he has eaten them he'll not see nowt at all.

4   She bought a stone of marrowbones and made him eat them all.
      The old man said: I am so blind I can't see nowt at all.

5   The old man broken-hearted, he unto her did say:
      I'm sure that I would drown myself if I could find the way.

6   If you will go and drown yourself and that without delay
      If you will go and drown yourself then I'll show you the way.

7   So they both went hand in hand unto the river's brim.
      The old man wouldn't drown himself unless she shoved him in.

8   So she stepped back a yard or two to push him o'er the brim.
      The old man quickly stepped aside and she went tumbling in.

9   Good Lord O she did holler, good Lord O she did bawl.
      The old man said: I am so blind I can't see nowt at all.

10   She swam until she floated unto the river's brim.
      The old man took his walking stick and shoved her further in.

11   So now my song is ended and what do ye all think?
      He is a damned poor singer if he doesn't earn a drink.

THE FARMER IN LEICESTER

1. For there was an old far-mer in Leice-ster
And to mar-ket his daugh-ter did go,
Not think-ing of an-y great dan-ger
For she'd been on the high road be-fore.

2   She met with a bold young robber.
Six chambers he drew from his breast,
Saying money and clothing I ask for
And then you may die in disgrace.

3   He stripped the young lady stark naked
And he gave her the bridle to hold.
And there she stood shivering and shaking
And freezing to death by the cold.

4   She put her left foot in the stirrup
And she mounted his horse like a man.
Over hedges and ditches she galloped,
Saying: Catch me bold rogue if you can.

5   She rode to the gates of her father
And she shouted all over the farm,
Saying: Father I've been in great danger
But the rogue he has done me no harm.

6   She put the grey mare in the stable
And she laid a white sheet on the floor
And she counted her money twice over.
She had five thousand pound there or more.

THE PENNY WAGER

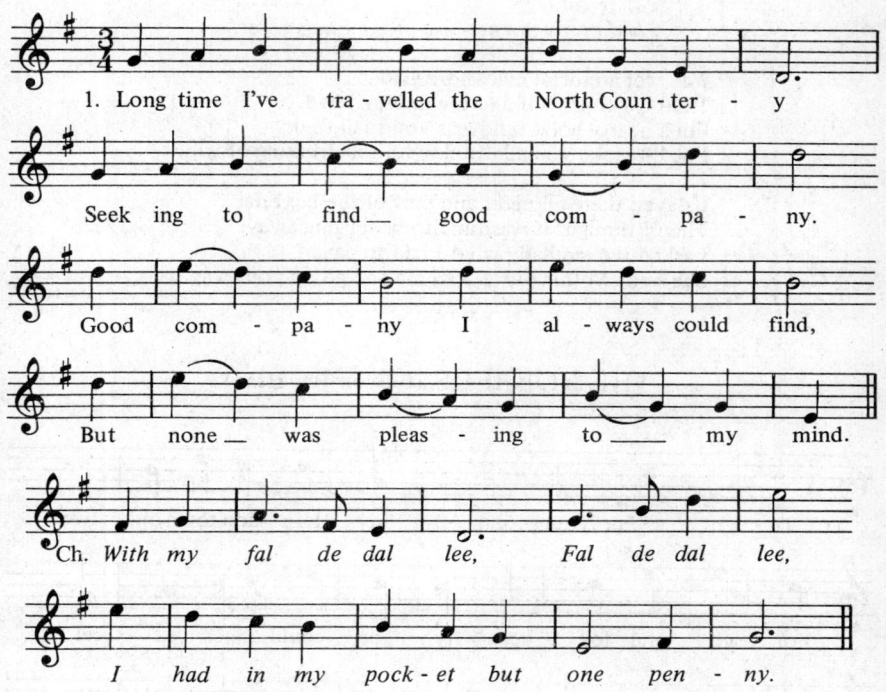

1. Long time I've tra-velled the North Coun-ter-y
Seek ing to find — good com-pa-ny.
Good com-pa-ny I al-ways could find,
But none — was pleas-ing to — my mind.
Ch. With my fal de dal lee, Fal de dal lee,
I had in my pock-et but one pen-ny.

2 I saddled my horse and away I did ride
  Till I come to an alehouse beside the roadside.
  I called for a pint of good ale that was brown
  And along with it I took myself and sat down.

3 I saw three gentlemen playing at dice.
  I took them to be some noble knights.
  They were at play and I looking on.
  They took me to be some nobleman.

4 They asked of me if I would play.
  I asked of them what bets would they lay.
  One said a guinea and I said five pound.
  The bets they were laid but no money put down.

5 I took up the dice and I gave them a spin.
  It happened to be my good luck for to win.
  If they had a-won and I had a-lost,
  I should have had to have pawned my little grey horse.

With my fal de dal lee,
Fal de dal lee,
I had in my pocket now five pounds three.

6   Was ever a mortal man more glad
       Than I with myself and the money I had.
       I'm a hearty good fellow as you shall find
       For I'll make you all drunk with the drinking of wine.

7   I stayed there all night and part of the next day.
       Then I thought it was time to be jogging away.
       I asked the landlady what I had to pay.
       She said: Nothing love, kiss me and go on your way.

THE ROBBERS (Box on Her Head)

1. 'Tis of a fair young dam-sel in Lon-don town did dwell,
For wit and for beau-ty none could her ex-cel.
Her mas-ter and her mist-ress she ser-ved se-ven years o
And what fol-lowed af-ter you quick-ly shall hear.

2   She put her box upon her head and gang-ed along.
       The first one she met was an able-bodied man.
       Says he: My pretty fair maid where are you going this way,
       I'll show you a nearer road across the counterie.

3   He took her by the hand and led her to a lane
       And says: My pretty fair maid I mean to tell you plain.
       Deliver up your money with neither fear nor strife o
       Or else this very moment I'll take your sweet life.

4   The tears from her eyes like two fountains did flow
Saying where shall I wander or where shall I go?
And while this young robber was feeling for his knife o
This beautiful young damsel she takes away his life.

5   She put her box upon her head and gang-ed along.
The next one she met was a noble gentleman.
Says he: My pretty fair maid where are you going so late o
And what was that noise that I heard at yonder gate?

6   Your box upon your head to yourself do not belong.
To your master or mistress you have done something wrong.
To your master or mistress you have done something ill o
For one moment from trembling you cannot stand still.

7   My box upon my head to myself it do belong.
To my master or mistress I have done nothing wrong.
To my master or mistress I have done nothing ill o.
But I fear in my own heart a young man I've killed.

8   He demanded my money and I soon did let him know
And tell this young robber I'd prove his overthrow.
She takes him by the hand and led him to the place o
Where this noble young fellow lies bleeding on his face.

9   The gentleman stepped off his horse to see what he had got
He had three loaded pistols some powder and some shot.
He had three loaded pistols some powder and a ball o
A knife and a whistle the robbers for to call.

10   He put the whistle to his mouth and he blew both loud and shrill.
And four young able fellows came tripping o'er the hill.
The gentleman shot one of them and that most speedily o
The beautiful young damsel she shot the other three.

11   And now my pretty fair maid for what you have done
I'll make you my own dear bride before 'tis very long.
I'll make you my own dear wife before 'tis very long o
For taking of your own part and firing off a gun.

NOTES

The Pear Tree (p. 80)   Sung by Frank Hinchliffe,   near Sheffield, South Yorkshire. Collected by Mike Yates, Ruairidh and Alvina Grieg, 1976.

It is rare that an unknown song turns up in oral tradition. 19th- and early 20th-century collections contain versions of nearly every song that has been collected since then, but 'The Pear Tree' is a pleasant newcomer. It was first reported in the 1960s in the Fens, and has turned up a few times since in areas as widely scattered as Kent and Scotland.

The Broomfield Hill (p. 82)   Sung by Walter Pardon, Knapton, Norfolk. Collected by Sam Richards and Tish Stubbs, November 1977.

This ballad is a treasure chest of ancient folkloric beliefs for those who enjoy decoding symbols and magical activities. It dates from the 16th century, although the old story is more detailed and complete than the versions that have lasted into recent years. A favourite of English gypsy singers, this song must vie with 'Barbara Allen' as the most popular ballad still in circulation. Unfortunately, most of the collected texts are very jumbled. As usual, the superb Norfolk singer Walter Pardon's version is an exception.

Young Maidenhead (p. 84)   Sung by George Collier, location unknown. Collected by George Gardiner, between 1906-10.

This is not a common song. It was printed occasionally and we have taken our verse 5 from a broadside to complete the sense of the narrative. The last line of verse 6 in George Collier's version does not appear in print and we surmise that he sang a decorous version for the visiting folklorist. The last line of the song poses a problem. The usual version is: 'Before I'll buy a maidenhead I'd rather have a whore', but the singer had 'If ever I buy any maidenhead I'll go and repent full sore' which we have recomposed unaided by broadsides.

The Old Woman in Yorkshire (p. 85)   Sung by Arthur Wood, Middlesborough, Yorkshire. Collected by Colin Wharton, c. 1960. In the archives of the Institute of Dialect and Folk Life Studies, Leeds University.

This genial ballad of marital bliss has lasted well, although older collections rarely included it. Mr Wood's tune fits well into the tradition of splendidly lively melodies associated with this narrative.

The Farmer in Leicester (p. 86)   Sung by Nelson Penfold, Westlake, Devon. Collected by Sam Richards, Tish Stubbs and Paul Wilson, 1974.

In the West Country we have never encountered a good gypsy singer who didn't know this song, and many, who know only a handful of songs, number this one in their repertoire. Other collectors across the south of England have found the same thing. Child refers to it in his note to 'The Crafty Farmer' (283), another version of this song, the principal difference being the sex of the one who is robbed. All versions could be grouped under the heading of 'The Highwayman Outwitted'. Nelson Penfold's tune is surprising and a delight to sing.

The Penny Wager (p. 87)   Sung by George Dunne, Cradley Heath, Quarry Bank, Staffordshire. Collected by Ewan MacColl and Peggy Seeger, 1971.

The singer's text closely follows the Pitts broadside 'The Adventures of a Penny', which in turn derives from an 18th-century text printed in London. Although extremely popular in England, we know of no Scots version, and have not seen it in North American collections. One Australian version has been in print. Songs of this type are known as 'biter bit' songs, and if the song itself has stayed mainly in England, its theme has turned up in gambling scenes in popular films and westerns.

The Robbers (Box on her Head) (p. 88)   No singer or date mentioned.   Taken down by M. A. Luard at Birch, Essex, and in the Vaughan Williams Mss, Cecil Sharp House, London.

A dashing tale of a liberated woman from an earlier century, full of action, and sufficiently widespread to appear in very recent collections.

LOVERS

There are few abstract love songs in folk literature. Unlike the featureless lover suspended in timeless space, a common enough stereotype in the romantic popular song of today and sometimes encountered in formal poetry and song as well, the lovers in folk-song are different altogether. Most of them have names and work, and the background to their meetings is usually defined — 'down by a riverside', 'old green lane', 'amongst the barley rakings', 'one evening so clear', 'in the month of May'.

Usually there is a very clear story and the lovers' feelings are expressed through their actions; even in purely lyrical songs some narrative unfolds. Tragedies and jiltings abound and lovers are left rocking the cradle. But there are happy endings too, and whether or not the lovers work things out for themselves, we feel there is a realism in the folksong, reflected in the language, allowing an involvement with the lovers that is missing from the romantic popular song.

I WISH THAT THE WARS WERE ALL OVER

1. It was down in the mea-dows where vio-lets are blue.
I saw pret-ty Pol-ly a - milk-ing her cow.
And the song that she sang made all the grove to ring.
O __ Bil - ly's gone from me to serve George the __ king.
And I wish that __ the __ wars were all o - ver,
Cry - ing O that __ the wars were all o - ver.

2   I stepped up to her and I made this reply.
I said pretty Polly what makes you to cry?
My Billy is gone from me that I love so dear
And the 'mericans will kill him so great is my fear.
And I wish that the wars were all over,
Crying O that the wars were all over.

3   I said pretty Polly can you fancy me?
I'll make you as happy as happy can be.
O no pretty sir I can never love you
To my Billy alone am I constant and true.
And I wish that the wars were all over,
Crying O that the wars were all over.

4   I now for my parents no longer can stay.
To seek for my Billy I'll haste and away.
To see if my Billy will make me his wife
So free for his sake I will venture my life.
And I wish that the wars were all over,
Crying O that the wars were all over.

5   O now to some tailor I'll haste and away
     To rig myself out in some young man's array.
     And like a bold fellow so neat and so trim
     So free for his sake I will go serve the King.
     And I wish that the wars were all over,
     Crying O that the wars were all over.

THE PRETTY FACTORY BOY

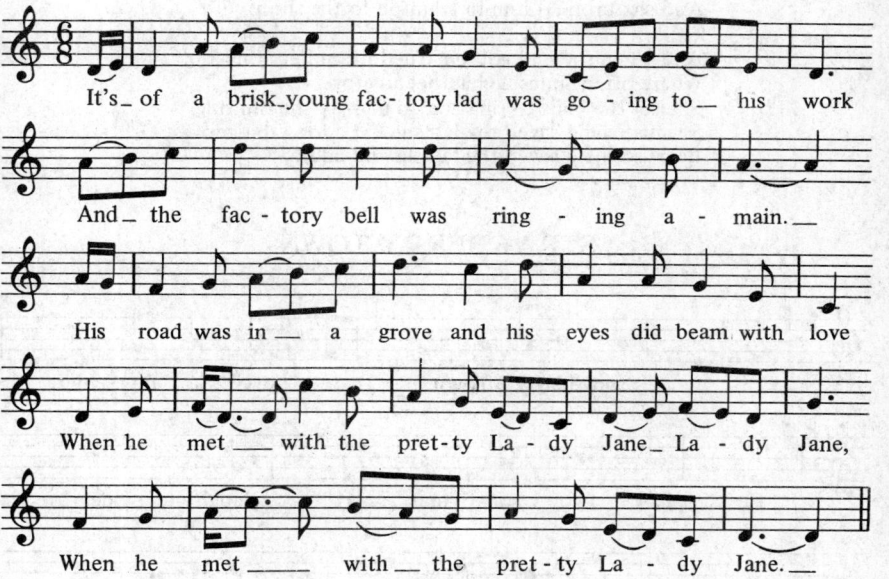

It's of a brisk young fac-tory lad was go-ing to his work
And the fac-tory bell was ring-ing a-main.
His road was in a grove and his eyes did beam with love
When he met with the pret-ty La-dy Jane, La-dy Jane,
When he met with the pret-ty La-dy Jane.

2   And this was his song as he walked along,
     Sweet maid you are of a high degree.
     If your parents get to know that my heart is fixed on you
     I much fear they will greatly frown on me, frown on me,
     I much fear they will greatly frown on me.

3   It chanced her aged parents they came for to know
     That the factory lad did court their daughter Jane.
     A pressgang they did send and pressed the factory lad away
     For to send him to the wars to be slain, to be slain,
     For to send him to the wars to be slain.

4   Then this pretty maid dressed herself all in her best
     Her pockets she well lined with gold.
     From seaport town to town she did travel up and down
     In search of her factory lad so bold, so bold,
     In search of her factory lad so bold.

5   At last she got a clue where her true love was taken to
      And travelled till the vessel she espied.
      She then did give some gold unto a young sailor bold
      For to row her in his boat to the ship side, the ship side,
      For to row her in his boat to the ship side.

6   So then unto the captain the case she did make known
      Who refused for to take her golden store.
      But quickly did discharge and set her factory boy at large
      And she brought him in triumph to the shore, to the shore,
      And she brought him in triumph to the shore.

7   And when she had got her true love in her arms
      Where often times he had been before,
      She set the bells to ring and so merrily she did sing
      Because she'd saved the lad she did adore, did adore,
      Because she'd saved the lad she did adore.

STRAWBERRY TOWN

1. In Strawberry Town there lived a farmer,
He had two sons and a daughter dear.
By day and night they were contriving
To fill their poor sister's heart with fear.

2   One brother said unto the other,
      See how our sister do sport and play
      With that young servingman, her lover.
      We'll send him silent to his grave.

3   A match of hunting it was prepared
Through woods and valleys where briars grow
And there they did this young man murder
And in the brake his body throw.

4   When they returned home from hunting
She asked them for her servantman.
I ask because I've seen you whisper
So tell me brothers now if you can.

5   O sister, sister, you do offend us
And why do you so examine me?
We left him in the fields of hunting
And no more of him did we see.

6   Then straight to bed went this fair young woman
Lamenting for her own true love.
She dreamt she saw her own true lover
A-covered all over in a gore of blood.

7   You rise early tomorrow morning
And straightway early to that brake you go
And there you'll find my body laying
A-covered all over in a gore of blood.

8   Then she rose early the next day morning
And straightway early to that brake did go
And there she found her own true lover
A-covered all over in a gore of blood.

9   She took her handkerchief from her pocket
And wiped his eyes though he was blind.
She often kissed him, sometimes crying,
Here lies the dearest friend of mine.

10   And since my brothers have been so cruel
To take your tender sweet life away,
One grave shall hold us both together
And along with you until death I'll lay.

A SAILOR BY MY RIGHT

1. I am a sailor by my right
And on the sea take great delight.
'Tis of two girls did I beguile
And both of them they proved of child.

2 He promised to be true to both
And bound himself with a sacred oath
To wed with both if he had life
And one of them he made his wife.

3 The other she being left alone,
She said: You false deceitful man
You've done the deed a wicked thing,
A public shame on me thou'dst bring.

4 A public shame all to prevent
It's into some little wood she went.
All for to end her further strife
She cut the tender thread of life.

5 She hung herself up to a tree.
Two men a-hunting did her see.
Her flesh by small birds was beastly tore
Which grieved those young men's hearts full sore.

6 They ran with speed to cut her down
And in her bosom a note they found.
I write these lines all out at large
Bury me not I do you charge.

7 Here on the ground then let me lie
For every one that do pass by.
And every one a warning take
And see what folly young men do make.

8   While he's on earth I will be just,
        While he's on earth I shall take no rest.
        And as she said she did haunt him so
        Till to the seas he was forced to go.

9   This young man climbed the mainmast high
        A little boat he chanced to spy,
        A little boat, a large crew of men
        And the female ghost she stood up between.

10   Down to the deck the young man did go
        And told the captain of his foe,
        Saying: Captain, captain stand my defence
        This spirit coming will fetch me hence.

11   'Twas up on deck the captain he did go
        All for to face this young man's foe.
        Captain, she said, you must and can
        Help me with speed to this young man.

12   In some little town your young man died
        And there his poor dead body lies.
        O captain captain don't say you so
        He's dwelling in thy ship below.

13   If you do stand in his defence
        Here is a spirit will fetch you hence.
        I will cause you and your men to weep,
        I'll leave you sleeping all in the deep.

14   'Twas up on deck they forced him to go
        To save the goodly ship and crew.
        She fixed her eyes on him so grim
        Which made him tremble in every limb.

15   Don't you remember when I was a maid
        You caused my poor trembling heart to bleed?
        Now I'm a spirit have come for thee.
        You deceived me once but I've got you now.

16   Down in her boat she forced him,
        Down in her boat he was forced to go.
        They sunk away in a flame of fire
        Which caused all sailors to admire.

AS I WAS OUT A-WALKING

1. As I was out a - walk - ing
Down by the ri - ver - side, _____
I heard a fair maid sing - ing
I wish I was ___ a bride a bride,
I wish I was ___ a bride. _____

2 So I gently stepped up to her
   And I thanked her for her song.
   For the answer that she gave to me
   Was: I am I am too young too young,
   I am I am too young.

3 The younger you are the better for me
   More suited to be my bride.
   Oh when I grow old I'll be able to say
   Well I married my wife a maid a maid,
   I married my wife a maid.

4   So I kissed her once and I kissed her twice
And ever so tenderly,
And I finally got it into her mind
To lay one night with me with me,
Just to lay one night with me.

5   So we lay one night till morning
Till daylight did appear.
Then Johnny arose and he on with his clothes
Saying: fare thee well my dear,
Saying fare thee well my dear.

6   Oh that's not the promise you made to me
When you laid by my side.
You promised me you'd marry me
And make me your own sweet bride,
And make me your own sweet bride.

7   Is that the promise I made to you
Which I never intend to do?
For I never intend to marry a girl
Whose heart's too easy to woo,
Whose heart is too easy to woo.

8   My parents will confine me up
Like a small bird in a cage.
Here I'm a poor girl in child by thee
Not eighteen years of age,
Not eighteen years of age.

9   Well if you are in child by me,
Which I may suppose you be,
Just wrap it up in its petticoats warm
And doddle it on your knee,
Just doddle it on your knee.

10   While other farmers daughters
To market they do go
Here I'm a poor girl must stay at home
Singing hushy bye baby - i - o,
Singing hushy bye baby - i - o.

11   Then if that you must stay at home
Singing hushy bye baby - i - o,
You just think back how it all came about
And you blame your own free will,
Just blame your own free will.

THE LITTLE BACK PARLOUR

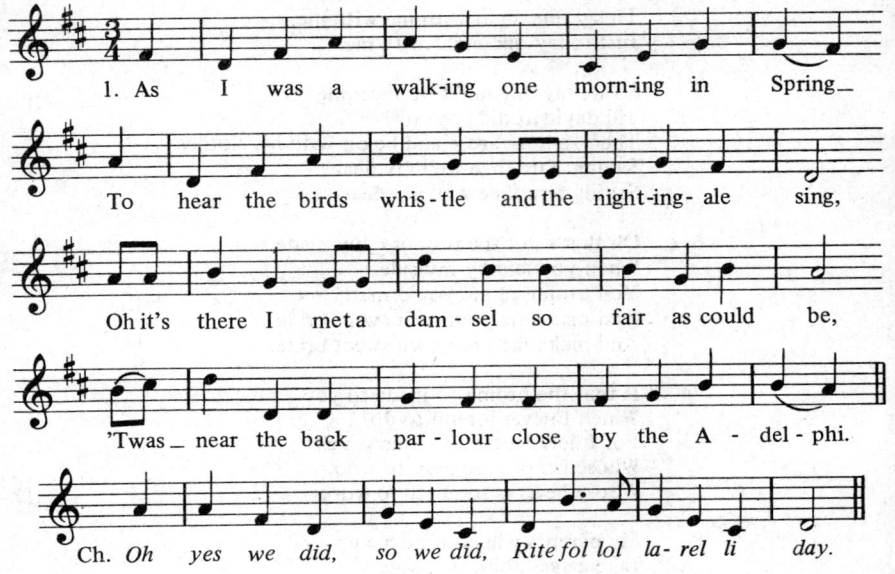

1. As I was a walk-ing one morn-ing in Spring—
To hear the birds whis-tle and the night-ing-ale sing,
Oh it's there I met a dam-sel so fair as could be,
'Twas— near the back par-lour close by the A-del-phi.
Ch. *Oh yes we did, so we did, Rite fol lol la-rel li day.*

2 I says my dearest fair maid if my bride you will be
It's from these dark arches I will then take thee.
Oh no kindest young man that never can be
For the Ratcliffe High bobbies is spying for me.

3 Now it's all of a moment she gave her consent
And straight to the alehouse oh there we both went.
Five shillings in oysters and lobsters it cost me
In the little back parlour close by the Adelphi.

4 Now in comes a luby, black eyes and thick sticks.
He drunk up my brandy and smoked my pickwick.
And in comes another and bonneted me
In the little back parlour close by the Adelphi.

5 They tore off my coat, my watch they pulled out.
They pitched into me and damaged my snout,
They stripped me of everything, then rolling sent me
Down by the dark arches close by the Adelphi.

6 I woke from my slumber at five the next morn
As naked as ever a mortal was born,
When four kind policeman on a stretcher took me
Down by the dark arches of the Adelphi.

7   Now I sent to my mother for money and clothes
     And likewise for a doctor to patch up my nose
     And away then they took me, you quickly shall see
     From the little back parlour close by the Adelphi.

THE *NIGHTINGALE*

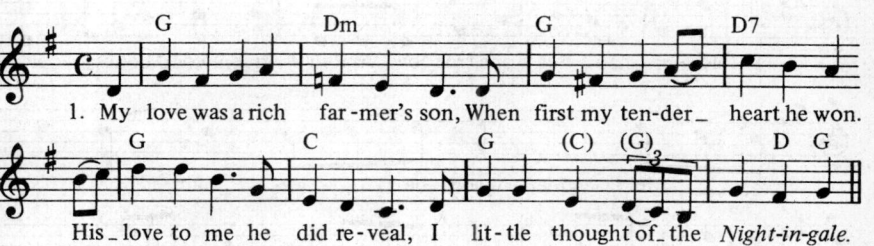

1. My love was a rich far-mer's son, When first my ten-der heart he won.
His love to me he did re-veal, I lit-tle thought of the *Night-in-gale*.

2   My cruel father contrived it so
     That my true love should quickly go.
     He told a press gang who did not fail
     To press my love in the *Nightingale*.

3   The fourteenth of November last
     The wind did blow a dreadful blast.
     My love he was in the dreadful gale
     And went to the bottom in the *Nightingale*.

4   The very night my love was lost
     He appeared to me a deadly ghost,
     His hair erect, his face was pale:
     Thy love was drowned in the *Nightingale*.

5   My dearest Nancy don't be surprised
     In the Bay of Biscay my body lies
     Became a prize for some shark or whale,
     'Twas my sad fate in the *Nightingale*.

6   My father's dwelling I will forsake.
     Some lonesome valleys I will take.
     And there my lover I will bewail,
     He lost his life in the *Nightingale*.

THE UNQUIET GRAVE

1. How cold the winds do blow dear love, — And sprink-ling falls the rain. —
I nev-er had — but one true love, And in green-wood he — was slain,
And — in green - wood he ___ was slain, ___
I nev-er had—but one true love, And in green-wood he—was slain. —

2   I'll do as much for my true love
As any young girl may.
I'll sit and mourn all on his grave
For a twelvemonth and a day,
For a twelvemonth and a day,
I'll sit and mourn all on his grave
For a twelvemonth and a day.

3   When a twelvemonth and a day was over
This young man he arose,
Saying: Who is this sits on my grave
And will not let me rest,
And will not let me rest,
Saying: Who is this sits on my grave
And will not let me rest?

4   'Tis I, 'tis I your own true love
Your own true love, she said.
A sweet little kiss from your clay cold lips
And that's all I want from thee,
And that's all I want from thee,
A sweet little kiss from your clay cold lips
And that's all I want from thee.

5   My lips are cold as clay sweetheart,
My breath smells heavy and strong,
If you were to kiss my clay cold lips
Your time would not be long,
Your time would not be long,
If you were to kiss my clay cold lips
Your time would not be long.

6   · Don't you remember the garden love
     Where you and I used to walk?
     For the finest flower that ever growed there
     Is withered to a stalk,
     Is withered to a stalk,
     For the finest flower that ever growed there
     Is withered to a stalk.

7   They're withered up and gone dear love,
     Oh they're withered up so brown.
     And you and I and the whole wide world
     Must go into the ground,
     Must go into the ground,
     And you and I and the whole wide world
     Must go into the ground.

SEVENTEEN COME SUNDAY

1. Where_ are you go-ing _____ my fair pret-ty maid __

Where are you go-ing my ho - ney? _____

she____ ans-wered me, yes quite cheer-ful - ly

On an er - rand for my mam - my.

Ch. With my rue dum a day, Fol the did-dle ay,

Whack fol the lau - rel - i - doh.

2   Can I come too my fair pretty maid
     Can I come too my honey?
     She answered me, yes quite cheerfully
     Well you can for me and welcome.

3   For she was tall and her clothes were smart
       And her hair hung down in ringlets.
    Her eyes were blue and her shoes were black
       And her buckles shone like silver.

4   How old are you my fair pretty maid
       How old are you my honey?
    She answered me, yes quite cheerfully
       I'll be seventeen come Sunday.

5   What is your father my fair pretty maid
       What may he be my honey?
    She answered me, yes quite cheerfully
       My father he's a farmer.

6   Will you marry me my fair pretty maid
       Will you marry me my honey?
    She answered me, yes quite cheerfully
       Well I'll have to ask my mammy.

7   Now if you come down to my daddy's farm
       When the moon shines bright and clearly,
    I'll come down and I'll let you in
       And my mammy will not hear me.

8   Now I goes down to her daddy's farm
       And the moon shone bright and clearly.
    She came down and she let me in
       And her mammy did not hear me.

(To second part of the tune)
Yes she came down and she let me in
    And I lay in her arms till morning.

MOWING THE BARLEY

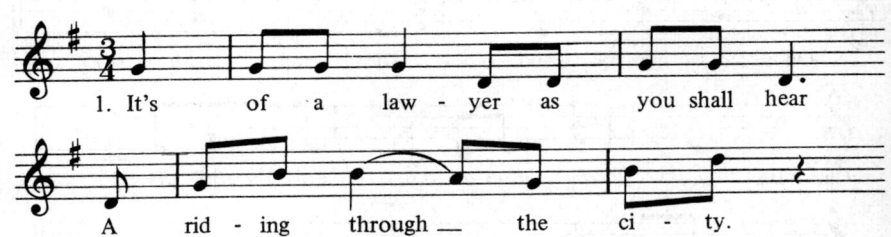

1. It's of a law-yer as you shall hear
A rid-ing through the ci-ty.

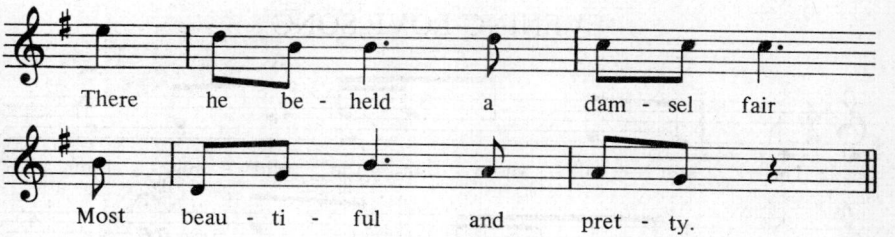

There he be-held a dam-sel fair
Most beau-ti-ful and pret-ty.

2 Where are you going my fair pretty maid,
Where are you going my honey?
To yonder meadow she replied
My father's there a-mowing.

3 Shall I go with you my fair pretty maid
Shall I go with you my honey?
She answered me right cheerfully,
My father will be angry.

4 Then quickly I tripped over the plain
And soon I overtook her.
I whispered these kind words to her ears,
A lady I will make you.

5 And up in London you shall dwell.
I'll dress you like some lady.
Fine silken gowns you shall have on,
Fine ribbons, strings, and laces.

6 Besides I'll give you money too,
I'll give you gold and silver,
If you'll consent to go with me
Unto the town of Dover.

7 Then it's keep your gold and silver too
And carry on where you're going.
There's many a false young man like you
Has brought poor girls to ruin.

8 I'd rather be a ploughman's wife
Sit at my wheel a-spinning
Than I'd be a lawyer's bride
Sit in some alehouse drinking.

9 Come all young maids a warning take
In country town or city.
You never should listen to what a lawyer says
For a lawyer's got no pity.

EVENING LOVE SONG

1. The sun will shine in the mid - night hour,
The stars through a sum - mer's day,
The se - ven seas will burn be - fore
My love will fade a - way,
Be - fore my love will fade a - way.

To weave our lov - ers'

*
* more often (e.g. verse 2):

2   Down by Cathedral Yard we met
        Just as the evening fell.
    Our day's work done and time our own
        To weave our lovers' spell,
        To weave our lovers' spell.

3   The spires rise to the twilight skies
        And straight and tall they stand.
    But the love that rests deep in my breast
        Is a thousand times as grand,
        Is a thousand times as grand.

4   And arm in arm we crossed the green
        Down to the river side.
    We kissed, embraced, and talked of love
        Where the waters gently glide,
        Where the waters gently glide.

5   Oh come my love and lie with me
        The evening's almost done.
    We went to bed in the midnight hour
        Till morning lay as one,
        Till morning lay as one.

6   The birds begin to sing my love,
       The daylight's coming on
       And you and I must part until
       Another day is done,
       Another day is done.

THE GAME OF ALL FOURS

1. As I were a-walk-ing one bright sum-mer's morn-ing,
I were all a-lone on the King's high-way,
And who should I meet but a fair pret-ty dam-sel
To the sweet town of Glas-gow were mak-ing her way.

2   So we walked and we talked just a few miles together
    Until we did come to that shady green tree,
    Where she sat herself down and I sat down beside her
    And the game that we played was one two and three.

3   So it's she cut the cards, it were his turn to deal them
    Well he dealt himself one trump in his hand.
    Then she chucked down the ace and she stole the jack from him
    And that's what you calls high, low, jack, and the game.

4   So he picked up his hat and he bid her good morning
    And he bid her good morning again and again.
    For he said: O fair maid, will you own I have beat you
    Or else the same game we'll play over again?

5   So she picked herself up and she bid him good morning
    And she bid him good morning again and again.
    O she said: There, young man, I'll be this way tomorrow
    And then that same game we'll play over again.

THE BANKS OF THE TYNE

1. As — I walked out— one sum-mer day to view the fields so green
The bush-es they were— in full bloom so love-ly to be seen.
When po-sy bush-es— was a-dorned so bright-ly they— did shine—
There I met my love-ly Nan-cy down— by the banks of Tyne.

2 And with a joyful harmony she made the valleys ring.
The lofty larks descending when this maid began to sing.
The pretty little small birds in chorus they did join.
O they filled the air with melody all around the banks of Tyne.

3 Her hair was like the links of gold this charming beauty bright.
Her eyes did glow like diamonds or the shining stars of night.
I says: My pretty fair maid if that you will be mine
O we'll spend our days in harmony all on the banks of Tyne.

4 Oh, she says, my jolly sailor bold how can you make so free?
I think by your appearance you're lately come from sea.
Come sit you down along with me if that you do incline
For I love a sailor's company all on the banks of Tyne.

5 For once I loved a sailor bold as ever crossed the main.
He was proper tall and handsome I think you are the same.
O yes my lovely Nancy it's hand in hand we'll join
And we'll have peace and unity all round the banks of Tyne.

6 When in the midst of dangers all round on every side
Where cannon balls did fly like hail all on the ocean wide
I was thinking of my Nancy the girl I left behind
That I shall see my own true love all on the banks of Tyne.

7 Come come my lovely Nancy to church let us away
And we will quickly married be without the least delay
And afterwards my own true love we'll crown the day with wine
And we'll have a joyful night my love all on the banks of Tyne.

THE OLD MISER

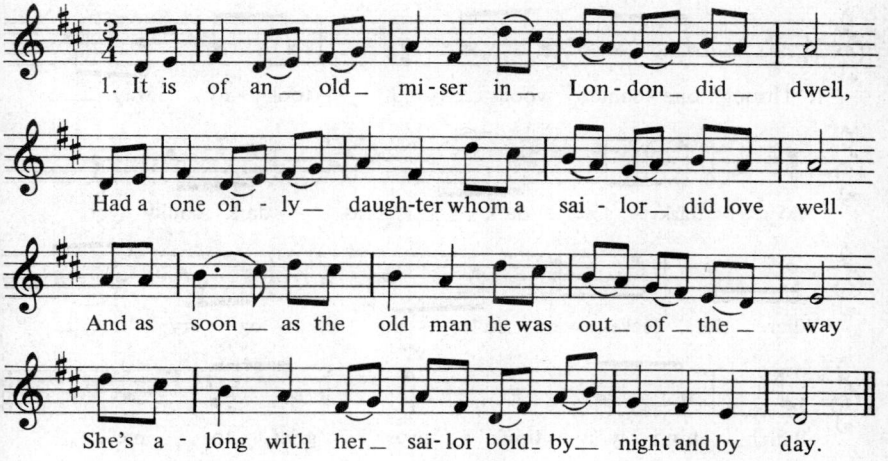

1. It is of an old miser in London did dwell,
Had a one only daughter whom a sailor did love well.
And as soon as the old man he was out of the way
She's along with her sailor bold by night and by day.

2   Now as soon as the old man he heard of the news
Down to a sea captain he immediately goes,
Saying: Captain, noble Captain, good news I have to tell
I have got a young sailor bold as a transport to sell.

3   Now what will you give me? This old miser did say.
I will give you ten guineas and I'll send him away.
I will take him, I will send him straight over the main
That he'll never come to England to court her again.

4   Now as soon as the lady she heard of the news
Down to the sea captain she immediately goes,
Saying: Captain, noble Captain, bad news I have to tell
You have taken my sweetheart whom I love so well.

5   She put her hands in her pocket, pulled out handfuls of gold
Down on the main table ten hundred she throwed,
Saying: Captain, noble Captain, I'll give you twice as much more
To release my young sailor bold, he's the lad I adore.

6   O no, says that Captain, o no, such a thing.
I have sent your love a-sailing right over the main,
I have sent your love a-sailing right over the main
Where he never will come back to England again.

7   O cursed be my father, o cursed be he.
I am sure in my own heart he has quite ruined me.
I'll go to my little cot and I'll lay myself down
And all through the long night for my William I'll mourn.

THROUGH LONESOME WOODS

1. Through lone - some woods___ I took my way, ___
So dark so dark ___ as dark could be,
Where the leaves were shiver - ing on ev - ery tree, ___
Which don't you think 'twas grief for me?

2   As I was going up Dibden town
      I saw my true love a-sitting down,
      I saw her sitting on another man's knee
      Which don't you think 'twas grief for me?

3   I called to my love by her name
      Then up she rose and to me came.
      I gave her kisses by one two three
      But none so sweet as she gave me.

4   Now the winter's gone, the summer's come
      The small birds from the nest is sprung.
      I'll tell you plainly unto your face
      You're not the young man that I love best.

5   Now the winter's gone, the summer's come
      The small birds from their nest is sprung.
      I'll neither borrow nor I'll lend
      But I'll keep my heart for a better friend.

THE NAVVIE MAN

1. I am a roving navvie man I rove from town to town
And when I get a job of work I'm willing to sit down,
With my kit upon my shoulder my grafting tool in hand
So up to London I did go like a roving navvie man.

2 O when I came to London town the girls did jump for joy,
Saying one with the other: Here comes a navvie boy.
Some treats me with a bottle, another with a dram
So it's round the country I do go like a roving navvie man.

3 I had not been in London town above two days or three
Before my master's daughter she fell in love with me.
She asked of me to dine with her, I tooked her by the hand
And so slyly told her mother that she wooed a navvie man.

4 O daughter, dear daughter how can you say so?
To love a roving navvie man you never saw before.
O hold your tongue dear mother, it's do the best you can
For it's round the country I will go with my roving navvie man.

FREDDIE MATHEWS

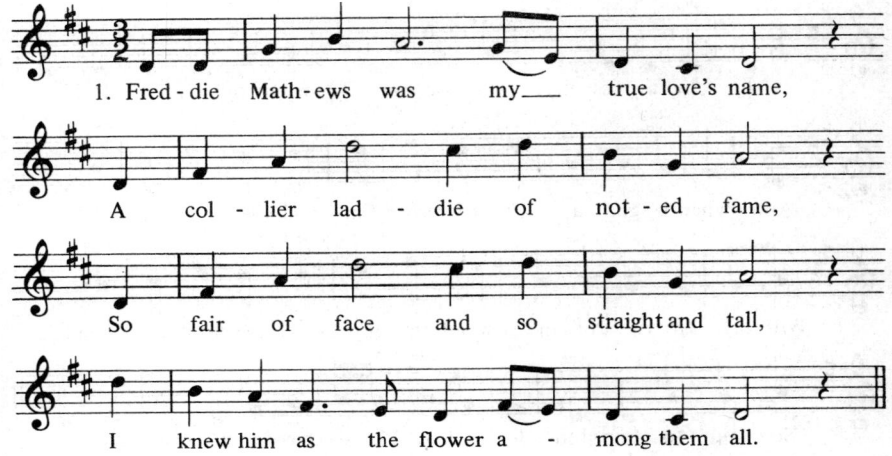

1. Fred-die Math-ews was my___ true love's name,
A col-lier lad - die of not-ed fame,
So fair of face and so straight and tall,
I knew him as the flower a - mong them all.

2   He was not taken by fire or flood
Or by the dust that blackens a collier's blood.
It was not by gas or a fall of stone
That he is dead and I lie here alone.

3   As a collier lad and a union man
On picket duty my love did stand.
On the picket line my lad took his place
Them cold and hungry February days.

4   Long days and nights while the frost lay hard
At the Keadby station there he stood guard
To stop the drivers who came that way
To ask them: Turn around and not betray.

5   The miners' plea they could not ignore.
Most turned around and were seen no more,
But one man swore not to turn around,
My lad stepped up to him and stood his ground.

6   So firm and sure as he stood there
With his breath like smoke on the frosty air,
Then the crash of gears and the engine's roar
And my sweet collier lad he breathed no more.

7   The snow may melt and the frost depart
But the breath of winter is on my heart.
The flowers may rise with the soft spring sun
But the fairest flower of all is dead and gone.

YOUNG RAMBLE-AWAY

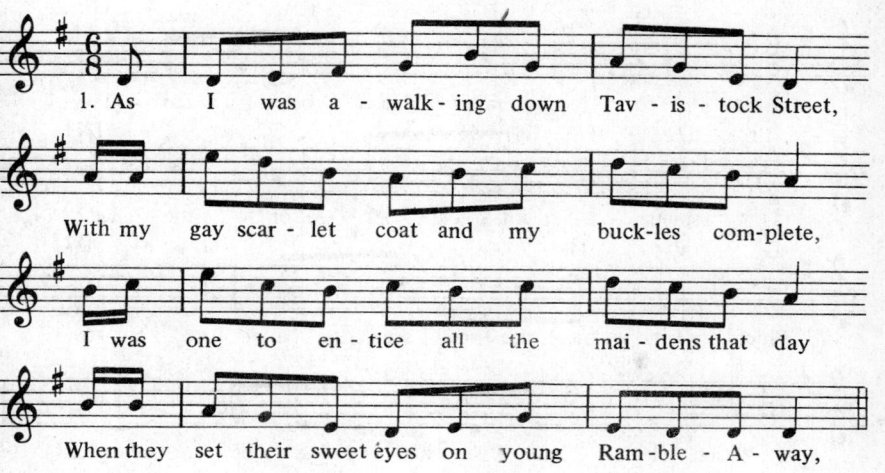

1. As I was a-walk-ing down Tav-is-tock Street,

With my gay scar-let coat and my buck-les com-plete,

I was one to en-tice all the mai-dens that day

When they set their sweet eyes on young Ram-ble - A - way,

2 As I was a-walking through Tavistock Fair
I saw pretty Nancy a-combing her hair.
With my cap and my ribbons so bright and so gay
She could not but look at young Ramble-Away.

3 As I was a-walking that night in the dark
I stood at her door and I shone as her spark.
I whistled, she looked from her window to say
Are you the young lad they call Ramble-Away?

4 When twenty four weeks they were over and past
This fair pretty maiden did sicken at last.
Her gown would not meet nor her apron string stay
And 'twas all through the love of young Ramble-Away.

5 My dad and my mammy from home they are gone
And when they return I will sing them a song.
I will sing them a song and I'll learn them to say
Alas, you've been playing with Ramble-Away.

6 So come pretty maidens where ever you be
With courting young fellows don't make yourselves free,
For if you should do so you'll rue the sad day
When you met with the likes of young Ramble-Away.

FORTY MILES

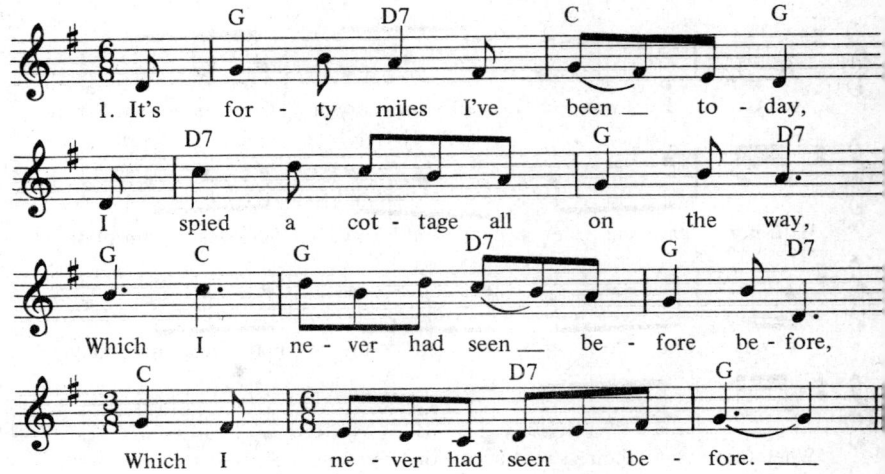

1. It's for - ty miles I've been __ to - day,
I spied a cot - tage all on the way,
Which I ne - ver had seen __ be - fore be - fore,
Which I ne - ver had seen be - fore. __

2 I boldly rattled all on the pin.
A bonnie young maid she heard the din
And she cried: Is anyone there, o, there?
And she cried: Is anyone there?

3 For pity's sake love open the door.
I've come a long journey ower the moor.
And I pray you let me in, o in,
And I pray you let me in.

4 To let you in that may not be
There's nobody here at home but me,
And I dare not let you in, you in,
And I dare not let you in.

5 See how it rains, it hails, it snows,
The night is dark, the cold wind blows,
And I'm soaking to the skin, the skin,
And I'm soaking to the skin.

6 To let you in, that may not be
My dad's gone lambing and ta'en the key,
And I may not let you in, you in,
And I may not let you in.

7 I turned to go but she said: Nay,
'T would be a sin to send you away.
And she up and she let me in, me in,
And she up and let me in.

8   In sport and play that night we spent
And she confessed her sweet content,
When I up and I entered in, o in,
When I up and I entered in.

NANCY FROM LONDON

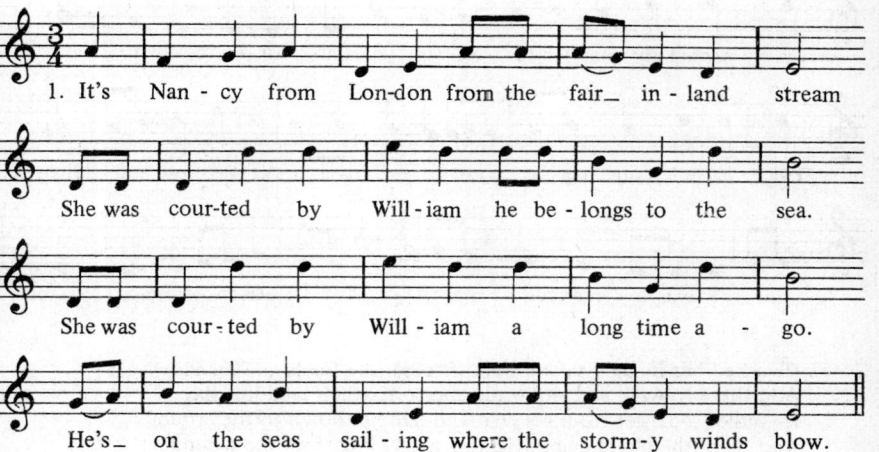

1. It's Nan - cy from Lon-don from the fair_ in - land stream
She was cour-ted by Will - iam he be - longs to the sea.
She was cour-ted by Will - iam a long time a - go.
He's_ on the seas sail - ing where the storm-y winds blow.

2   Oh the stormy winds blow boys and make my heart ache.
They make my room window for to shiver and shake.
God knows where my love lies so far from the shore.
I'll pray for his welfare — what can I do more?

3   When the sailors are sailing drink a health to their wives
For they love their sweethearts as they love their lives.
Here's a punch going round my boys, here's a full glass in hand,
Here's a health to loving Nancy that I leave on dry land.

4   Oh it's Nancy my jewel, my joy and heart's delight.
Here is one lovely letter I'm going for to write.
Here is one lovely letter for to let you know
That I'm on the seas sailing where the stormy winds blow.

THE PRENTICE BOY

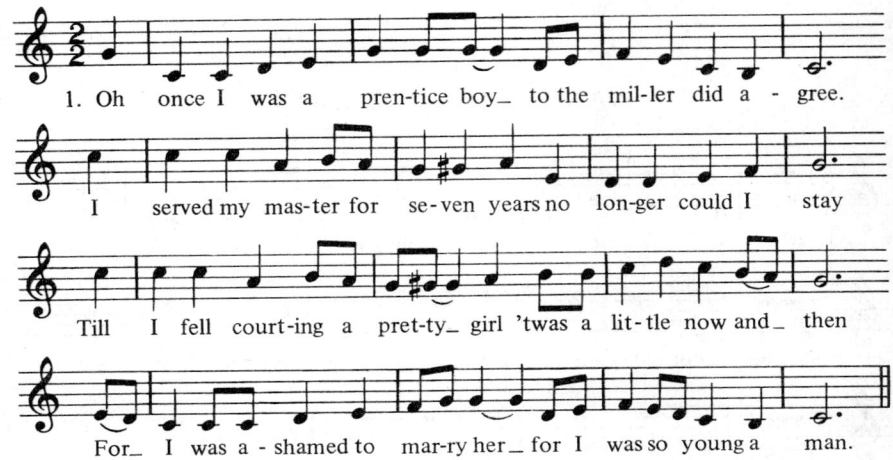

1. Oh once I was a pren-tice boy_ to the mil-ler did a - gree.
I served my mas-ter for se-ven years no lon-ger could I stay
Till I fell court-ing a pret-ty_ girl 'twas a lit-tle now and_ then
For_ I was a-shamed to mar-ry her_ for I was so young a man.

2   He asked her if she'd take a walk through the fields and meadows gay
And there to walk and sit awhile and to fix their wedding day.
He pulled a dagger from his coat and laid her down to the ground
And there the blood came trickling a-trickling from the wound.

3   He grabbed her by her curly locks and he dragged her to the stream.
There he bides a-thinking when at last he throws her in.
He watched her float yes he watched her float he watched her go down with the
        tide,
Saying that poor girl's got a watery grave when she ought to have been my bride.

4   He goes home to his master's house twelve o'clock that night.
His master rose and let him in by striking of a light.
He asked him and he questioned him what had stained his hands and his clothes
And the answer that he gave to him was the bleedings from his nose.

5   It was a few days after that poor young girl was missed.
They took him on suspicion for a-doing all of this.
They sent him on to Newgate there to be tried for his life
For the murder of that honest young girl that ought to have been his wife.

6   It was a few days after that poor young girl was found.
She came floating down the river near by Wesley town.
The judge and the jury they set themselves to agree
For a-murdering of that honest young girl and a-hanged you shall be.

THE KNIFE IN THE WINDOW

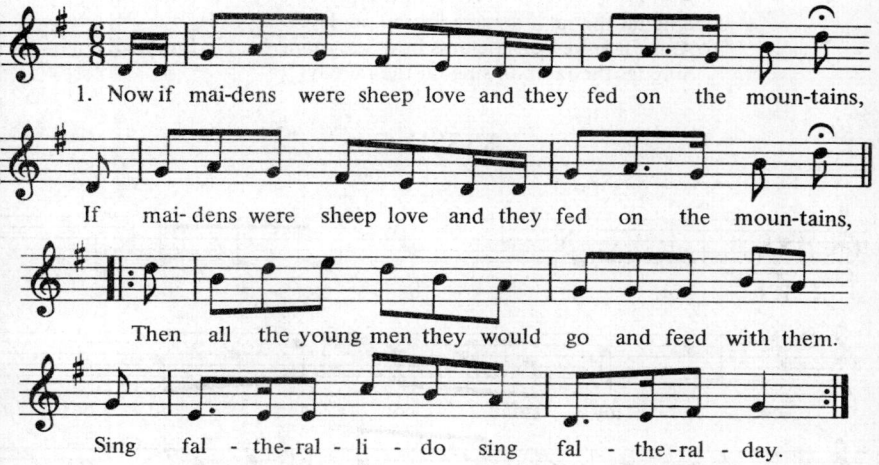

1. Now if mai-dens were sheep love and they fed on the moun-tains,

If mai-dens were sheep love and they fed on the moun-tains,

Then all the young men they would go and feed with them.

Sing fal - the-ral - li - do sing fal - the -ral - day.

2   O Molly my true love may I come to bed to you?
O Molly my true love may I come to bed to you?
O yes, she replied, you can come to bed with me.
Sing fal the ral li do sing fal the ral day.
O yes, she replied, you can come to bed with me.
Sing fal the ral li do sing fal the ral day.

3   Now the door it is bolted and I cannot undo it.
The door it is bolted and I cannot undo it.
O now, she replied, you must put your knee to it.
Sing fal the ral li do sing fal the ral day.
O now, she replied, you must put your knee to it.
Sing fal the ral li do sing fal the ral day.

4   So I put my knee to it and the door flew asunder,
So I put my knee to it and the door flew asunder,
And upstairs I went like lightning and thunder.
Sing fal the ral li do sing fal the ral day.
And upstairs I went like lightning and thunder.
Sing fal the ral li do sing fal the ral day.

5   Now your small things are tight love and I cannot undo it.
Now your small things are tight love and I cannot undo it.
There's a knife in the window and you can take it to it.
Sing fal the ral li do sing fal the ral day.
There's a knife in the window and you can take it to it.
Sing fal the ral li do sing fal the ral day.

6   Now her small things fell off her and I into bed tumbled.
Now her small things fell off her and I into bed tumbled.
And I'll leave you to guess how we young couple fumbled.
Sing fal the ral li do sing fal the ral day.
And I'll leave you to guess how we young couple fumbled.
Sing fal the ral li do sing fal the ral day.

KISSING

1. It's how can I be mer - ry and free
And in my mind — con - tent - ed be?
The bon - ny young lad I love so dear - ly
He — is ban -ished quite out of my com - pa - ny.
Vs. 2. young —— mans arms ———— I'd

2   Kissing is a silly thing.
It'll bring poor lasses into sin.
I wish I was in the young man's arms.
I'd care not whether I sink or swim.

NOTES

I Wish That the Wars Were All Over (p. 92)   Sung by Sam Fone, Mary Tavy, Devon. Collected by Sabine Baring-Gould, 1893. Last two verses from *A Sailor's Songbag,* Ed. George C. Carey, University of Massachusetts Press, 1976.

This song is something of a rarity. Sam Fone, a Dartmoor miner, gave our first three verses to Baring-Gould, and we have completed the text from another source. It is not untypical of a certain class of song from the time of the American Wars of independence. Many English people had little sympathy with the wars — the Americans' ambitions were shared by English radicals and Americans were regarded as their own blood. Polly, therefore, sings an eloquent protest against the removal of thousands of young men to fight in wars many cared little about.

The Pretty Factory Boy (p. 93)   Broadside ballad printed by Harkness, Church Street, Preston.

Country singers of the 19th century had a particular affection for 'The Pretty Plough-boy' — a love song which turns up in all major collections. 'The Pretty Factory Boy' is a close parody, practically the only difference being in the type of work the young man does. The rural versions are usually associated with good flowing, flowery tunes which lend themselves to decoration. We've used a Newfoundland tune from Peacock's *Songs of the Newfoundland Outports.*

Strawberry Town (p. 94)   Sung by George Whitcombe, Westhay Meare, Somerset. Collected by Cecil Sharp 1906 and 1907, JFSS vol. 5, p. 126.

The MS text has a few gaps and awkward transitions, so we have taken the liberty of adding a few verses from other versions, as well as lightly editing George Whitcombe's own verses. The history of this song has often been told. The story first occurs in Boccaccio's *Decameron* as 'Isabella and the Pot of Basil'. It must have been a current European folk-tale before that, dating back possibly over 700 years. In England, as a folksong, it has circulated both in a fairly similar form to the one we give here, and in a slightly weaker broadside remake 'The Constant Farmer's Son'.

A Sailor by my Right (p. 96)   Sung by Mrs Betsy Pike, Somerton. Collected by Cecil Sharp, 1906. Collated with versions from Newfoundland and Labrador — *Songs of the Newfoundland Outports,* Peacock; *Folk Ballads and Songs of the Lower Labrador Coast,* MacEdward Leach.

This ballad is very rare in English tradition, and in all collated versions there is something lacking in the text. Consequently, we have had to look across the Atlantic for texts to use in collation. The song has survived much more healthily in Canada.

As I Was Out A-Walking (p. 98)   Sung by Jack Gard, Calverleigh, Devon. Collected by Sam Richards, Tish Stubbs, and Paul Wilson, 1977.

We have given all the singer's melodic variations because they were used so freely, and so integrally, that it is impossible to designate one set as the tune. Jack Gard is a magnificent singer, who emigrated to Canada in the 1920s. We were lucky enough to catch him on a visit to his native Devon. He has remembered his English songs perfectly over a period of more than 50 years. This one has been collected often in English tradition.

The Little Back Parlour (p. 100)   Sung by James Brown, details unknown. Collected by George Gardiner, pre-1910.

In 19th-century east London, prostitutes, pimps, bullies, bawds and thieves all made the Ratcliffe Highway the centre for the lowest of low life. Henry Mayhew, in the 1860s, observed that there was little beauty there: 'It might have been hiding under a bushel, but it was not patent to the casual observer. Yet I must acknowledge something prepossessing about the countenances of the women, which is more than could be said of the men.' He might have been describing the professionals in this song. It is quite rare in oral tradition, but was perhaps widespread at one time judging by the number of printed versions.

The Nightingale (p. 101) Sung by Mr Lolley, near Howden, Yorkshire. Collected by Frank Kidson pre-1891. Text completed from Catnach broadside. Tune first published in *Traditional Tunes* 1891, republished by SR Publishing, Wakefield, Yorkshire 1970.

Mr Lolley knew only the first two verses when Kidson published the songs in *Traditional Tunes* (1891), and Kidson himself remarked, 'We have not been able to recover more than the two verses here presented.' We have completed the text from a broadside in Kidson's own collection, presumably one which came into his possession after the publication of *Traditional Tunes*.

The Unquiet Grave (p. 102) Sung by James Brown, details unknown. Collected by George Gardiner, pre-1910.

Mourn for the dead, but not overmuch or they will not be able to rest in the grave. This simple folkloric belief is embodied in this song which Child included in *The English and Scottish Popular Ballads*, but which would more accurately be termed a lyric. Bronson speculates, on good evidence, that it might originate from the end of the 15th century, but also points out that no definite versions are known until the 19th century.

Seventeen Come Sunday (p. 103) Sung by Amy Birch, near Bampton, Devon. Collected by Sam Richards, Tish Stubbs and Paul Wilson, 1975.

One of the most widespread love songs, not only in England, it is often found in the repertoire of all good traditional singers. Nearly always attached to a good, singable tune, the words normally turn up in sets similar to this one. Sometimes the singer adds a verse at the end, showing that the man is a soldier and a false lover. Whether or not this was added by broadside poets we don't know, but we prefer the song as it is here.

Mowing the Barley (p. 104) Sung by Charles Chivers, details unknown. Collected by George Gardiner, pre-1910.

This song may be best known in a version with an insipid ending published by Cecil Sharp in *English Folk Songs for Schools*, in which the young woman becomes the lawyer's wife and the song ends in a shower of confetti. We prefer the story as Gardiner collected it, with the woman's spirited. It's an interesting tune, too.

Evening Love Song (p. 106) By Sam Richards, Totnes, Devon. Written in 1978.

The Game of All Fours (p. 107) Sung by Phoebe Smith, Woodbridge, Suffolk. Collected by Rod and Danny Stradling, 1960s.

The collectors actually recorded Phoebe Smith singing at a folksong club in London. The song is very well known in southern England, especially with gypsy singers (Phoebe Smith is a gypsy). It is a classic example of erotic symbolism, in this case based on a card game the object of which is to win high, low and jack.

The Banks of the Tyne (p. 108) From the MS of Thomas Hepple, Kirkwhelpington. From Beamish Museum Music Collection, Beamish, Durham.

The Old Miser (p. 109) Sung by Mrs Ursula Ridley, West Hoathley, Sussex. Collected by Ken Stubbs, 1962.

This was a well-known broadside ballad. The tune is a fine example of the power of tasteful decoration. The passing notes seem to have been added and they soften what is perhaps otherwise an unremarkable melodic line.

Through Lonesome Woods (p. 110) Sung by Henry Perkes, details unknown. Collected by George Gardiner, pre-1910.

The Navvie Man (p. 111) Sung by William Nott, Meshaw, Devon. Collected by Cecil Sharp, 1905.

There are a number of remakes of a song known in the folksong revival as 'The Little Beggarman' — usually in an Irish version. Most common in England is 'The Roving Journeyman', although 'The Navvie Man' is a close second. Nearly all the songs Sharp collected from William Nott have character and completeness. Sharp himself once commented that Nott was one of the best singers he had come across.

Freddie Mathews (p. 112) By Ron Elliott. Written in 1973. Printed in *Garland.*

Freddie Mathews was killed on picket duty during the 1972 miners' strike. The flying picket at power stations and coal depots asked the lorry drivers to turn back. The song tells the tragic tale of what happened when one refused.

Young Ramble-Away (p. 113) Sung by James Parsons, Lew Down, Devon. Collected by Sabine Baring-Gould, 1891.

A wonderful, wild tune to a fairly well-known set of words. The singer, James Parsons, seems to have been one of those inexhaustible suppliers of songs who now belongs to a bygone age. He sang for evenings on the trot without repeating himself, and was known, like his father, as 'The Singing Machine'.

Forty Miles (p. 114) Sung by Mark Anderson, Teesdale, Yorkshire. Collected by Ewan MacColl, 1947.

An enormously popular love lyric, found all over England, but perhaps mostly in the Yorkshire area where it still turns up regularly. Baring-Gould and Sharp also had good versions from the West Country. Usually, the tale ends with church bells, but Ewan MacColl's singer had an earthier liberated ending.

Nancy From London (p. 115) Sung by Mr J. Elliot, Todber, Dorset. Collected by H. E. D. Hammond, 1905. JFSS vol. 3, p. 101.

Nancy of Yarmouth/Weymouth/London seems to have been celebrated throughout the English countryside, particularly in the south. A version with an identical tune was collected in Newfoundland only in 1977, where the song is also popular.

The Prentice Boy (p. 116) Sung by Amy Birch, near Bampton, Devon. Collected by Sam Richards, Tish Stubbs and Paul Wilson, 1975.

A song originating in the 18th century and supposedly based on a real murder that took place on the Oxfordshire/Berkshire border. The theme caught the imagination of broadside poets and country singers; it was printed many times and established itself as one of the classic, later murder ballads. Amy Birch actually starts her performance with line 3 of verse 2, 'He pulled a dagger from his coat'. We have added verse 1 and the beginning of verse 2 from other versions. Although it leaves part of the background to the story incomplete, Amy Birch's beginning has a stunning effect. Singers who prefer the original might like to edit our version. The rest is exactly as she sang it.

The Knife in the Window (p. 117) Sung by Bill Whiting, Longcott, Berkshire. Collected by John Faulkner.

Verse 1 of this song derives from 'Hares on the Mountains', itself a more recent variety of the ballad 'The Two Magicians'. This lusty little encounter illustrates the theme in all these songs that whatever young women do, young men will get to them.

Kissing (p. 118) Sung by Mrs Lizzie Welch, Langport, Somerset. Collected by Cecil Sharp, 1904.

MARRIAGE

Happy, uneventful marriages do not produce enough conflict for drama or song, so it is hardly surprising how few songs of marital bliss there are.

There are many songs about young men and maidens with wedding bells ringing in their ears, but once the knot is tied the songs are of adultery, drunken or henpecked husbands, and babies bawling in the cradle. Some are even quite malicious.

Despite their humour, a wish-fulfilment stalks between the lines of songs like 'The Gypsy Laddie' or the broadside 'Timothy Briggs the Barber' and especially the wonderfully wry tale of 'The Poor Old Couple'.

HECKETTY PECKETTY

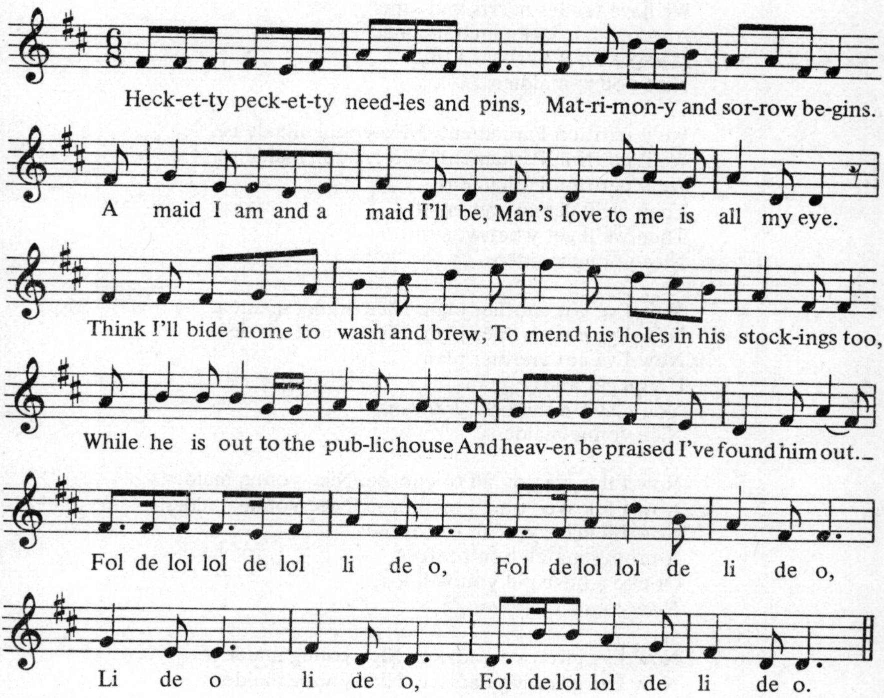

Heck-et-ty peck-et-ty need-les and pins, Mat-ri-mon-y and sor-row be-gins.

A maid I am and a maid I'll be, Man's love to me is all my eye.

Think I'll bide home to wash and brew, To mend his holes in his stock-ings too,

While he is out to the pub-lic house And heav-en be praised I've found him out.

Fol de lol lol de lol li de o, Fol de lol lol de li de o,

Li de o li de o, Fol de lol lol de li de o.

NICE YOUNG MAIDENS

1. Here's a pret-ty set of us. Nice young mai-dens.

Here's a pret-ty set of us. Nice young mai-dens.

Here's a pret-ty set of us, All for hus-bands at a loss.

Shall we long con-tin-ue thus? Nice young mai-dens.

123

2   We have tender hearts and kind. Nice young maidens.
We have tender hearts and kind. Nice young maidens.
We have tender hearts and kind
And for marriage much inclined
If we can but husbands find.
Nice young maidens.

3   We'll petition Parliament. Nice young maidens.
We'll petition Parliament. Nice young maidens.
We'll petition Parliament
Then we'll get an argument,
Then we'll get what we want.
Nice young maidens.

4   Now I've got another plan. Nice young maidens.
Now I've got another plan. Nice young maidens.
Now I've got another plan
If you get a little man
You may do the best you can.
Nice young maidens.

5   Now I'll leave you all to choose. Nice young maidens.
Now I'll leave you all to choose. Nice young maidens.
Now I'll leave you all to choose
A proper match don't refuse
Or else a husband you will lose.
Nice young maidens.

6   Now I've given you advice. Nice young maidens.
Now I've given you advice. Nice young maidens.
Now I've given you advice
If you are not over nice
You'll get husbands in a trice.
Nice young maidens.

THE DRUNKEN MAN

1. A couple got married for better or worse
But the woman had reason the man to curse
For never did he give her a good word
But came home at night as drunk as a lord.

Ch. So women I hope you'll follow this plan
If you should be plagued with a drunken man.

2   Next morning she went off in a flirt.
She pawned his waistcoat breeches and shirt.
And before she returned again to him
She spent three parts of the money in gin.

3   Then he came home in a terrible rage
But she was ready the foe to engage.
She plucked up her spirits and he did begin
She knocked him down with a rolling pin.

4   He hollered aloud, she tore his clothes,
She blacked his eyes and broked off his nose.
You villain, she cried, no more of your airs
And slap she bundled him over the stairs.

5   O wife dear wife, he then did say
On your husband have compassion, pray.
If you will me this time forgive
I'll never get drunk so long as I live.

JOAN TO JAN

1. I long to be mar-ried says Joan to Jan.

I have no boots for to get mar-ried in.

An old pair of boot-legs will do says Joan to Jan An Joan to Jan.

Ch. O what an 'or-rid thing for to get mar-ried in says Jan to Joan.

Good as oth-er poor folks says Joan to Jan.

O what an 'or-rid thing for to get mar-ried in says Jan to Joan.

(After verse 1 line 1 'I long to be married. . . . ' is dropped.)

2   I've no stockings for to get married in.
      I've no stockings for to get married in.
      A fleece of wool will do says Joan to Jan.
      A fleece of wool will do says Joan to Jan.
      O what an 'orrid thing for to get married in says Jan to Joan.
      Good as other poor folks says Joan to Jan.
      Good as other poor folks says Joan to Jan.
      O what an 'orrid thing for to get married in says Jan to Joan.

3   I've no breeches for to get married in.
      An old bull's hide will do says Joan to Jan.

4   I've no waistcoat for to get married in.
      An old sheepskin will do says Joan to Jan.

5   I've no jacket for to get married in.
      An old lime bag will do says Joan to Jan.

6   I've no necktie for to get married in.
     The tail of your shirt will do says Joan to Jan.

7   I've no hat for to get married in.
     An old bee butt will do says Joan to Jan.

I'LL BE NO SUBMISSIVE WIFE

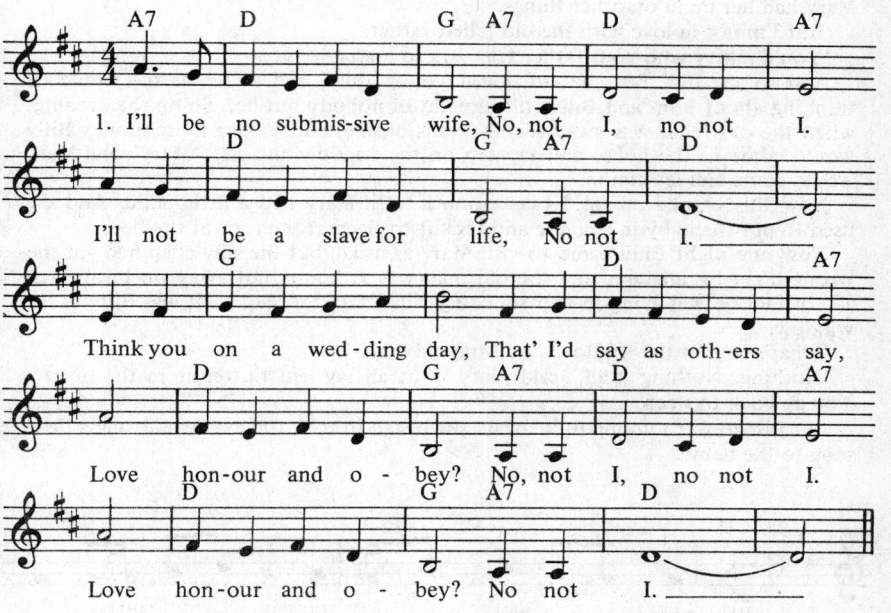

1. I'll be no submis-sive wife, No, not I, no not I.
I'll not be a slave for life, No not I. _____
Think you on a wed-ding day, That' I'd say as oth-ers say,
Love hon-our and o-bey? No, not I, no not I.
Love hon-our and o-bey? No not I. _____

2   I to dullness don't incline.
        No not I, no not I,
     Go to bed at half-past-nine.
        No not I.
     Should a humdrum husband say
     That at home I ought to stay,
     Do you think that I'll obey?
        No not I, no not I.
     Do you think that I'll obey?
        No not I.

127

GO FROM MY WINDOW

There was once a young woman called Mary, and she was courted by two men. One of the men was old and rich, and the other one was young and poor, and Mary loved the poor young man and didn't fancy the rich old codger at all.

Now when it was time for Mary to be married her father insisted that she married the rich old feller. Of course, he was only thinking of the money, but Mary had her mind on other things.

'But I'm not in love with the old feller, father.'

'You'll marry who your father tells you to marry.'

And so she did. But she still loved young Billy, and at nights she would lie thinking about him, and Billy still thought of nobody but her. So on the evenings when the old feller was away seeing to his business or making more money Billy would come to the house and tap tap on the window and call 'Mary', and Mary would come and let him in.

Now this carried on for a twelvemonth until Mary had a little child. And she used to put the baby in a cradle and rock it to sleep at the foot of the bed.

Now one night Billy came to visit Mary as usual, but the silly chap had got the wrong night by mistake, and the old man was at home, not away on business at all. In fact he was lying in bed snoozing when tap, tap, tap. . . It was Billy at the window.

'What's that at the window?' said the old man.

'Nothing. Nothing at all,' said Mary, 'but an ivy leaf fluttering in the breeze. You go back to sleep.'

But just to warn young Billy away, she began to rock the cradle and sing a little song to the baby:

Be - gone be - gone my___ Wil - ly my __ Bil - ly ___
Be - gone my _____ love and my dear.
O the wind _ and the rain have _ sent him back a - gain
And you can - not have a lodg - ing here.

But Billy called out 'Mary', and the old feller woke up again.

'What's that? What's going on out there?'

'Nothing, nothing at all. Only the owls calling and hooting through the night. You go back to sleep.'

But she sang again:

> Begone, begone, my Willie, my Billy
> Begone my love and my dear,
>   O the wind and the rain
>   they have sent him back again
> And you cannot have a lodging here.

But still Billy called and tapped, and the old feller woke up again.

'What's that? What's going on out there? There's somebody there. I know it. . . .'

'It's nothing. Nothing at all. Just a bat flying against the window, and the owls calling, and the ivy leaves falling. You go back to sleep.'

And she sang again:

> Begone, begone, my Willie, my Billy
> Begone my love and my dear.
>   For the wind is in the west
>   And the cuckoo's in his nest
> And you cannot have a lodging here.

But still he tapped, and Mary leapt up and threw open the casement and sang out:

> Begone, begone, my Willie, thou silly
> Begone my fool and my fear.
>   Oh the devil's in the man
>   That he cannot understand
> That tonight he cannot lodge here.

NEVER MARRY AN OLD MAN

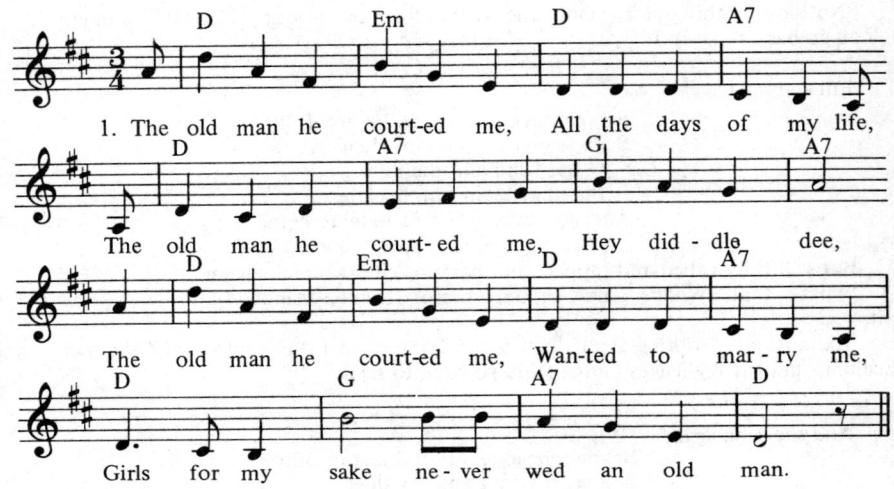

1. The old man he court-ed me, All the days of my life,
The old man he court-ed me, Hey did-dle dee,
The old man he court-ed me, Wan-ted to mar-ry me,
Girls for my sake ne-ver wed an old man.

2   When he got into church,
All the days of my life,
When he got into church,
Hey diddle dee,
When he got into church,
All the money he begrudged,
Girls for my sake never wed an old man.

3   When we sat down to dine,
All the days of my life,
When we sat down to dine,
Hey diddle dee,
When we sat down to dine
He said I looked too fine,
Girls for my sake never wed an old man.

4   When we sat down to sup,
All the days of my life,
When we sat down to sup,
Hey diddle dee,
When we sat down to sup
He said I eat too much,
Girls for my sake never wed an old man.

5   When it was ten-o-clock,
       All the days of my life,
       When it was ten-o-clock,
       Hey diddle dee,
       When it was ten-o-clock,
       All the doors he did lock,
       Girls for my sake never wed an old man.

6   When he got into bed,
       All the days of my life,
       When he got into bed,
       Hey diddle dee,
       When he got into bed
       He lay like a lump of lead,
       Girls for my sake never wed an old man.

7   When he was fast asleep,
       All the days of my life,
       When he was fast asleep,
       Hey diddle dee,
       When he was fast asleep
       Out of bed I did creep,
       Into the arms of a nice young man.

8   Then we did sport and play,
       All the days of my life,
       Then we did sport and play,
       Hey diddle dee,
       Then we did sport and play
       Until the break of day
       Then I went back to the silly old man.

9   For a young man is my delight,
       All the days of my life,
       A young man is my delight,
       Hey diddle dee,
       For a young man is my delight
       All the days of my life,
       Girls for my sake never wed an old man.

THE POOR OLD COUPLE

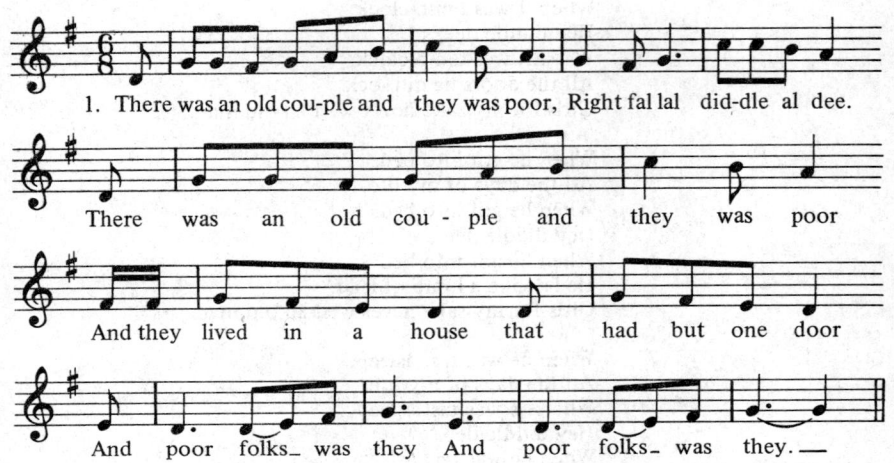

1. There was an old cou-ple and they was poor, Right fal lal did-dle al dee.

There was an old cou-ple and they was poor

And they lived in a house that had but one door

And poor folks_ was they And poor folks_ was they. —

2   Now the little old man he went from home.
Right fal lal diddle al dee.
Now the little old man he went from home
And he leaved this little old woman alone
And that was hard, said she,
And that was hard, said she.

3   There was a town clerk who lived close by.
Right fal lal diddle al dee.
There was a town clerk who lived close by
And he was resolved with her to lie
And that was kind, said she,
And that was kind, said she.

4   Now eight-o-clock and a little o'er.
Right fal lal diddle al dee.
Now eight-o-clock and a little o'er
A gentle knock came to the door.
Who is that, said she,
Who is that, said she.

5   O 'tis the town clerk, O don't be afraid.
Right fal lal diddle al dee.
O 'tis the town clerk, O don't be afraid.
Come down and open the door he said.
O yes I will said she,
O yes I will said she.

6 At twelve-o-clock and a little o'er.
Right fal lal diddle al dee.
At twelve-o-clock and a little o'er
Another knock came to the door.
Who is that, said she,
Who is that, said she.

7 It is your dear husband, O don't be afraid.
Right fal lal diddle al dee.
It is your dear husband, O don't be afraid.
Come down and open the door, he said.
O yes I will, said she,
O yes I will, said she.

8 Now fetch me an apple from yonder tree.
Right fal lal diddle al dee.
Now fetch me an apple from yonder tree
And I will come and let in thee.
O yes I will, said he,
O yes I will, said he.

9 Now as he was a-grabbing under the tree
Right fal lal diddle al dee.
Now as he was a-grabbing under the tree
Up jumped the town clerk and away runned he.
That's very well done, said she,
That's very well done, said she.

10 O I have been sick since you have been gone.
Right fal lal diddle al dee.
O I have been sick since you have been gone,
My sickness was all for the want of a man.
Poor wife, said he.
Poor cuckold, thought she.

A COLLIER LAD

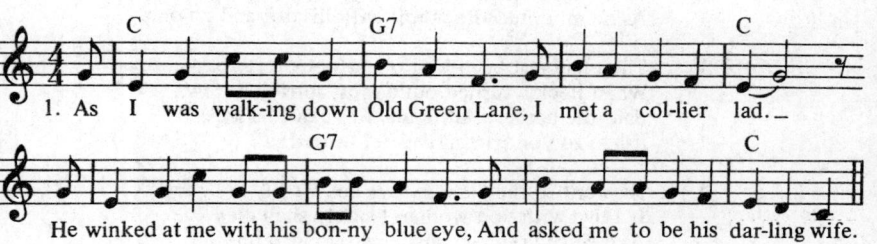

1. As I was walk-ing down Old Green Lane, I met a col-lier lad.
He winked at me with his bon-ny blue eye, And asked me to be his dar-ling wife.

2 I said: No no I'm far too young
Far too young for you.
The younger you are the better for me
Not quite sixteen years of age.

3   He took me away and he locked me up
Just like a bird in a cage
And now I'm the mother of a child
Not quite seventeen years of age.

4   Now all you lassies take a tip from me
Never let a feller an inch above your knee.
If you do you'll be just like me
Always having kids on your knee.

TIMOTHY BRIGGS THE BARBER

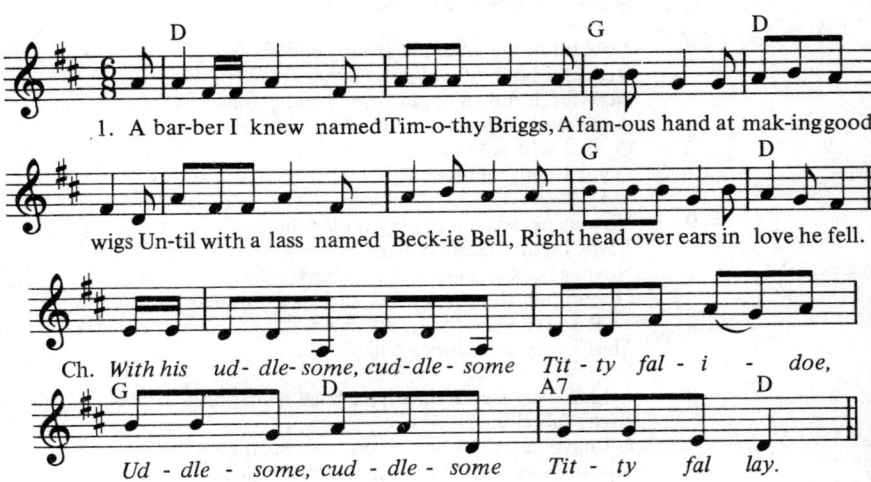

1. A bar-ber I knew named Tim-o-thy Briggs, A fam-ous hand at mak-ing good
wigs Un-til with a lass named Beck-ie Bell, Right head over ears in love he fell.
Ch. With his ud-dle-some, cud-dle-some Tit-ty fal-i-doe,
Ud-dle-some, cud-dle-some Tit-ty fal lay.

2   They went to the church the knot to tie
To a wooden-legged parson named Jonathan Sly.
You would have laughed to have seen the fun
As he mounted the pulpit with his dot and go one.

3   They had not been wed o'er a week or two
When Beckie turned out a most terrible shrew.
Said the barber: A life like this can't be led
I'll go to yon parson and get unwed.

4   He went to the parson, says he: Mr Sly
If I live with yon woman I surely shall die
And since you have made us two into one
I've come for to see if we can't be undone.

5   Oh, the parson says he, that's a thing rather new,
I have not the power my flock to undo,
So you must go home, lead a happier life,
And I'll call in the morning and tick off your wife.

6   Now the parson quite pleased after taking a glass
Stepped into the house and he lectured the lass
And the barber returned and what did he see?
Why, the parson with Betsy on top of his knee.

7   Now the barber he bristled up every hair.
Says he: Mr Sly, what are you doing here?
Oh you said that you wanted undoing, my man.
Don't you see I'm a-trying as fast as I can?

8   I think I am done as I ne'er was before
And he kicked Mr Sly clean out of the door.
He laid in the street with his wooden leg stuck
Like a spade sticking up in a cartload of muck.

9   And now they live more reconciled
Until at last she brought forth a child.
And the parson he hung himself on a peg
When he heard it was born with a new wooden leg.

THE GYPSY LADDIE

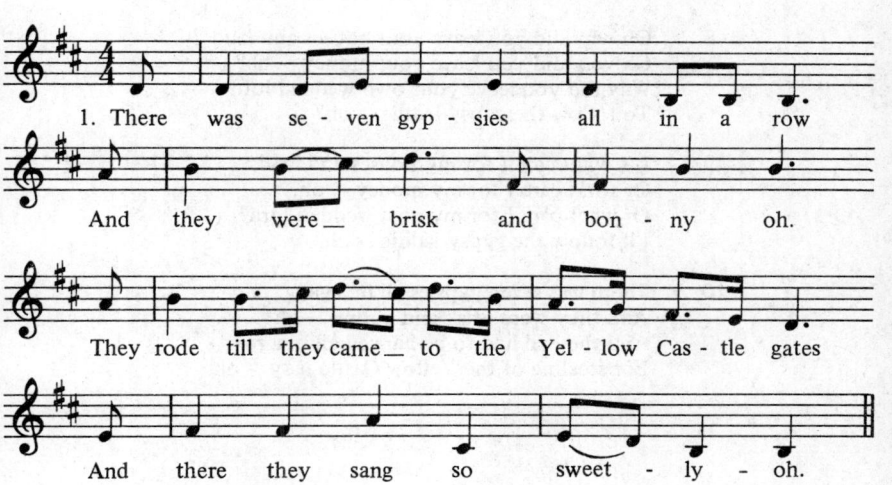

1. There was se-ven gyp-sies all in a row

And they were brisk and bon-ny oh.

They rode till they came to the Yel-low Cas-tle gates

And there they sang so sweet-ly oh.

2   The Yellow Castle lady she came down
With a waiting maid beside her — oh.
They gave to her a nut brown bowl.
It was made the best of any — oh.

3   She gave to them a bottle of wine,
        She gave to them some money — oh,
        She gave to them a far better thing,
        The ring from off her finger — oh.

4   And she pulled off her high-heeled boots,
        They was made of Spanish leather — oh
        And she put on her Highland brogues
        To follow the gypsy laddie — oh.

5   Now when the lord came home that night
        Enquiring for his lady — oh
        The waiting maid made this reply
        She's following the gypsy laddie — oh.

6   Then saddle me my milk white steed
        And bridle him so sweetly — oh
        That I might find my own wedded wife
        That's following the gypsy laddie — oh.

7   Then he rode all that summer's night
        And part of the next morning — oh
        And then he spied his own wedded wife
        Both cold and wet and weary — oh.

8   Oh why did you leave your houses and lands?
        Oh why did you leave your money — oh?
        Why did you leave your own wedded lord
        To follow the gypsy laddie — oh?

9   It's what care I for my houses and lands
        Or what care I for my money — oh,
        Or what care I for my own wedded lord?
        I'll follow the gypsy laddie — oh.

10   There was seven gypsies all in a gang
        And they were brisk and bonny — oh
        And they all had to be hanged all in a row
        For stealing of the Yellow Castle lady — oh.

NOTHING BETWEEN US NOW

1. I was walk-ing a-long some side street, see, down Brock-ley
When I 'eard this wo-man sing-in' some-'ing sof'-ly.
She was think-in' a-bout the 'us-band she 'ad done with-out
Since the day 'e wen' a-way and then 'e ne-ver come back.
Sing-in' to 'im she was, a lit-tle too late be-cause
Las' thing 'e ev-er done for 'er was leave 'er flat
'N' these are the words she was sing-in', I can 'ear 'em now.

2 Can't 'ardly believe you really loved me did yer
Though your mates all say you swore you'd 'ave me, didn' yer.
Well you 'ad me too, an' I loved you.
Thought you was 'appy with me.
Didn' we get married and didn' I carry
Them two kids of ours you give me?
We made 'em between us, ain't that nothin' between us now?

137

3   Not a lot between us that Sat'day night I met yer
     'Cept for the girl who come with yer, you soon 'ad to ditch 'er.
     Never said much — didn' 'ave to,
     We done alright without it.
     You fancied me and I fancied you
     That was all there was about it.
     Are them days all over? No never, they're between us now.

4   Nothing much between us first night we slept together
     Naked and achin' to be one another's lovers for ever.
     If you'd been honest you wouldn' 'ave promised,
     Now there's a new 'ead on your pillow.
     She don' know you yet the way I do.
     Time she does it'll likely kill 'er.
     Your bird come between us, is that nothin' between us now?

5   Not much love lost between us, precious little left, like.
     We ain't together no more, but the wounds'll never 'eal till death, right.
     'Cause there's been things said and there's been things done.
     P'raps you could 'ave 'it me 'arder.
     There's 'alf an empty bed and your clothes all gone
     And two kids with no father
     But you writ me a letter saying 'nothin' between us now'.

6   You've walked out the door for good and all then, ain't yer?
     Left yer past and yer wife and yer kids and their future be'ind yer.
     One week in four yer cheque falls through the door,
     It's the least you can get away with,
     Rolled up so small, can't 'ardly find it at all.
     Are we jus' things you play with?
     'Atin' an' 'urtin', that's what's between us now.

7   Was it the kids come between us? Didn' 'alf make yer jealous.
     I really believe you'd rather I went out with other fellers.
     One day you was off to a new job up north
     Where you went and met and fell in love with someone.
     Three years you been gone, I've 'ad to soldier on
     An' I'm learnin' to be me own woman
     But 'ow can you tell me there's nothin' between us now?

NOTES

Hecketty Pecketty (p. 123) Sung by Mrs Harper, Hambridge, Somerset. Collected by Cecil Sharp, 1904.

What better introduction to a selection of songs about marriage? In Sharp's manuscript this is the complete song, although broadsides exist such as 'The Old Maid of 95', in which these words occur as part of a longer song. However, it can be argued that what the broadsides take six verses to say 'Hecketty Pecketty' does just as well in one.

Nice Young Maidens (p. 123) From the MS of Thomas Hepple of Kirkwhelpington. Beamish Museum Music Collection, Beamish, Durham.

The tune and the verse formula suggest the children's game 'We are the Roman Soldiers', although there appears to be little link other than the possibility that this is a game song as well. It's refreshing to find a version of a song in which young women are looking for husbands instead of the more familiar old maid's laments. 'Over nice' in the last verse means 'over particular'.

The Drunken Man (p. 125) Sung by William Nott, Meshaw, Devon. Collected by Cecil Sharp, 1908.

The image of the tolerant wife sitting at home patiently suffering her husband's waywardness is quite rare in folksong — more common in the classics. The subject of this song — a married woman who meets her inconsiderate husband on his own ground — is more typical. This song is not very common in oral tradition but was well known to broadside printers.

Joan to Jan (p. 126) Sung by William Nott, Meshaw, Devon. Collected by Cecil Sharp, 1904.

We know of no more unusual tune than this one in our folk tradition. The dialogue between the couple about to get married is common enough, and the country humour is rough and managed well enough, but to sing it accurately is a feat of virtuosity. It's worth persisting — even if it sounds odd at first — especially with two singers. Sharp has this to say in JFSS vol. 1-2: 'Mr. Nott, who is an old man, said of this song: "It is very difficult to sing, for you must show the two voices." It certainly gave me considerable trouble to note correctly. The Rev. A. de Gex and I have listened to it on three different occasions. At first we thought that the two changes of key in the middle of the song were unintentional, and I accordingly noted that passage, as it was undoubtedly sung on its repetition at the end of the verse. But on the last occasion we went to the piano in the next room while Mr. Nott sang the song twice over, and we found that he sang it as here printed, and that he kept his pitch with perfect accuracy. I do not think there are many singers who could do the same.'

In the light of this definitive evidence from Sharp himself, it seems a pity that the song was straightened out when more recently published.

I'll Be No Submissive Wife (p. 127) From a Pitts broadside. Baring-Gould collection, British Museum.

Unfortunately, we have only seen these two verses of this song. Independent ladies are not rare in folksong, but this is an unusually explicit and spirited declaration. No tune was given, but it is not difficult to spot the distinctive verse formula that has been used in the past for everything from political creeds to hymns and goodnight ballads.

Go From My Window (p. 128) Sung and spoken by John Woodrich, Thrushelton, Devon. Collected by Sabine Baring-Gould, 1890.

An elegant cante-fable of ancient lineage. The tune and verses have remained remarkably consistent from the late 16th century when it was printed first. Often the spoken part seems to have been omitted, but it seems a shame to elevate the song at the expense of the story. For accuracy's sake we should point out that our spoken parts are not to be found in Baring-Gould's MS. His tale is in staid language and we get the impression that he simply wrote out the bones of the story. Our version is transcribed from Tish Stubbs' own performance.

Never Marry An Old Man (p. 130) Sung by Mrs Overd, Langport, Somerset. Collected by Cecil Sharp, 1904.

One of the best-known examples of a 'May and December' song. For the sake óf fluency we altered Mrs Overd's last line 'And back to the cottage of that old man' and for sense we added our first verse. Mrs Overd's title 'The Old Man He Courted Me' was perhaps from a half-forgotten first verse.

The Poor Old Couple (p. 132) Sung by Henry Reed, Axbridge, Somerset. Collected by Cecil Sharp, 1908.

This often collected, often unnoticed song seems to have an ancient ring to it, despite a modern touch in the last line when the wife's thoughts are neatly revealed.

A Collier Lad (p. 133) Sung by Mrs Lilly Hill, Castleford. Collected by A. E. Green.

Timothy Briggs the Barber (p. 134) Sung by Arthur Wood, Middlesborough, Cleveland. Collected by Colin Wharton, early 1960s. In the archives of the Institute of Dialect and Folk Life Studies, Leeds University.

An uncommon song that has circulated on broadsides but rarely been collected. We know of only this one version from the field. The parson is often the butt of the joke in traditional tales.

The Gypsy Laddie (p. 135) Sung by James Watson, Portsmouth Workhouse. Collected by George Gardiner, 1907.

This is an excellent version of a ballad which probably needs little introduction. Speculation has died down now as to whether or not it is based on some real incident, although the song itself shows no sign of disappearing from tradition. Older sets frequently contain the final detail about the gypsies being hanged, although more recent singers have dropped this unfortunate conclusion.

Nothing Between Us Now (p. 137) By John Pole, London. Written in 1977.

Like the tunes for many of John Pole's songs this one needs to be varied a little to accommodate the words. It is worth making the effort, for his use of London idioms is impressive. We have written the words exactly as the composer sang them, although they don't have to be adhered to rigidly.

BAWDY SONGS

In recent years bawdy songs have received some of the attention denied them in earlier, more prudish days of folksong study. There are numerous bawdy songs and the fact that they still live a vigorous life is a testament to general demand.

The bawdy song can be broadly defined as a humorous song involving sex or excreta, but the boundaries of taste are difficult to draw and are always subjective. We have included some of what we feel are the wittier pieces, but not erotic songs, verbally witty though many are, since we feel they do not belong. The symbolic erotic song is intimate, inviting the listeners into the singer's thoughts and emotions, while the bawdy song is usually thrown out to the listeners with the object of creating hilarity.

THE CRABFISH

1. There was a lit-tle man and he had a lit-tle wife
And he loved her as dear as he loved his life.
Ch. Mash a row dow dow dow did-dle all the day.
Mash a row dow dow dow did-dle all the day.

2   Now the wife's with child and she's fallen sick
And all that she wanted was a little crabfish.

3   So her husband arose and put on his clothes
And down to the seaside he followed his nose.

4   O fisherman, fisherman can you tell me
Have you got a little crabfish you'll sell to me?

5   O yes, sir, yes sir, I've one, two, and three
And the best in the basket I'll sell to thee.

6   So he took the little crabfish, he took it by the horn
He slung it on his back and toddled off home.

7   But when he got it home he couldn't find a dish
So into the chamberpot he put the crabfish.

8   And early in the morning the wife she arose
She felt beneath the bed for to use the so-and-so.

9   She took up her clothes and she began to squat
And the crabfish got her by the you-know-what.

10   So loudly did she scream, so loudly did she grunt
The devil's in the room and he's got me by the nose.

11   Wife, dearest wife, you must be going mad
That you can't tell the devil from an old sea crab.

12   If it be a sea crab or fish of any kind
       It'll let go its hold if you blow it from behind.

13   Se he's knelt down and lifted up her clothes
       But it took its other pincher and got him by the nose.

14   Curse the very hour that I brought the thing hither
       For it's joined my nose and my wife's tail together.

15   So you'd better have a look before you have a squat
       Make sure there's nothing swimming in the old pee-pot.

TH'OWD CHAP COME OWER T'BANK

1. Th'owd chap come o-wert' bank   bawl-ing for his tea,

Saw a muck-y pair o' clogs where his owd clogs should be.

Come here wife, come here wife, what's this here I see?

How come this muck-y pair o' clogs where my owd clogs should be?

Y' owd bug-ger, you daft bug-ger, it's plain as plain can be,

They're just a coup-le o' pick-le jars me owd mam sent to me.

I've been o'er hills and dales, me lass, and man-y a gras-sy moor

But girt hob-nails on a pick-le jar I've ne-ver seen be-fore.

2   Th'owd chap come ower t' bank bawling for his tea,
Saw a coat on 't back o't' door where his owd coat should be.
Come here wife, come here wife, what's this here I see?
How come this coat on 't back o't' door where my owd coat should be?
    Y'owd bugger, you daft bugger, it's plain as plain can be
    It's just an owd pudding clout me owd mam sent to me.
I've been o'er hills and dales, me lass, and many a grassy moor
But buttons on a pudding clout I've never seen before.

3   Th'owd chap come ower t' bank bawling for his tea,
Saw a head on 't pillow where his owd head should be.
Come here wife, come here wife, what's this here I see?
How come this head on 't pillow where my owd head should be?
    Y'owd bugger, you daft bugger, it's plain as plain can be
    It's just a girt big turnip me owd mam sent to me.
I've been o'er hills and dales, me lass, and many a grassy moor
But a girt big turnip full of teeth I've never seen before.

4   Th'owd chap come ower t' bank bawling for his tea,
Saw a pair of hairy cods where his owd cods should be.
Come here wife, come here wife, what's this here I see?
How come this pair of hairy cods where my owd cods should be?
    Y'owd bugger, you daft bugger, it's plain as plain can be,
    It's just a couple of garden spuds me owd mam sent to me.
I've been o'er hills and dales, me lass, and many a grassy moor,
But garden spuds with hairs on I've never seen before.

5   Th'owd chap come ower t' bank bawling for his tea,
Saw a great big standing prick where his owd prick should be.
Come here wife, come here wife, what's this here I see?
How come this great big standing prick where my owd prick should be?
    Y'owd bugger, you daft bugger, it's plain as plain can be,
    It's just a home-grown carrot my owd mam sent to me.
I've been o'er hills and dales, me lass, and many a grassy moor,
But a carrot diggin' a great big hoyle I've never seen before.

THE TAILOR'S BREECHES

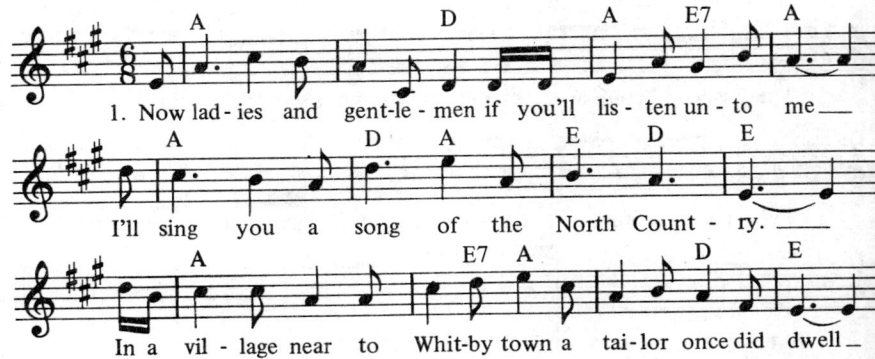

1. Now lad-ies and gent-le-men if you'll lis-ten un-to me
I'll sing you a song of the North Count-ry.
In a vil-lage near to Whit-by town a tai-lor once did dwell

And wo-men, wine and com-pan-y he loved them right well. ___

2   A dance one New Year's evening the tailor did attend
I'm sure that he would ne'er have gone if he had seen the end.
The jolly little tailor he will ne'er forget that night
For never yet was tailor seen in such a sorry plight.

3   Oh he danced and he sang and had whisky many a tot,
The jolly little tailor was the merriest of the lot.
To a lady he was dancing with the tailor then declared
If you'll lend to me your petticoats I'll dance like a maid.

4   Oh his breeches he put off and her petticoats put on.
The maid the tailor's breeches she quickly did adorn.
The fiddler he played to them a merry merry tune.
She danced his money, watch, and breeches clean out of the room.

5   O bring me my breeches back, the tailor loud did call.
O bring me my breeches back, my money, watch and all.
All the company there assembled with laughter they did roar
When the little tailor's petticoats fell down upon the floor.

6   O Lord, said the tailor, where ever Thou may be.
O Lord, said the tailor, take pity now on me.
Well the little tailor didn't know the best thing for to do
For his little shirt was far too short to cover all below.

7   'Twas then the fiddler played a tune for all that he was worth.
The tune he played the tailor was the famous Cock o' the North.
All the ladies were delighted and they loudly shouted: No
When the tailor took his trilby hat to cover Uncle Joe.

8   When at last the little tailor got out into the street
A bevy of fair damsels he chanced for to meet.
All the ladies screamed with laughter when the tailor did appear
They wished him a Merry Christmas and a Happy New Year.

9   The poor little tailor those ladies did address
Says he: It is not ladylike to laugh at man's distress.
Said the ladies to the tailor: Give us no more of that
If you call yourself a gentleman why don't you raise your hat?

10   In that village near to Whitby town there's old men living yet
They'll tell you of that famous dance they never will forget.
Old ladies too will tell to you the dance they loved the best
Was the dance where the tailor he did show his cuckoo's nest.

11   Now that jolly little tailor from that day unto this
Oh women, wine, and company he gave them all a miss.
At a dance that little tailor they never more did catch
Since the lady pinched his breeches, his money, and his watch.

COTTAGE FOR SALE

1. Come all you rak-ish ba-che-lors, come lis-ten to my tale.

I've got a cot-tage neat and snug I'm put-ting up for sale.

It's in a pleas-ant val-ley with a ris-ing hill a-bove

And a cry-stal stream of wa-ter is a-run-ning through a grove.

Ch. *Then oc-cu-py my cot-tage for it is in good re-pair.*

It has a plea-sant en-trance and will suit you to a hair.

2   The first was a rich old alderman the cottage did engage.
He thought himself so stiff and strong though eighty years of age.
He fumbled long till he was tired and said: My dear I'm sure
I'm doubled up and cannot stand nor yet find out the door.

3   Oh the next was a fat old quaker all with his Thee and Thou
And for to take the cottage O the spirit moves me now.
But he could not get in at all for such a paunch had he
And from his breeches pocket he could not pull the key.

4   Oh the next was a brave young sailor bold with golden locks in store
And soon within that cottage that jolly tar was moored.
He roamed the cottage up and down and turned the things about
Until he got quite giddy — and then he tumbled out.

5   Oh the next was a brave young soldier that cottage did desire
And he demanded entrance or else he said he'd fire.
He marched in like a hero bold, the door was opened wide,
His pouch and ammunition and his balls he left outside.

6   So all young men and bachelors come hasten, be in time.
Come and view my cottage for you'll find it snug and prime.
The roof is well thatched over and the entrance neat and plain
And all whoever entered there have wished to go again.

COCK-A-DOODLE-DOO

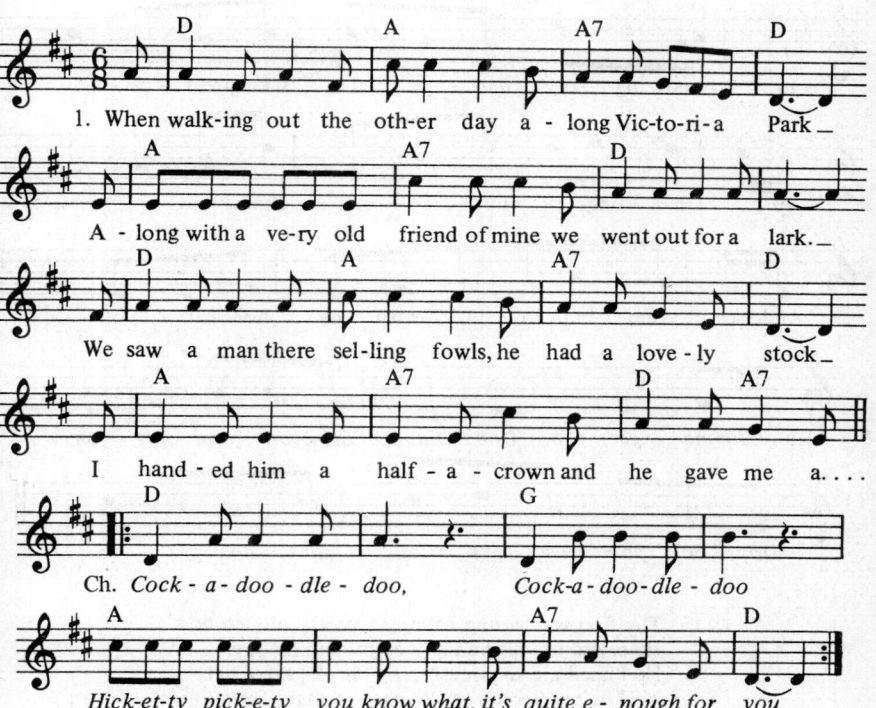

1. When walk-ing out the oth-er day a - long Vic-to-ri-a Park _

A - long with a ve-ry old friend of mine we went out for a lark. _

We saw a man there sel-ling fowls, he had a love-ly stock _

I hand - ed him a half - a - crown and he gave me a. . . .

Ch. Cock - a - doo - dle - doo,   Cock-a - doo-dle - doo

Hick-et-ty pick-e-ty you know what, it's quite e - nough for you. _

2   I put the old cock under my arm a-walking along the street.
Along with a very old friend of mine my judy I did meet.
She put her arm around me and she gave me quite a shock.
She put her hand right up my coat and then she got hold of my. . . .

3   I took the old cock home with me and I put him in a cage.
Along with another old hen of mine and they went in a rage.
Some lady friends was passing by and thought it quite a lark
And one of them she said to me: The hen had got hold of the. . . .

4   Kind friends what I am telling you is only a bit of chaff.
The reason why I'm here tonight is just to make you laugh.
And when I come this way again I'll have a better stock
And just to please you one and all I'll show to you my. . . .

THE BUXOM DAIRY MAID

1. I am a young dair-y maid bux-om and bright.
In mind-ing my dair-y I take great de-light.
In __ mak-ing of but-ter and cheese that is new
And a young man to play with my how-d'-you-do.
Ch. With me gee ho Dob-bin, Drive on your wag-gon
Drive on your wag-gon, Gee - up and gee - ho.

2   The first was young Johnny a pretty plough boy.
He called me his honey, delight and his joy.
He kissed me so sweetly, my cheek gave a pat
And he's welcome at all times to shave for all that.

3   The next a young shepherd a buxom young lad
And many's the frolic together we had.
He used me so kindly he shoved it in tight
And he played a sweet tune on his tapering pipe.

4   The waggoners they are all jolly blades,
They know very well how to please the young maids.
They are hearty and willing, good natured and free
And those are the boys that shall do it for me.

5 My mother she told me of men to beware
  Unless they should draw my poor heart in a snare
  But for all advice still I care not a fig
  For young men shall play with my hairy wig.

6 My snatch is my own and the ground is the king's.
  It is free for a young man that brings a good thing.
  So let him be strong or ever so stout.
  I'll warrant I'll make him to quickly give out.

JUST AN OLD FASHIONED PUSH BIKE

It's just an old fash-ioned push bike ＿ with an old fash-ioned frame ＿

And a bell gives a warn-ing to you. ＿＿＿

An old fash-ioned sad - dle that I used to strad-dle,

When the toil of the long day was through. ＿＿

It has no Dun-lop ty - res I just ride the rims,

Mind, there's some-thing that makes it di - vine, ＿＿＿

On a cob - ble - stone hill I can still get a thrill

On an old fash - ioned push bike like mine.

NOTES

The Crabfish (p. 142)   Melody and four verses of text from Mrs Overd, Langport, Somerset. Collected by Cecil Sharp, 1904. Our version from Sharp's MS. Other verses collated from other versions including Bishop Percy's Folio MS and C. K. Sharpe *A Ballad Book*, 1824.

Gershon Legman claims that this song has the longest unbroken genealogy of any English bawdy song. As far as we know it was first written down in Italy by Sacchetti, *c.* 1400 as a prose tale. The English-language version, though, is always in verse, and our earliest-known text is from Bishop Percy's Folio Manuscript *c.* 1620. It is usually encountered today as 'The Lobster Song'. F. J. Child did not include it in his *The English and Scottish Popular Ballads,* probably because of the same prudishness which caused Cecil Sharp to note down only a handful of verses from his singer, Mrs Overd. Her melody for this song is the most exciting we have come across.

Th' Owd Chap Come Ower T'Bank (p. 143)   Sung by Harold Sladen, Openshaw, Manchester, Lancashire. Collected by Ewan MacColl, 1933.

F. J. Child called this song 'Our Goodman' (Child 274). A very ancient piece, it has been suggested that it may be a section from a longer narrative. There is no evidence for this assertion in English-language tradition, but the song has been known all over Europe for centuries and enjoys a vigorous life in North America and Australia. Everywhere it settles it picks up local details. This Lancashire version is one of the best we have heard, for its rich vernacular language, conversational melody and explicit denouement. The singer was 18 in 1933 when the song was collected and learnt it from his grandmother who lived in Wigan.

The Tailor's Breeches (p. 144)   Sung by Arthur Wood, Middlesborough, Teesside. Collected by Colin Wharton, 1962. In the archives of the Institute of Dialect and Folk Life studies, Leeds University.

Arthur Wood, in his 80s in the early 1960s when he sang to Colin Wharton, claimed the words as his own and the collector notes that this incident happened at a dance in a village near Whitby many years ago. The traditional song about the tailor losing his breeches was known to Thomas Hardy in Dorset years before, and versions of the song have occasionally turned up ever since. None are as detailed or superbly ridiculous as Mr Wood's version, and our justification for his claim to authorship is that he reworked the existing song in his own, very inventive way. It is not rare to hear of traditional tales being referred to as actual occurences.

Cottage for Sale (p. 146)   Sung by Henry King (75), Lyndhurst, Hampshire. Collected by J. G. Guyer, 1906. The George B. Gardiner MS.

Often printed on broadsides, rarely collected in the field, this piece is the typical concoction of a Seven Dials poet, slightly wordy, but witty, and full of *double-entendre.* The singer's tune is usually associated with 'The Handsome Cabin Boy', although in his version he simply repeated the tune for lines 3 and 4 throughout verses and chorus. We have given it a first phrase and also a last verse from a broadside.

Cock-A-Doodle-Doo (p. 147)   Sung by Walter Pardon, Knapton, Norfolk. Collected by Tish Stubbs and Sam Richards, 1977.

Another bawdy piece that has been in the folksong repertoire for years but ignored by collectors. It is still enormously popular throughout the English-speaking world; just as often remembered by women as men.

The Buxom Dairy Maid (p. 148)   Broadside from the Harris Library collection, Preston, Lancashire. Printer's name not given.

Very similar in style to 'Cottage For Sale' and, again, frequently encountered in print but not in oral circulation. The melody, 'Gee Ho Dobbin', is 18th century and was popular for humorous and light-hearted broadsides.

Just an Old Fashioned Push Bike (p. 149)   Sung by Bert Draycott, Fishburn, Durham. Collected by Ian Scott Massie, 1970s. Beamish Music Collection.

CHILDREN'S SONGS

There's a world of difference between rhymes sung by adults to children and the rhymes children sing themselves. A few adults' songs appear elsewhere in this anthology — the dandling song 'Did You See My Man?', for instance, or 'Dance To Your Daddy' — but we are concerned here with those scraps of rhyme which punctuate playground activity, are sung on tops of buses, on the way to swimming or football, or bawled out raucously as an affront to authority anywhere and everywhere.

A separate anthology could be compiled from the rich folklore of children, especially modern urban children. Our selection is necessarily small, but it gives the flavour.

DOWN MARSH LANE

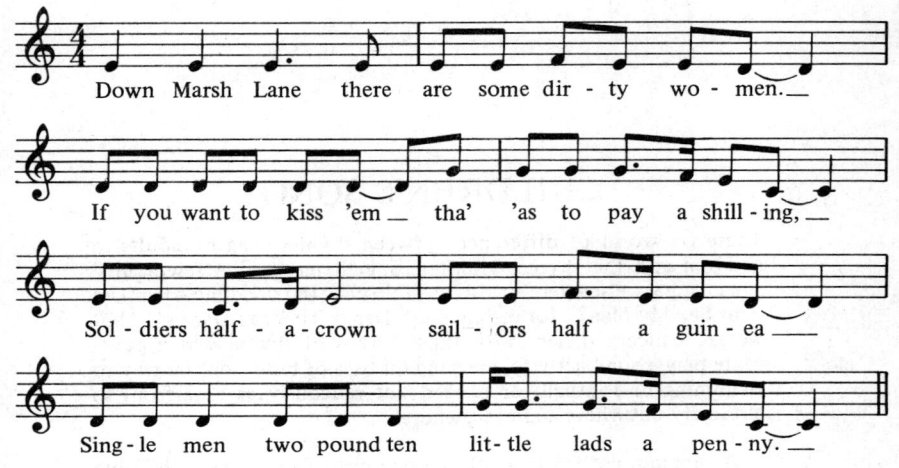

Down Marsh Lane there are some dir - ty wo - men.

If you want to kiss 'em tha' 'as to pay a shill - ing,

Sol - diers half - a - crown sail - ors half a guin - ea

Sing - le men two pound ten lit - tle lads a pen - ny.

MOLLY RILEY

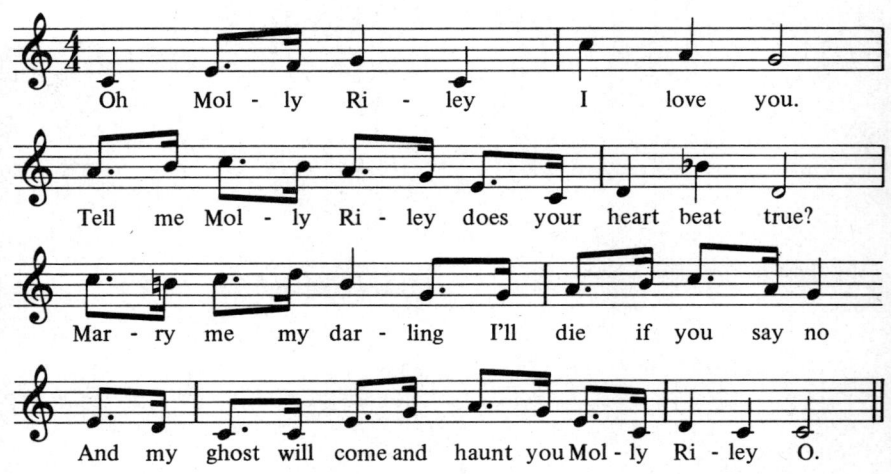

Oh Mol - ly Ri - ley I love you.

Tell me Mol - ly Ri - ley does your heart beat true?

Mar - ry me my dar - ling I'll die if you say no

And my ghost will come and haunt you Mol - ly Ri - ley O.

THREE POPEYE RHYMES

1. I'm Pop-eye the sail-or man, ___ I come from the land of Ja - pan ___
I climb on the stee-ple and pee on the people, I'm Popeye the sailor man.

2   I'm Popeye the Eskimo,
I come from the land of the snow.
I lie on my belly and shiver like jelly,
I'm Popeye the Eskimo.

3   I'm Popeye the sailor man.
I sat in a pot of jam.
The jam was so sticky it stuck to my dicky,
I'm Popeye the sailor man.

DO YE KNOW MY FATHER?

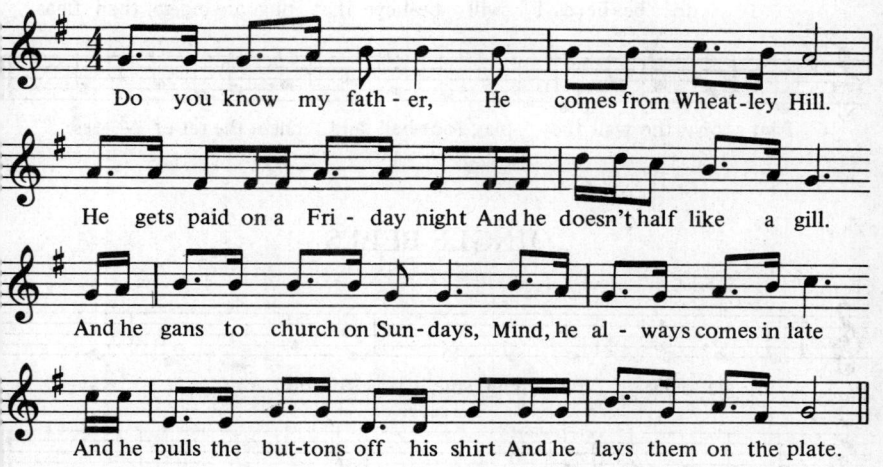

Do you know my fath-er, He comes from Wheat-ley Hill.

He gets paid on a Fri - day night And he doesn't half like a gill.

And he gans to church on Sun-days, Mind, he al - ways comes in late

And he pulls the but-tons off his shirt And he lays them on the plate.

153

B I BUY

1. B I Buy, B E Bee, Be I bick-y buy, bee bo bo,

Bick-y buy bo bee you boo, Bick-y buy bo bee you boo.

2   D I Die, D E Dee,
D I dicky-die, dee doe doe,
Dicky die doe dee you do,
Dicky die doe dee you do.

3   Fee I fie, fee E fee,
Fee I ficky fie, fee foe foe,
Ficky fie foe fee you foo,
Ficky fie foe fee you foo.

BUGS ARE BIGGER THAN FLEAS

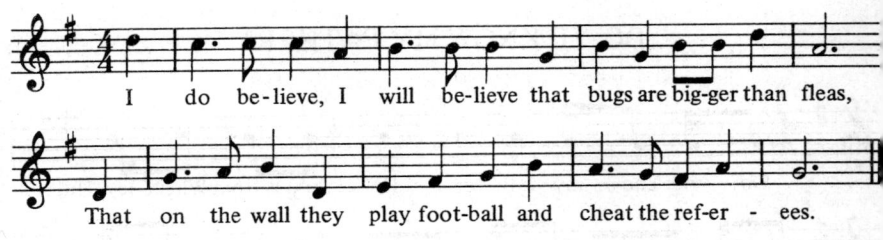

I do be-lieve, I will be-lieve that bugs are big-ger than fleas,

That on the wall they play foot-ball and cheat the ref-er - ees.

JINGLE BELLS

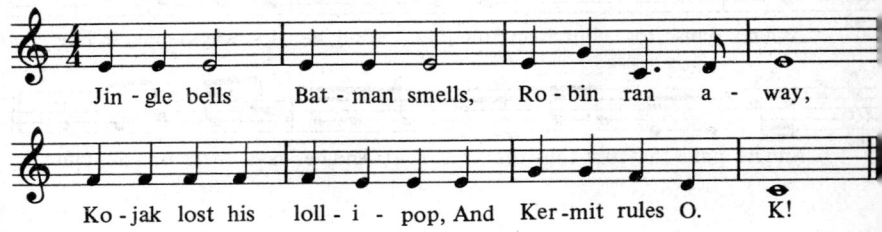

Jin - gle bells Bat - man smells, Ro - bin ran a - way,

Ko - jak lost his loll - i - pop, And Ker - mit rules O. K!

154

GUY FAWKES SONG

Guy Fawkes Guy, Poke him in the eye,

Hang him on a lamp - post and there let him die.

A pen-n'orth o' cheese to choke him, A jol ly good fire to roast him,

Guy Fawkes Guy.

We knock at your knock-er, We ring at your bell, —

To see what you give us for sing - ing so well.

BATMAN AND ROBIN

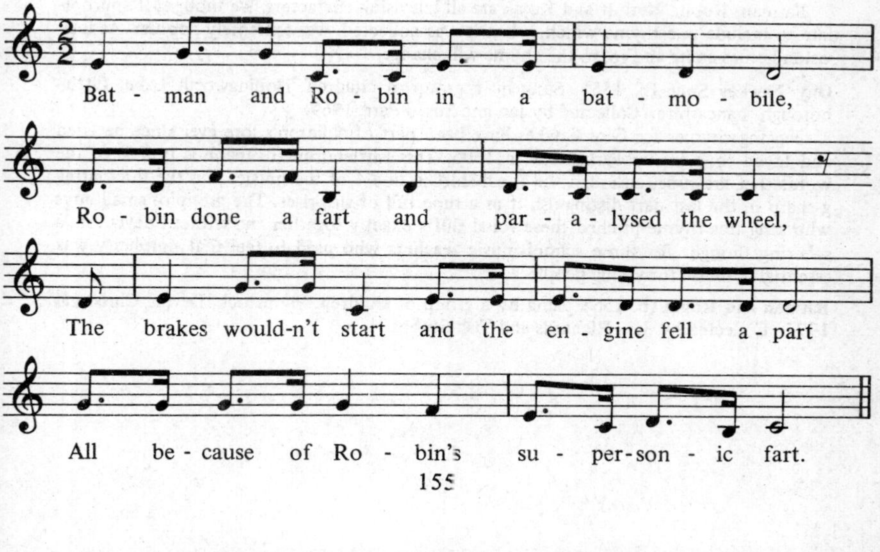

Bat - man and Ro - bin in a bat - mo - bile,

Ro - bin done a fart and par - a - lysed the wheel,

The brakes would-n't start and the en - gine fell a - part

All be - cause of Ro - bin's su - per - son - ic fart.

NOTES

Down Marsh Lane (p. 152) Sung by Margaret Cowell, Preston, Lancashire. Collected by Sam Richards and Tish Stubbs, 1977.

Few of the children's rhymes given here were actually recorded from children themselves. This one, for instance, comes from a woman in her 60s and is remembered from childhood. There appears to be no evidence as to the existence of 'dirty women' in Marsh Lane, Preston. The rhyme was just used as a taunt.

Molly Riley (p. 152) Sung by Mrs Osborne and Miss Ross, sisters, Appledore, Devon. Collected by Tish Stubbs and Paul Wilson, 1975.

There is the definite ring of an Irish popular song here, but so far we haven't placed it. Whatever its origins it was a childhood song of two older ladies in the old seafaring community of Appledore.

Popeye Rhymes (p. 153) First two rhymes from the collection of Ewan MacColl, 1960 and 1961. Third rhyme from children, Totnes, Devon, 1978.

Children's lore, ever adaptable, makes use of the characters of films and television, invents new words and continually changes. Popeye the sailorman, for some reason, frequently figures in slightly obscene verses.

Do Ye Know My Father? (p. 153) Sung by Bert Draycott, Fishburn, Cleveland. Collected by Ian Scott Massie, 1977. Beamish Museum Music Collection.

B I Buy (p. 154) Sung by Doreen Elliott Henderson, Birtley, Durham. Collected by Ewan MacColl and Peggy Seeger, May 1961.

In many living folksong traditions we meet odd pieces, nonsense in themselves, but fun to sing, which demand a certain amount of concentration and virtuosity. We surmise that where traditions are more alive than in this country, these pieces provide a kind of basic training for singers, especially when, as in this case, they are sung from an early age. Revival singers would do well to accumulate a stock of such 'exercises'. The verses given here are examples. Singers can continue to change the consonants until they have exhausted the alphabet. When consonants run out compound consonants can be tried, i.e. sh, ch, th, fr, pr.

Bugs Are Bigger Than Fleas (p. 154) Sung by James Lyons, Batley, Yorks, 1965. Collected by A. E. Green. In the archives of the Institute of Dialect and Folk Life Studies, Leeds University.

Jingle Bells (p. 154) Mary Moreton, Chagford, Devon. Collected by Sam Richards and Tish Stubbs, 1978. Generally current in many parts of England.

Batman, Robin, Kermit and Kojak are all television characters. We thought it appropriate to include one rhyme which, when it was collected, was extremely popular. As television heroes come and go, so the rhyme will change.

Guy Fawkes Song (p. 155) Sung by a group of children, Hollingworth Lake, Littleborough, Lancashire. Collected by Ian and Susan Parr, 1969.

Begging rhymes for Guy Fawkes have been part of children's lore ever since he tried and failed to blow up Parliament in 1605. This Littleborough version is typical of the words that are sung, although the tonal shift in line 4 of the music, plus the fluctuating g sharp in the last part distinguish it as a tune full of surprises. The group of small boys who sang this rhyme pitched these tonal shifts exactly together and without deviation, a sobering thought for those school music teachers who used to feel that simplicity was essential in music for young people.

Batman and Robin (p. 155) Sung by a group of children, Plymstock, Devon, Christmas 1977. Collected by Sam Richards and Tish Stubbs.

HISTORICAL EVENTS

Relatively few ballads of historical events survive in oral tradition today. In view of the vast numbers that were churned out by the urban printing houses this deserves some comment.

A high proportion was hackwork, doomed to a short life by its limited poetry, although some sold like wildfire as it was hawked on the streets by patterers and singers with names that read like the cast of 'The Threepenny Opera'.

Many were short-lived due to their subject matter; and although the historian may prefer to record certain events, the traditional singer is just as likely to value a good semi-accurate, blood-and-thunder song.

In some ways oral tradition is capricious. Why has a florid, slightly high-flown account of the death of Wolfe at Quebec, for example, survived as opposed to 'Wolfe and Saunders'? Perhaps the distribution of one ballad was not as extensive as another. Maybe, as seems to be the case with the Tolpuddle Martyrs, some ballads were simply not written.

There are songs, however, hidden in broadside collections, which do deserve to be sung. We have revived two and fitted melodies to them ourselves. Apart from the two recent songs, the rest of this section comes from standard folksong collections. Many are songs of piracy and sea battles, a subject area which evolved for itself its own conventions and deserves detailed study; many are songs like the magnificent broadside ballad of Peterloo, which comment polemically but their main intent is to record events.

THE *MARGARET* AND THE *MARY*

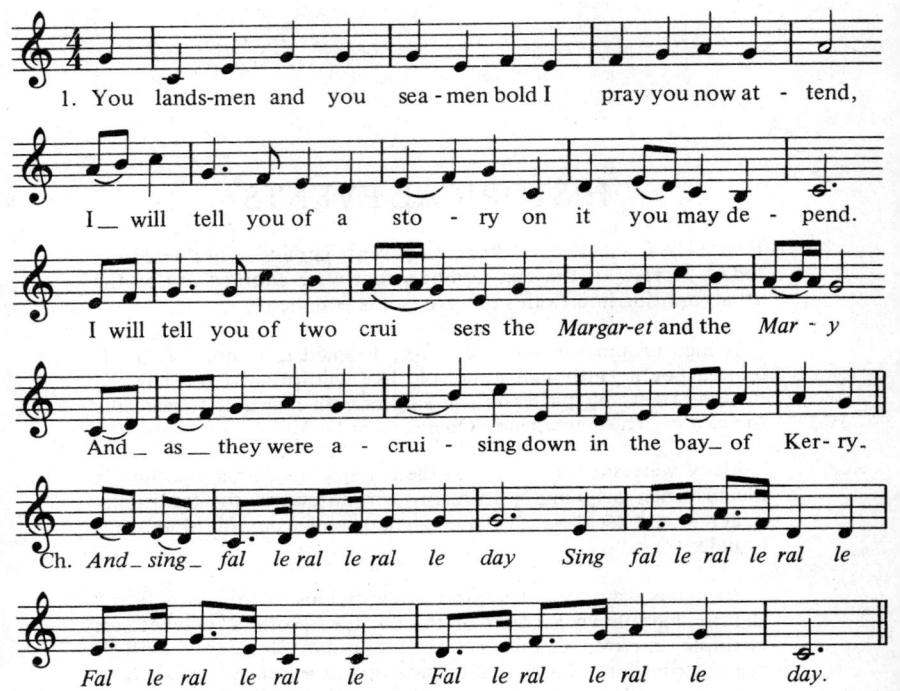

1. You landsmen and you seamen bold I pray you now attend,
I will tell you of a story on it you may depend.
I will tell you of two cruisers the *Margaret* and the *Mary*
And as they were a-cruising down in the bay of Kerry.

Ch. And sing fal le ral le ral le day Sing fal le ral le ral le
Fal le ral le ral le Fal le ral le ral le day.

2   Said the *Margaret* to the *Mary*: It's time to make a move
For yonder lies a smuggler all ready for to land
We boldly sailed up to them and unto them did say
Pray are you that bold smuggler that sails from Kerry Bay?

3   Oh yes I'm that bold smuggler that sails from foreign land.
From France unto old Ireland my cargoes for to land.
I'll not show you my papers free nor where I land my cargo
And if you come alongside of me damned little I'll reward you.

4   Then the action it began and it last from ten till one
We beat these saucy cruisers and gave them gun for gun.
'Tis true we beat these cruisers and made them to give o'er.
We've surely sunk the *Margaret* and the *Mary*'s run on shore.

5   The people of Kerry they all did see the fight.
All on the banks, all on the hillsides stood many a Shannon bright.
'Tis true they all did see the fight, they heard our cannons roar
They've surely sunk the *Margaret* and the *Mary*'s come on shore.

6   Now landlord fill a bumper and let the toast go round
    We will drink to all good people that dwells in Kerry town.
    Here's to me and my bold shipmates that never was afraid
    Bad luck to all you cruisers, success to the smuggling trade.

THE *QUAKER*

1. Come all — you bold he-roes where-so-ev-er you may be —
If — you have got a good — mind to cross the salt — sea.
You go on board the *Qua-ker* and soon you shall find —
Our ship she is well rig-ged and — sails with the wind.

2   Our ship is built like waxwork in every degree.
    Our ship she is well rigged and fitted for the sea.
    Nine hundred and twenty bright seamen's on board
    And by those little French dogs we'll never be controlled.

3   We fought them for hours till they could no longer stay.
    The big guns and small ones how sweetly they did play
    Till the dead lay on the deck boys, both wounded and slain
    Till the blood ran down the scupper holes like showers of rain.

4   And now the wars are over and homeward we will steer,
    Home to our wives and sweethearts and the girls we love so dear.
    Here is a good health to the girl that is so true.
    Here is a good health to the *Quaker* and her crew.

PAUL JONES

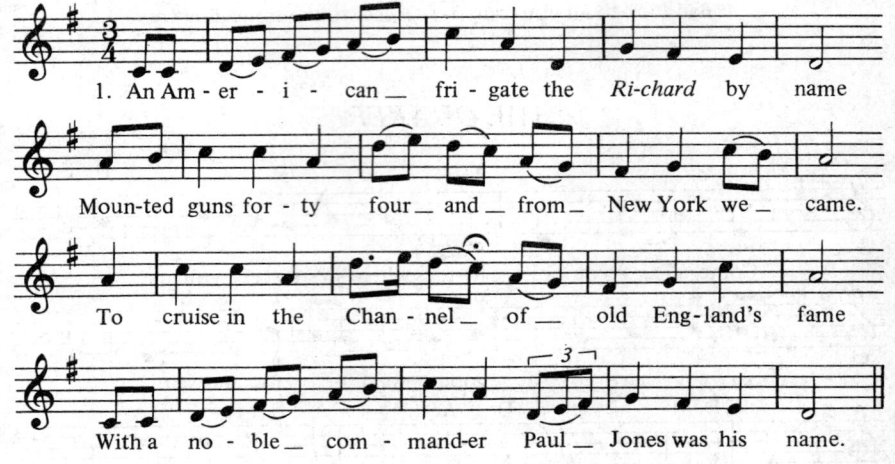

1. An Am-er-i-can _ fri-gate the *Ri-chard* by name
Moun-ted guns for-ty four _ and _ from _ New York we _ came.
To cruise in the Chan-nel _ of _ old Eng-land's fame
With a no-ble _ com-mand-er Paul _ Jones was his name.

2   We had not cruised long when two sails we espies
With forty four guns and a twenty likewise.
Some fifty bright shipping well loaded with stores
And the convoy did sail by the old Yorkshire shores.

3   It was seven-o-clock when we came alongside
With a long speaking trumpet: Whence came you, they cried.
Come answer me quickly I hail you no more
Or else it's a broadside into you I will pour.

4   We fought them four hours for four hours so hot
Till forty brave seamen lay dead on the spot
And fifty five more wounded lay bleeding in their gore
While the thundering large cannons of Paul Jones did roar.

5   Our carpenter being frightened to Paul Jones he came,
Our ship she leaks water and is likewise in flame.
Paul Jones he made answer unto him replied
If we can do no better we'll sink alongside.

6   Paul Jones he then turned to his men and did say,
Let every man stand the best of his play.
For broadside for broadside they fought on the main
And like true buckskin heroes we returned it again.

7   The *Serapis* wore round then our ship for to rake
And many proud hearts of the English did ache.
The shot flew so hot and so fierce and so fast
And the bold British colours were hauled down at last.

8   Oh now my brave boys we have taken a rich prize
      A large forty four and a twenty likewise,
      With fifty bright merchant-men all loaded with store
      So we'll alter our course to the American shore.

THE MEETING AT PETERLOO

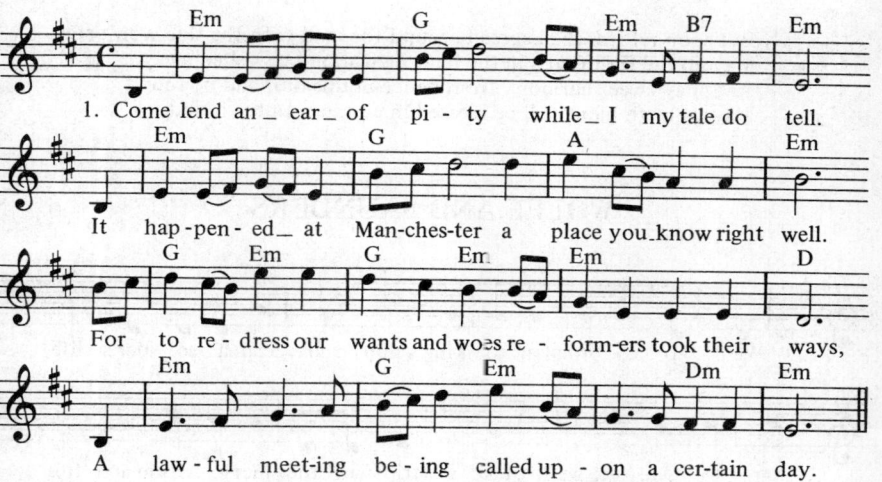

1. Come lend an ear of pi-ty while I my tale do tell.
It hap-pen-ed at Man-ches-ter a place you know right well.
For to re-dress our wants and woes re-form-ers took their ways,
A law-ful meet-ing be-ing called up-on a cer-tain day.

2   The sixteenth day of August eighteen hundred and nineteen
      There many thousand people on every road were seen
      From Stockport, Oldham, Ashton and from other places too,
      It was the largest meeting that reformers ever knew.

3   Brave Hunt he was appointed that day to take the chair.
      At one-o-clock he did arrive, our shouts did rend the air.
      Some females fair in white and green close by the hustings stood
      And little did we all expect to see such scenes of blood.

4   Scarcely had Hunt begun to speak: Be firm, he said, My friends.
      But little still did we expect what was to be the end
      For around us all so hard and cruel regardless of our woes
      Our enemies surrounded us on the plains of Peterloo.

5   The soldiers came unto the ground and thousands tumbled down
      And many armless females lay bleeding on the ground.
      No time for flight was gave to us, still every road we fled.
      There were such heaps were trampled down, some wounded and some dead.

6   Brave Hunt was then arrested and several others too.
They marched us to the New Bailey, believe me it is true
And numbers there was wounded and many there was slain
Which makes the friends of those dear souls so loudly to complain.

7   Oh God above look down on those for Thou art just and true
And those that can no mercy show thy vengeance is their due.
Now quit this hateful mournful scene, look forward with this hope
That every murderer in this land may swing upon a rope.

8   But soon reform shall spread around for sand with the tide won't stay.
May all the filth that's in the land right soon be washed away.
And may sweet harmony from hence in this our land be found
May we with plenty all be blessed in all the country round.

WOLFE AND SAUNDERS

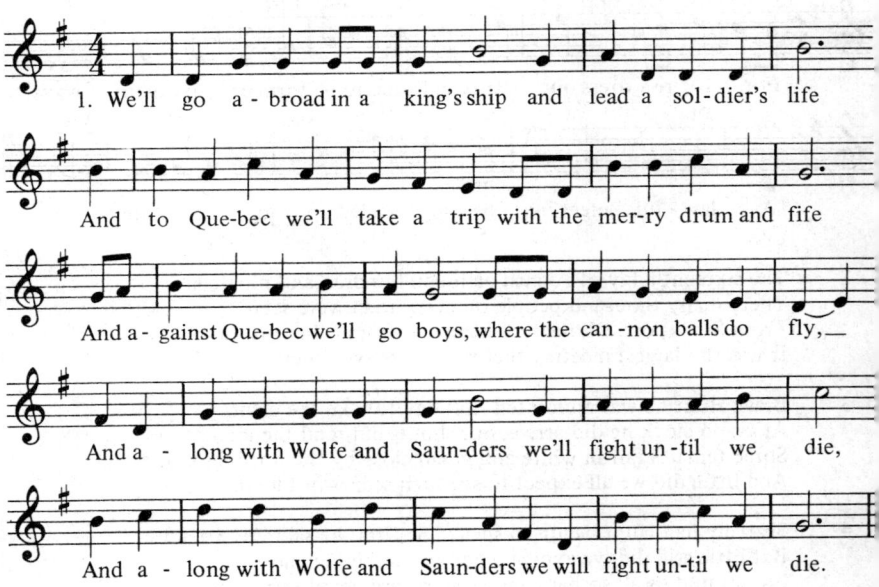

1. We'll go a-broad in a king's ship and lead a sol-dier's life
And to Que-bec we'll take a trip with the mer-ry drum and fife
And a-gainst Que-bec we'll go boys, where the can-non balls do fly,—
And a-long with Wolfe and Saun-ders we'll fight un-til we die,
And a-long with Wolfe and Saun-ders we will fight un-til we die.

2   The thirteenth of September, the weather being clear
All on the plains of Abraham brave Wolfe he did appear.
At the head of his fine army so boldly he did cry,
Come follow me my country lads we'll fight until we die,
Come follow me my country lads we'll fight until we die.

162

3   Both armies did together meet the battle for to try
With drums and trumpets sounding to drown the dreadful cry.
Some of the French they ran away and some we overtook
And brought them to old Louis and presented to the court,
And brought them to old Louis and presented to the court.

4   Montcalm and all his army came tripping o'er the plain
Thinking brave Wolfe for to have killed and his army to have ta'en,
But they was much mistaken as plainly doth appear
And Montcalm for his rashness there paid with his life so dear,
And Montcalm for his rashness there paid with his life so dear.

5   Brave General Wolfe all at Quebec his death wound he received.
His men they hearing of the same it made them sorely grieve.
They being men of courage bold not daunted in the least,
They scorned to turn their backs my boys, brave Wolfe for to disgrace,
They scorned to turn their backs my boys, brave Wolfe for to disgrace.

6   Now here's a health to Saunders wheresoever he may be.
We've beat the French by land my boys, and beat the French by sea
And as for General Wolfe boys, his praises we will sing.
He's a credit to his country and an honour to his king,
He's a credit to his country and an honour to his king.

ADMIRAL NELSON

1. Draw nigh my friends and neigh-bours,
Good news to you I'll bring.
The fame of Admi-ral Nel-son
From shore to shore to sing.

2   For taking of the French fleet
Likewise the Spaniards too
Here's success to Admiral Nelson
And all his jovial crew.

3   The twenty first of October
      Our ships to wind did lie.
   A man from the topmast, my boys
      A sail did chance to spy.

4   A sail, a sail, full twenty sail
      There's thirty sail, there's more.
   I'm sure they are the French fleet
      Lying off the Spanish shore.

5   Down chests and up with hammocks boys
      Your match tubs now prepare
   And quickly form a line my boys
      To fight the proud Monsieur.

6   Fight on, fight on my jolly tars
      Bold Nelson he did cry
   And like a valiant hero
      With sword in hand did die.

7   Our jolly tars like lions bold
      Unto their quarters stood
   Until the deck was covered o'er
      With many a brave man's blood.

8   But now the battle is over
      Our ships are under way,
   Some we'll bring to Plymouth Dock
      And some unto Torbay.

9   And when that we have anchored
      Along the British shore
   We'll drink success to George our king
      And make the taverns roar.

THE BOLD *RICHARD*

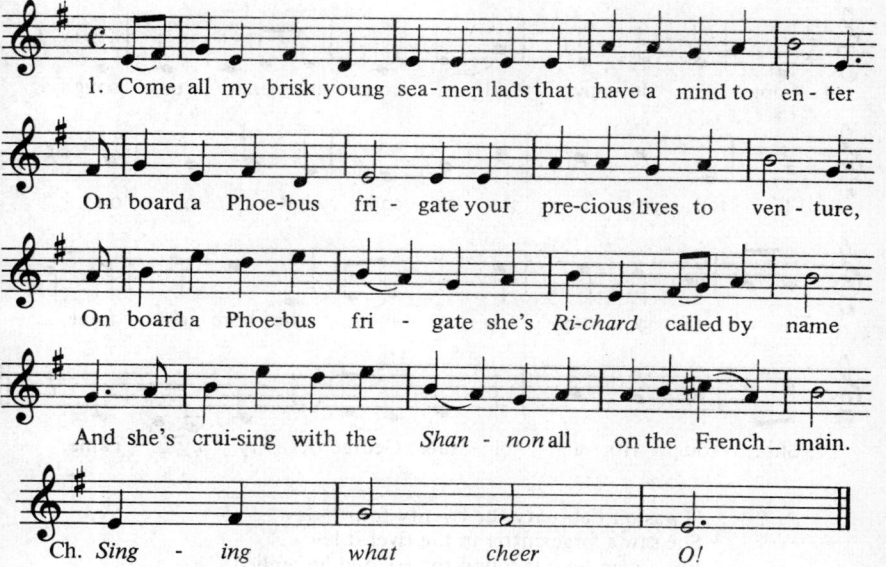

1. Come all my brisk young sea-men lads that have a mind to en-ter
On board a Phoe-bus fri - gate your pre-cious lives to ven - ture,
On board a Phoe-bus fri - gate she's *Ri-chard* called by name
And she's crui-sing with the *Shan - non* all on the French main.
Ch. *Sing - ing what cheer O!*

2   Now we'd not been sailing many leagues before we did spy
     Three lofty sails to windward they came bearing down so nigh,
     But two of them were merchant-men came bowling from the west
     But the *Conway* was a frigate that did sail out of Brest.

3   Now we bore down upon them with high and lofty sails.
     For broadside for broadside we soon made them prevail.
     Then he lashed his helm o' weather not thinking he could fly
     When they found their ship was sinking for quarters they did cry.

4   Now we launched out our long-boats and the others did likewise
     To save all those poor prisoners that ever we came nigh
     And those which we saved they vow and protest
     We sunk the finest frigate that did sail out of Brest.

5   So come all my brisk young fellows now to Kingston we have got.
     Let each of a hearty fellow drink out of a hearty pot,
     For some unto their sweethearts and some unto their wives,
     So we'll sing Hallelujah to all England my brave boys.

GEORGE KEARY

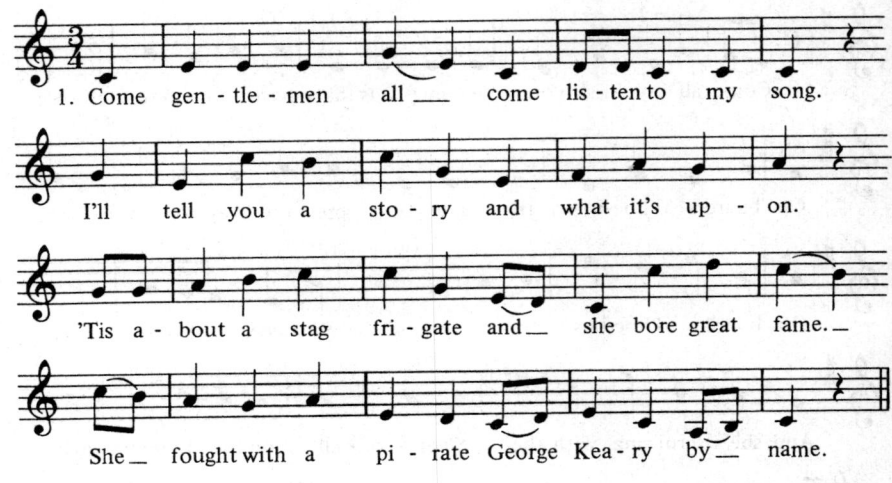

1. Come gen - tle - men all __ come lis - ten to my song.

I'll tell you a sto - ry and what it's up - on.

'Tis a - bout a stag fri - gate and __ she bore great fame. __

She __ fought with a pi - rate George Kea - ry by __ name.

2   'Twas on February the twenty fourth day
She saw a large cutter in the river it lay
But a man on our round top so loud he replied,
Saying: Yonder's a sail and she seems to lay by.

3   Then up stepped our captain for to look through the glass
Likewise our Lieutenant to see what she was.
Up steps our head commander who viewed her all round,
It's Keary the pirate I'll lay fifty pound.

4   Jump up and unreef boys, set all your guns clear,
Set a man at your helm and after them steer,
Get all things in order, make ready to fight,
I hope I shall come up with Keary tonight.

5   They sailed along after till they came within gunshot.
We saw the proud cutter seemed to value us not.
Then yard arm for yard arm so close they did lie.
The shot through each rigging so smartly did fly.

6   Oh now, replies Keary, my heart shall be stout.
I'll sink to the bottom before I give out.
For if we get taken you plainly may see
Like dogs in a halter all hanged we shall be.

7   Now a rich prize we have taken, you may ask for her name.
She is a bold Briton, from Dunkirk she came.
For to rob and to plunder, to kill and destroy
The bold Captain Cooper he did her defy.

THE *ELWOOD MEAD*

1. Oh the *El-wood Mead* was a freigh-ter boys Six-ty thou-sand tons or more
And she sailed on the sea on her mai-den run
With a car-go of ir - on_ ore brave boys, with a car-go of ir - on ore.

2   Oh she sailed from Western Australia.
On the ocean she did sail.
She was bound away for the port of Rotterdam
And she battled with the swell, brave boys,
And she battled with the swell.

3   Oh the proud, proud ship sailed across the world
With her crew of thirty four
Till she sailed into the English Channel
On a cold December morn, brave boys,
On a cold December morn.

4   Oh the ship struck a rock off Guernsey boys
And it was on Christmas Day,
And she lay in the sea fast bound to a reef
And stranded in Grand Rock Bay, brave boys,
And stranded in Grand Rock Bay.

5   The lifeboat put to the sea that day
From St Peter Port in the morn
And twelve of the crew they went on shore
And their shipmates followed soon, brave boys,
And their shipmates followed soon.

6   There was five million pounds of iron ore
Was on board the *Elwood Mead*
But try as they may by night and day
It was months before she was freed, brave boys,
It was months before she was freed.

7   Oh much of the cargo was lost that day
And it never could be saved.
That company can rule on the dry, dry land
But the sea won't be their slave, brave boys,
But the sea won't be their slave.

8   So here's to the crew of the *Elwood Mead*
With thanks that they all got free,
And here's to those Guernsey lifeboatmen
And here's to the rolling sea, brave boys,
And here's to the rolling sea.

THE TRICO STRIKE

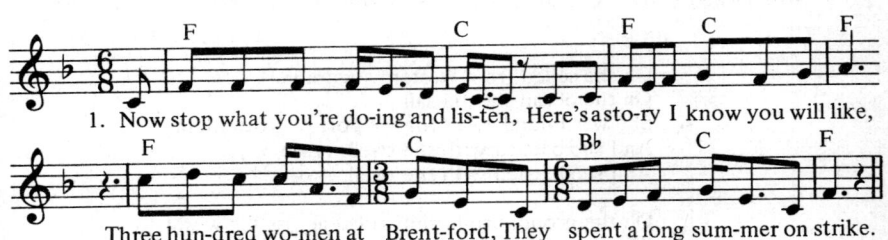

1. Now stop what you're do-ing and lis-ten, Here's a sto-ry I know you will like,

Three hun-dred wo-men at Brent-ford, They spent a long sum-mer on strike.

2   Trico's was where we were working,
We walked out one morning in May
And we didn't go back till October
Until we had won equal pay.

3   Born and brought up in West London
Been married for five years and more
And I don't think we've seen such ding-dong
In the history of Brentford before.

4   It was every day nose to the grindstone,
Eight hours of heaven and then
Got paid six quid less in my wages
For doing the same as the men.

5   We were getting cheesed off with this system
And we found that it wasn't just us.
For women all over the country
Were starting to kick up a fuss.

6   From John o' Groats right down to Dover
We chipped in and all had our say
Till six hundred blokes in Westminster
Gave in and gave us equal pay.

7   So as soon as the Pay Act was legal
Like lightning we bunged in our claim,
But the company said: Business as usual
So you lot work on just the same.

8   They said we had families and children
And couldn't work nights like the men,
But there'd been no nightshift at Trico
Since Jesus Christ only knows when.

9   Then they said: If the men take a wage cut
Then everyone's got equal pay.
Well we laughed till we cried and we damn nearly died.
Do you think we were born yesterday?

10   Down tools! was the cry that May morning,
There was white brown and black people too.
Jamaicans and Asians and some other nations
Told Trico's just what they could do.

11   We found we had plenty of backing
With pickets and blacking as well,
So the company said: A tribunal
Could settle this matter quite well.

12   To hell with your bloody tribunal!
It's rigged in the old British style.
We invited them down to the picket
And held up our slogans and smiled.

13   We were there every day through the summer
When the weather was scorching and hot.
There was threats, there was coppers and cowboys
But we stood against the whole lot.

14   The company nearly went hairless,
It encouraged us all to press on.
In October they had to give over
And the women of Trico had won.

15   Here's a health to those women of Trico
Who stuck it through thick and through thin.
The little that's given still has to be taken
So take it and make them give in!

NOTES

The Margaret and the Mary (p. 158) Sung by Frederick Fennemore, Portsmouth Workhouse, Hampshire. Collected by J. F. Guyer and George Gardiner, 1907.

Folksongs about smugglers are curiously rare. Instead of the more usual conflict between ships and pirates, this song concerns a battle between excisemen and smugglers. Presumably based on a real incident this song is hardly known in the English repertoire, tune and place names clearly indicating Irish origin. Gardiner collected another version in which *Mariner* was substituted for *Mary* and St Peters Bay for Kerry Bay.

The Quaker (p. 159) Sung by Harriet Young, West Chinnock. Collected by Cecil Sharp, 1905.

Fairly well known in Dorset and Somerset, this song was collected in the 1950s as a choral piece in a mummers play. Our version collected over 50 years earlier is substantially the same.

Paul Jones (p. 160) Sung by Sam Fone, Mary Tavy, Devon. Collected by Sabine Baring-Gould, 1888. Slightly collated with a version in Barrett's *English Folk Songs.*

Paul Jones was a real-life character who left his native Scotland in mysterious circumstances and after various romantic escapades enlisted in the American navy under the Revolutionary flag. He then became commander of an American privateer and administered the historic defeat of the English navy as told in our song. What encouraged traditional singers to sing this treasonable piece was widespread sympathy with the American cause and sneaking admiration for this hero. An element of comment is veiled behind a damned good blood-and-thunder piece.

The Meeting at Peterloo (p. 161) A Manchester broadside, set to a traditional tune – a Cornish version of 'The Loyal Lover' from the Gardiner manuscript.

This broadside describes the notorious massacre at St Peter's Field, Manchester, 16th August, 1819. Hunt, mentioned in several verses, was the main leader at this gathering of radicals and reformers, and in their book *The British Labour Movement, 1770-1920*, A. L. Morton and G. Tate give a grim picture of what took place: 'On August 16th 1819, contingents with bands and banners, and including many women, marched to the meeting ground in perfect order but with a discipline more terrifying to the authorities than any disorder could have been. As Hunt was beginning to speak, a troop of Huzzars and the Manchester Yeomanry were launched at the closely packed crowd. The soldiers seem merely to have obeyed their orders mechanically; it was the upper-class yeomanry who showed a positive enthusiasm for hacking and trampling the unarmed people. Very soon eleven were dead and some four hundred wounded.'

Wolfe and Saunders (p. 162) Text is a broadside printed in C. Firth's *American Garland*, set to a traditional tune – 'Chase the Buffalo' (our match).

In 1759 the protracted Anglo-French squabbles over Canada were settled on the Plains of Abraham. The British army under General James Wolfe and the navy under Admiral Saunders routed the French forces led by Montcalm, the French leader, Wolfe being killed in the process. The magnitude of Wolfe's achievement plus his heroic death, guaranteed him plenty of ballads, though this journalistic piece has not been found in oral circulation. Like many battle ballads it is almost accurate.

Admiral Nelson (p. 163) Source unknown.

This vivid ballad of Trafalgar turned up in an old book in a library in South Devon. Unfortunately, attempts to re-locate it have been unsuccessful. A note in our papers, written when the song was copied, attributes it to one Dick Tremuan, a street ballad singer of Plymouth who claimed to write all the songs he peddled. However, unknown source is no excuse for ignoring one of the best songs of the Napoleonic Wars that we have come across so far.

The Bold Richard (p. 165)   Sung by James Sutton, Winterton, Norfolk.   Collected by E. J. Moeran, July 1915. JFSS vol. 7, p. 1.

We know nothing of an actual battle between these ships, but the song is typical of rattling good broadside naval conflicts.

George Keary (p. 166)   Sung by Edmund Pack, Robertsbridge, Sussex.   Collected by Eva Ashton, October 1906. JFSS vol. 6, p. 34.

Lucy Broadwood suggested that the word 'stag' (stag frigate) which is slang for an informer, may mean a scout or spy, the frigate being a pirate-chaser.

The Elwood Mead (p. 167)   Written by Sam Richards, Totnes, Devon, 1974.

This event happened in December 1973. It took many months to move the ship off the rocks and the whole incident was the favourite pub story in Guernsey all that winter.

The Trico Strike (p. 168)   Written by Sam Richards, Totnes, Devon, 1977.

When the 1976 Equal Pay Act came into force in Britain there was a rash of strikes and tribunals to establish women's rights under it. Most failed until a dispute occurred at the windscreen-wiper factory of Trico-Folberth in Brentford, London. The success of the women there gave women in industry and the women's movement generally a shot in the arm.

COMMENT AND POLEMIC

There is a tradition of committed verse and song in England, from the royalist and anti-royalist ballads of the Civil Wars, the papal and anti-papal satires and squibs which litter our history, to the numerous Chapters of Cheats, songs about the rights of man, union songs, lamentations, petitions and requests of the poor, industrial parodies, and 20th-century satires.

These songs demand from the singer little melodic decoration, but clarity and precision, and a sense of humour, bitterness or vision (sometimes all three), are important. The songs put forward a direct argument. Their purpose is either to convince us of a cause or idea, or at least to draw our attention to it. Their topical and local references often date. They are never neutral or objective, always partisan, and it is this quality which gives them their immediacy.

THE MARE AND THE FOAL

1. The old clerk in this par - ish I know ver - y well.

He of - ten do toll __ the eight-o' - clock bell.

He __ went to the ale - house and got a full pot

And for - got the old church for to lock - a - lock lock.

Ch. *Ri - lo ri - lid - dle 'a - lid - dle* __

la did - dle le did - dle - i - day.

2   A mare and a foal they ran in great speed.
The mare from the bible began for to read.
Stay, said the foal, before you begin
Whatever you pray for I'll answer Amen.

3   We'll pray for the millers who grind us our corn
For they are the biggest rogues that ever were born.
Instead of one sackful they'll take two for toll.
May the devil take millers! Amen, said the foal.

4   We'll pray for the bakers who bake us our bread.
They'll take a small loaf and then hurl at your head.
They'll rip it and squeeze it at every roll.
May the devil take the bakers! Amen, said the foal.

5   We'll pray for the tailors for they are no men.
They'll buy an old coat and they'll sell it again.
They'll rub it and scrub it and darn up a hole.
May the devil take the tailors! Amen, said the foal.

6   We'll pray for the publicans who draw us our liquor.
Small measure they like they can fill us the quicker.
If you ask them for best beer they'll draw you the small.
May the devil take the publicans! Amen, said the foal.

7   We'll pray for the butchers for they are great cheats.
They'll buy an old cow and they'll sell it young meat.
May their fingers be burnt into cinders of coal.
May the devil take the butchers! Amen, said the foal.

STRIKE FOR BETTER WAGES

1. At the docks there is a strike that the com-pa-ny don't like
A tan-ner on the hour they'll have to pay.
Like slaves they'd have us work far more than an-y Turk
And make us sweat our lives out ev-ery day.

Ch. Strike boys strike for bet-ter wa-ges,
Strike boys strike for bet-ter pay.
Go on fight-ing at the docks, Stick it out like fight-ing cocks,
Go on fight-ing 'till the boss-es they give way.

2   Every morning there are flocks for employment at the docks,
Hard-working men who scarce can get a meal.
With wives and children dear it would make you shed a tear
If you only knew the hardships that they feel.

3   If it's slavery that you seek for about a quid a week,
They'll take you on as soon as you come near.
Sweat your guts out with a will or they'll try your job to fill
But that won't wash with working men it's clear.

4   We'll stand up for our rights and the company we will fight
Supported by our brothers everywhere.
For we have friends galore — the good old stevedores
And the seamen and the firemen they are there.

5   Starvation 'tis they bids to a man with seven kids,
When he brings home only fifteen pence a day.
For what can you get to eat on seven and six a week
When it often takes it all the rent to pay?

6   Here's a health to Mr Burns, he's done us all a turn
Ben Tillett, Mann, and Mr Toomey too.
We won't give in a bit for we've got them in a fit
And we've put the old dock company in a stew.

BYE BYE BLACKLEG

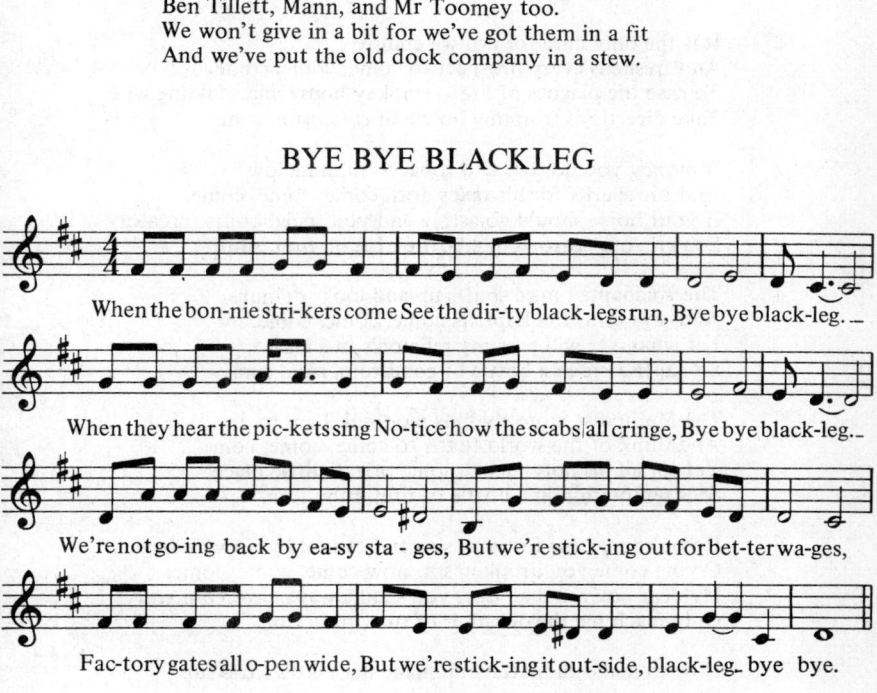

When the bon-nie stri-kers come See the dir-ty black-legs run, Bye bye black-leg. —

When they hear the pic-kets sing No-tice how the scabs all cringe, Bye bye black-leg. —

We're not go-ing back by ea-sy sta - ges, But we're stick-ing out for bet-ter wa-ges,

Fac-tory gates all o-pen wide, But we're stick-ing it out-side, black-leg. bye bye.

A BOTTLE OF GOOD RUM

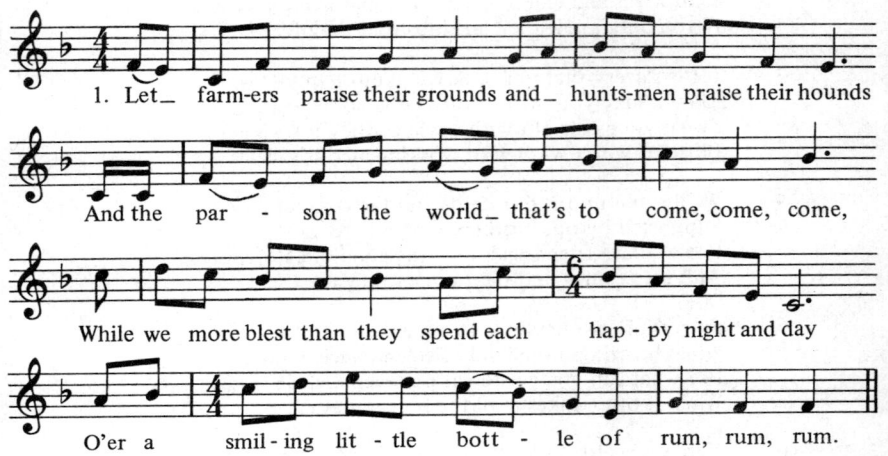

1. Let_ farm-ers praise their grounds and_ hunts-men praise their hounds
And the par - son the world_ that's to come, come, come,
While we more blest than they spend each hap - py night and day
O'er a smil - ing lit - tle bott - le of rum, rum, rum.

2   It is the only cure for evil we endure
    And freshens every prospect to come, come, come.
    To ease the plagues of life — smokey house and scolding wife
    Take directions from my bottle of rum, rum, rum.

3   If money you do owe and tobacco running low
    And the sheriff for his taxes doth come, come, come.
    If your horse should go astray and your neighbours run away
    Drown your sorrows in a bottle of rum, rum, rum.

4   The Anabaptist pure snuffs up and looks demure
    And says unto the Baptists come, come, come.
    Let what e'er will pass my religion's in a glass
    So baptise me in a bottle of good rum, rum, rum.

5   The Methodist more sly bids me think I am to die
    And think of the world that's to come, come, come.
    Yet for all his holy face in some private little place
    Sees temptation in a bottle of rum, rum, rum.

6   If you're married for your sins and to scold your wife begins
    Crying come you drunken sot, now come, come, come.
    My dear you scold all day, you shall always have your way
    Only reach me the decanter of rum, rum, rum.

7   Now to make all matters up make her take a little sup
    Come my loving creature, come, come, come.
    You will find she will prove kind if you take her in right mind
    Stop her prattling in a bottle of rum, rum, rum.

SEE IT COME DOWN

1. In the house where I was born first home I knew
There's cor-ru-ga-ted ir-on blind-ing all the win-dows.
In the gar-den Dad made round the lawn where green grass grew
There's muck and rub-ble and mud half-bricks and cin-ders.
For the de-ve-lo-pers have come to town
And soon we'll see it, see it come down, see it come down.

2   My old mum they've moved her to an 'igh-rise flat
Where she misses her mates and hopes she'll see us Sunday.
She lives alone with a lovely view and a clean door mat
Expecting death will catch her napping one day,
The lady with the meals-on-wheels the one friend she found,
She cries for the old place, she won't see it come down, see it come down.

3   Clouds of dust like smoke on a demolition site where I drive my crane,
It's swinging a big steel ball that smashes walls in.
Just winch her up careful till the cable's tight then let it swing again.
There's a little more no-man's-land as each brick falls in.
First a car-park then an office block well I've cleared the ground.
They paid me to see to it, well I've seen it come down, seen it come down.

4   We was all one like where we lived, wish we was now.
We 'ad debts and dole and kids but we did have neighbours.
Where our street was they wanna build some tombstone tower,
A monster concrete moneybox for strangers,
Every last square foot of it worth a hundred pound.
Some day we'll see it come tumbling down, see it come down.

THE CHARTIST SONG

1. Art thou poor but hon-est man Sore-ly op-pressed and a' that. —
A - tten-tion give to Chart-ist plan 'Twill cheer they heart for a' that. —
For a'— that and a'— that, Though land-lords gripe and a' that, —
I'll show thee friend be - fore we part The rights of men and a' that. —

2 Thy Bible friend will plainly show
  How God gave his laws and a' that.
 And land and springs he did bestow
  To families and a' that.
 Yes a' that and a' that
  To have and hold for a' that,
 That with his gift they should not part,
  The text will plainly show that.

3 The rights of man then's in the soil,
  An equal share and a' that.
 For landlords no one ought to toil
  'Tis imposition a' that.
 Yes a' that and a' that
  Their title, deeds and a' that,
 Howe'er they got them matters not
  The land is ours for a' that.

4 Cursed be he who shall remove
  The poor man's bounds and a' that,
 Or covet aught should he improve
  His house or stock and a' that.
 Yes a' that and a' that
  His cattle, goods and a' that,
 Could not be mortgaged for a term
  Till Jubilee and a' that.

5   Brave Chartist has shown the way to fix
       Man's happiness and a' that.
    His freedom with his interest mix
       Their Charter plan will show that.
    Yes a' that and a' that
       Divide the rent and a' that,
    What God has gave all should enjoy
       And all the world should know that.

6   Then let us pray that come it may
       As come it will for a' that.
    This Christian plan o'er a' the earth
       Shall bear the gree and a' that.
    Yes a' that and a' that
       As come it will for a' that.
    The man and man the world o'er
       Will brothers be for a' that.

TIME TO BE MOVING ON

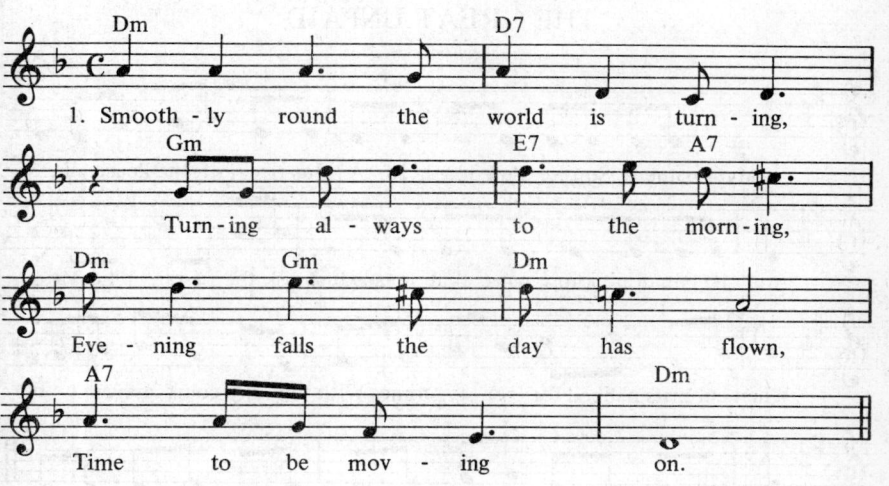

1. Smooth - ly round the world is turn - ing,
Turn - ing al - ways to the morn - ing,
Eve - ning falls the day has flown,
Time to be mov - ing on.

2   Two strong hands began the journey,
    Held a stone and started learning,
    Reached for the stars and made a home,
    Time to be moving on.

3   Turned the soil and built the bridges,
    Crossed the ocean, worked the factories,
    With hand and heart a world we won,
    Time to be moving on.

4   Through the bleak years, years of hunger,
Ours the pain and ours the danger,
From our fight a world has grown,
Time to be moving on.

5   Oil from far beneath the ocean,
Coal to burn in furnace fires,
Caught the heat from the very sun,
Time to be moving on.

6   Seeds of plenty we've been sowing,
Through each season they've been growing,
Time to reap what we have sown,
Time to be moving on.

7   Smoothly round the world is turning,
Turning always to the morning,
Shall we claim what we have won?
Time to be moving on.

THE GREAT UNPAID

1. My name is Squire Pudding-head, A Justice of the Peace, sir.

And if you don't know what that means Just ask the rural p'lice sir.

When culprits nabbed for petty crimes Within my court assemble

If I am sitting on the bench Oh don't the wretches tremble.

Ch. At the great un - paid

Ask any-thing but justice of the great unpaid.

2   The cases that I have to try
       Are mostly small transgressions.
     So small the court in which I sit
       Is called the Petty Sessions.
     A sort of legal small tooth-comb
       Th'offences are so tiny.
     You'd laugh at them — but you'd not laugh
       When I proceed to fine ye.

3   If Polly Brown but takes a stick
       From Farmer Giles's fences
     I fine her twopence as its worth
       And fourteen bob expenses,
     And if a tramp sleep in a field
       Such is my lordly bounty,
     I give him lodging for a week
       Provided by the county.

4   The Union leaders I would hang
       'Twould be a task delightful.
     But since I can't I am content
       To do the mean and spiteful.
     And if my colleague Captain Fair
       Would be the poor's protector
     The vilest things I dare to do
       Are backed up by the Rector.

5   So Policeman Hobbs and Snobs my clerk
       Their paltry charges trump up
     To vex and harass Union men
       And don't I make 'em stump up.
     What good to me to be JP
       Over my wretched drudges
     If I can't strain and twist the law
       To pay off all the grudges.

THE HONEST PLOUGHMAN

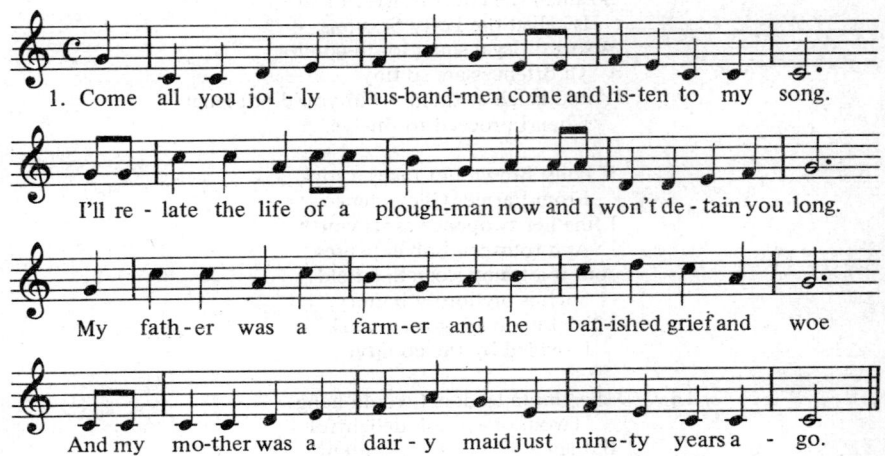

1. Come all you jol-ly hus-band-men come and lis-ten to my song.
I'll re-late the life of a plough-man now and I won't de-tain you long.
My fath-er was a farm-er and he ban-ished grief and woe
And my mo-ther was a dair-y maid just nine-ty years a-go.

2   O to drive the plough my father he did a boy engage
Until that I had just arrived to seven years of age.
My father did no servant want, my mother milked the cows
And with the lad each morn he rose to go and drive the plough.

3   O the farmer's wives in every part the cows themselves did milk.
They did not wear the dandy veils nor gowns made out of silk.
They did not ride blood-horses as farmer's wives do now.
Their daughters went to milking and their sons went out to plough.

4   When I was twenty years of age I could manage well a farm,
To hedge and ditch and reap and sow and thresh all in a barn.
At length when I was twenty-five I took myself a wife
Compelled to leave my father's house and then to change my life.

5   There was nothing then upon a farm but what that I could do.
As daily as a husbandman to labour I did go.
The rent tithes then was not half so dear as what that they are now.
My father though all very poor could keep a pig and cow.

6   My wife could set to net and spin and I the land could plough.
But I find things very different now to ninety years ago.
When a man have laboured all his life and done his country good,
He's respected just as much when old as a donkey in a wood.

7   I can no longer labour and for relief apply
Or else go in the Union House and end my days and die.
I can no longer labour since I no power have
So then at last just like a dog they'll lay me in my grave.

DRINKING

1. Some peo-ple will tell you that drink-ing's a curse,

While oth-ers will tell you it's quite the re-verse.

Some drink all their days their time to em-ploy,

Some drink when in sor-row and some drink for joy.

Some drink when their christ-ened and some when they're wed,

Some are drink-ing your jol-ly good health when you're dead.

Some drink on all these oc-ca-sions like I, For I drunk at my birth and I'll drink till I die.

Ch. For I mean to get jol-ly well drunk, I do. I mean to get jol-ly well drunk, I do.

As long as I'm he-re I'll stick to my be-er, For I mean to get jol-ly well drunk, I do.

2 I'll drink till the high price of coals becomes small,
  Till ale and roast beef they cost nothing at all.
  I'll drink till we have no more reasons for strikes,
  Till a man values work just as much as he likes.
  I'll drink till the law gives a man no denial
  For taking a wife out a month upon trial,
  Till the dukes and the lords have to sort clean from dirt
  And the big Prince of Wales has to clean his own shirt.

3   I'll drink till all landlords choke as they guzzle.
I mean to keep drinking till bobbies are muzzled.
Till dandies are worth nowt but the clothes they put on.
I'll drink till old Peabody's money is gone.
I'll drink till the laws of the land are made fair
That punish a man for killing a hare.
I'll drink till all wealth is shared out amongst men
And I'll drink and I'll drink till it's shared out again.

EARLY ONE EVENING

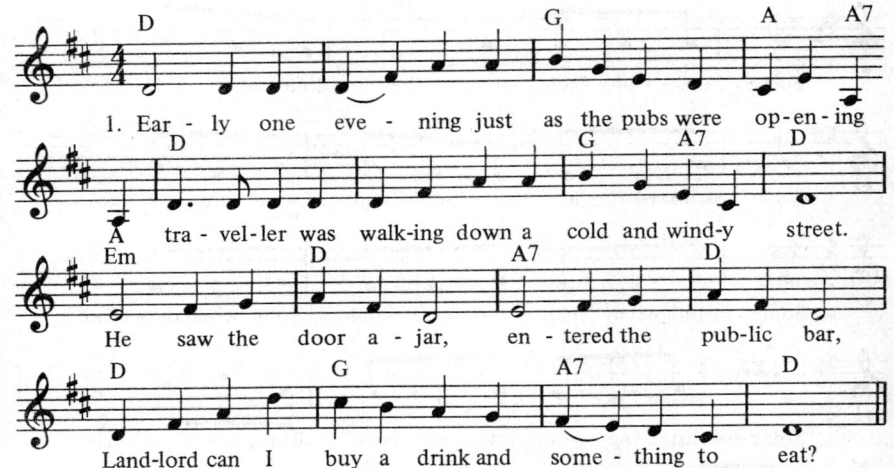

1. Ear-ly one eve-ning just as the pubs were op-en-ing
A tra-vel-ler was walk-ing down a cold and wind-y street.
He saw the door a-jar, en-tered the pub-lic bar,
Land-lord can I buy a drink and some-thing to eat?

2   I fancy some crusty bread and roast beef of old England,
Fresh butter from the churn and a pickled onion too.
And if you think you could draw some bitter from the wood
I'd be quite content to sip a gentle pint or two.

3   I'll sit by your fine log fire and ponder on the infinite.
The quiet of your hostelry shall seep into my heart.
And if a regular should come into the bar
Maybe I'll entice him to a contest with a dart.

4   Come in, said the landlord, I've got pre-packed fish-paste sandwiches
And tasty instant sausage which I purchase by the ton.
So if you fancy it I could defrost a bit,
Serve it up with ketchup in a supermarket bun.

5   I'll serve you a plastic pint of quaint old English Reddibrew
It's advertised on telly by a famous rugby scrum.
No dirty barrels here, we serve hygienic beer,
Safely paralysed inside this aluminium drum.

6 Sit down by the fireside, I'll switch the logs on presently.
How about a game of pool or else the fruit machine?
Three cherries in a row, they'll set your heart aglow
How about some heavy rock to really set the scene?

7 The traveller sat down beside the polystyrene inglenook.
The plastic beams were jumping to an electronic sound.
Started to bite and chew, took a sip of Reddibrew
Gave a ghastly gurgle and fell dead upon the ground.

8 Oh dear, sighed the landlord as he switched his colour telly on,
Another fatal accident, the third this week I fear.
If they can't hold their own why don't they stay at home?
I must say we do get some funny customers in here.

WHO'S WHO

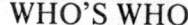

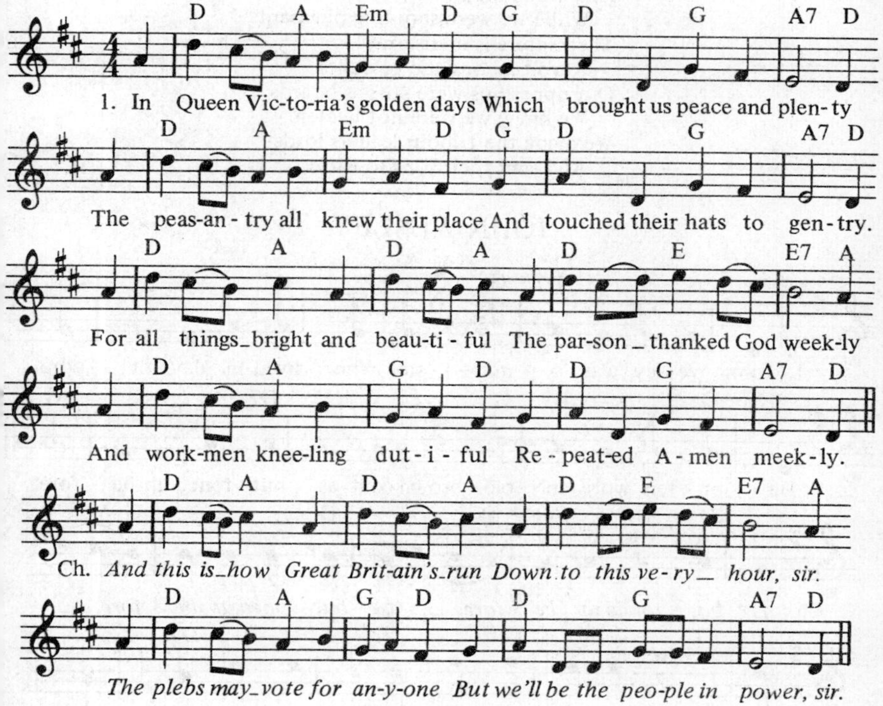
D A Em D G D G A7 D
1. In Queen Vic-to-ria's golden days Which brought us peace and plen-ty
D A Em D G D G A7 D
The peas-an - try all knew their place And touched their hats to gen-try.
D A D A D E E7 A
For all things_bright and beau-ti - ful The par-son _ thanked God week-ly
D A G D D G A7 D
And work-men knee-ling dut - i - ful Re - peat-ed A - men meek-ly.
D A D A D E E7 A
Ch. *And this is_how Great Brit-ain's_run Down to this ve - ry_ hour, sir.*
D A G D D G A7 D
The plebs may_vote for an-y-one But we'll be the peo-ple in power, sir.

2   The best of all we could afford
       And not have to be clever.
    We had an Empire there abroad
       On which the sun set never.
    With wogs, Babus and Blackamoors
       Who all required a saviour
    And so we taught them English.laws
       And public school behaviour.

3   We had some ill-bred Englishmen
       Who dipped their bread in gravy.
    We used to teach them discipline
       Between decks in the navy.
    And when some upstart blighter sought
       To broach our Empire's border,
    We'd send them to a foreign port
       To re-establish order.

4   And when the news was brought one day
       While-we were shooting pheasants
    The Empire is in disarray!
       Revolt among the peasants.
    Our upper lips were stiff as boards
       We knew we were not beaten.
    We made the Labour leaders lords
       And sent their sons to Eton.

JOHN WESLEY

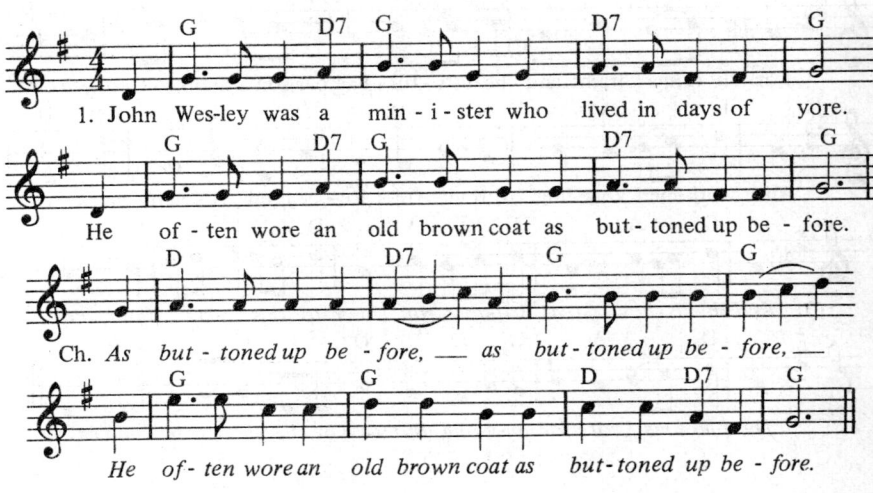

1. John Wes-ley was a min-i-ster who lived in days of yore.
He of-ten wore an old brown coat as but-toned up be-fore.
Ch. As but-toned up be-fore, — as but-toned up be-fore, —
He of-ten wore an old brown coat as but-toned up be-fore.

2   John Wesley had another coat of quite a different kind.
    Instead of buttoning up before, it buttoned up behind.
    It buttoned up behind, it buttoned up behind,
    Instead of buttoning up before, it buttoned up behind.

3   John Wesley had an old grey mare as rough as you could find
And each time he got on her back she kicked 'un off behind.
She kicked 'un off behind, she kicked 'un off behind,
And each time he got on her back she kicked 'un off behind.

4   John Wesley had a little ghost appeared all ghastly white.
It used to climb up his bed post and frighten him at night.
And frighten him at night, and frighten him at night,
It used to climb up his bed post and frighten him at night.

5   John Wesley had another ghost of quite a different hue.
Instead of clambering up the post it clambered down the flue.
It clambered down the flue, it clambered down the flue,
Instead of clambering up the post it clambered down the flue.

6   John Wesley had three daughters fair and they was tall and thin.
He took them to the river's bank and pushed the buggers in.
And pushed the buggers in, and pushed the buggers in,
He took them to the river's bank and pushed the buggers in.

7   There came along three farmers' sons and they was strong and stout.
They saw them struggling in the stream and pulled the buggers out.
And pulled the buggers out, and pulled the buggers out,
They saw them struggling in the stream and pulled the buggers out.

8   John Wesley had an old straw hat without nor crown nor brim.
It wouldn't have been much use to thee, and 'twas no use to him.
And 'twas no use to him, and 'twas no use to him,
It wouldn't have been much use to thee and 'twas no use to him.

THE LOFTHOUSE COLLIERY DISASTER

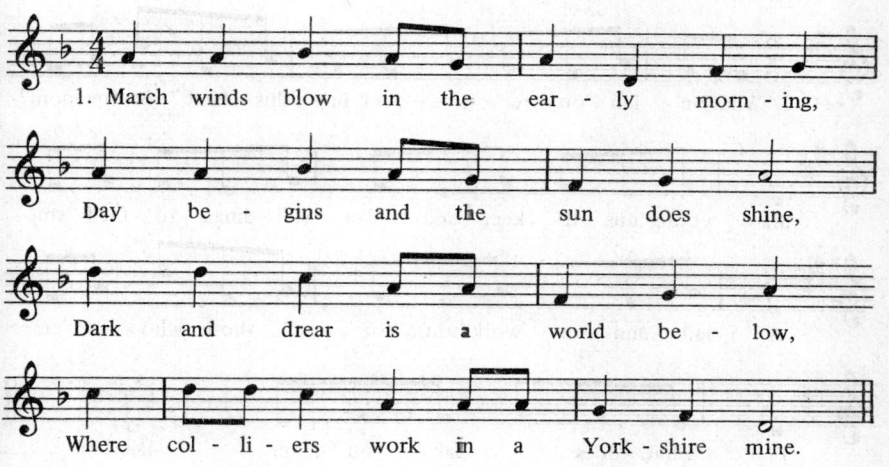

1. March winds blow in the ear-ly morn-ing,
Day be-gins and the sun does shine,
Dark and drear is a world be-low,
Where col-li-ers work in a York-shire mine.

2   Day begins and the mist is rising
     But there are eyes which cannot see.
     Seven men at the Lofthouse Colliery
     Flockton Seam Face South 9B.

3   Eighteen fifty was the year
     When Low Laithes Colliery was closed down,
     Leaving pit shafts, disused workings,
     Leaving tunnels underground.

4   A hundred years of coal black water
     Waiting to be a miner's tomb,
     Trapped in the silent earth and waiting
     A hundred years of rubble and stone.

5   Wednesday morning, Lofthouse Colliery,
     Water flooded into the mine.
     No one knew of the disused workings.
     Seven men died for that crime.

6   Keep on working, get the coal out,
     Safety takes up too much time.
     There's seven of those greedy miners
     Lying in a sea of grime.

7   March winds blow in the early evening.
     Seven men lost in their prime.
     Who can sleep, who can sit easy,
     Who'll be there to mourn next time?

OH DEAR WHAT'LL BECOME OF US?

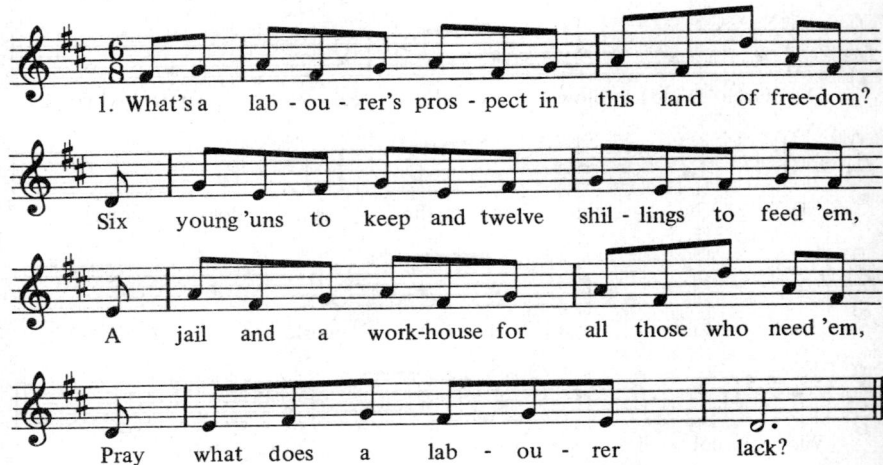

1. What's a lab - ou - rer's pros - pect in this land of free-dom?

Six young 'uns to keep and twelve shil - lings to feed 'em,

A jail and a work-house for all those who need 'em,

Pray what does a lab - ou - rer lack?

Ch. Oh dear what will be - come of us?
Oh dear what will be - come of us?
Oh dear what will be - come of us
If he should give us the sack?____

2   Twelve shillings a week it'll just fit one belly,
But Bill, Tom, and Hal, Polly, Susan, and Nelly
They eat all day long – my old woman'll tell ye,
    I only can just get a snack.

3   There came an old chap whom the Union engages
To show the poor man how to go for more wages.
Says he: Ask for more and if Farmer Grumps rages
    The Union will stand at your back.

4   Says Grumps: If you join it will end in disaster.
How dare you offend such an excellent master?
Says I: If you say so we'll join all the faster.
    Oh he looked awfully black.

5   He says: In the harvest we're putting him quite about.
Yet if he'd be just there'd be nothing to fight about.
But he swears he'll send us all to the right about
    When he begins to get slack.

6   There's plenty of work to be had by the willing
With wages at double the paltry twelve shilling
And land o'er the sea to be had for the tilling
    If he should tell us to pack.

CANTEEN TEA

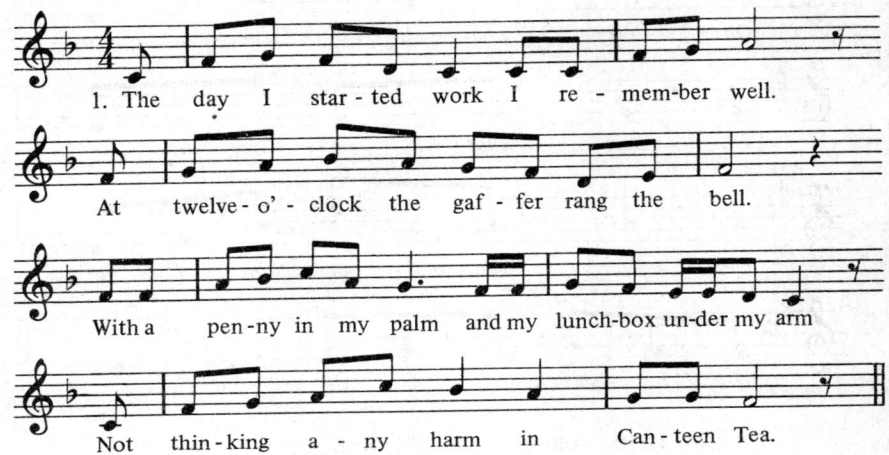

1. The day I star-ted work I re-mem-ber well.
At twelve-o'-clock the gaf-fer rang the bell.
With a pen-ny in my palm and my lunch-box un-der my arm
Not thin-king a-ny harm in Can-teen Tea.

2 The first taste that I took brought me to my knees,
Stewed maiden's water laced with anti-freeze.
I took that witches' brew and I poured it down the loo.
It's the best thing you can do with Canteen Tea.

3 I only stuck the job two days or three
Until the canteen got the better of me.
Down the road I made my way and I took a drop in pay
Thinking I'd get away from Canteen Tea.

4 But every job I took the tea got worse
And it followed me like Tutankhamen's Curse.
And for my punishment the secret ingredient
Was everywhere I went in Canteen Tea.

5 In the army then I served a six year spell
And I'll swear the tea had bromide in as well.
I was horrified to learn I couldn't do a turn
And I'd be glad to return to Canteen Tea.

6 Then I laboured for the rest of my working life
With the canteen lady who'd become my wife.
But on the day that I'd retired I fear my life expired,
Overworked and sick and tired of Canteen Tea.

7 And when at last they tolled my funeral knell.
I'd reckoned that I'd served my time in hell.
St Peter at the gate said: Welcome, come in mate
You're just in time for break and Canteen Tea.

NOTES

The Mare and the Foal (p. 173) Sung by George Hill, East Stonham, Suffolk. Collected by E. J. Moeran, 1921. JFSS vol. 8, p. 270.

Numerous versions of 'The Soldier and the Sailor' have been collected from tradition and are still part of many a singer's repertoire, but somehow this one is the most fanciful.

Strike for Better Wages (p. 174) Sung by George Hardy, South Norwood, April 1954. Collected by Ewan MacColl.

Previous to the 1880s the British Labour movement had been held back by weak leadership and countless defeats. In the London of the late 1880s a wave of London strikes, starting with one involving 700 match girls from Bryant and May, grew into an upsurge of militancy culminating in a strike by dock workers who were having to fight each other for low-paid jobs and who often knocked off work to buy food as soon as they had earned a few coppers. The strike began in the Southwest India Dock where Ben Tillet (one-time circus boy) was called upon to act as organizer. It spread along 50 miles of London docks, picketed by 16,000 workers, and involving over 60,000 various riverside workers, of whom many were previously unorganized. Every day there were marches and meetings involving speeches, songs, bands. The last verse mentions most of the important leaders of the strike which ended in the victory of the 'full, round, shining orb of the dockers' tanner'.

Bye Bye Blackleg (p. 175) From *Strike Songs,* published by United Clothing Workers Trade Union, 1928.

This parody originated during a garment workers' strike in 1928 at Rego and Polikoff's factories.

A Bottle of Good Rum (p. 176) Broadside ballad published by Catnach, Monmouth Court, London, 19th century.

We have never seen this song in collections from the field, although the style and meter of the text, plus the repeated words 'rum, rum, rum' give away the traditional tune to which this was intended to be sung. 'Dumb Dumb Dumb' is a jocular tale about a scolding wife, well known in Irish tradition. Our tune is from the MacPeakes of Belfast.

See It Come Down (p. 177) By John Pole, London. Written in 1974.

John Pole's song refers to East London, but it is a tale that could be told of many city areas in the 1960s and 1970s.

The Chartist Song (p. 178) Broadside ballad published by Pitts, 19th century.

Chartism began in the 1830s and for a short period in the mid-19th century provided a focus for progressive political ideas all over the country. Some would claim, with justification, that it was the first genuine mass movement to be infused with socialist principles. It was based on a six-point charter which called for male suffrage, annual parliaments, secret ballots, payment for MPs, the abolition of property qualifications for MPs, and equal electoral districts. The Chartist movement was well aware of the importance of the role of cultural activity, although much of its literature missed the mark by being couched in a language borrowed from the very culture it wished to remove. 'The Chartist Song', a broadside, is one of their best efforts, doubly enhanced, we feel, by being written to that stirring tune 'For A' That and A' That'.

Time To Be Moving On (p. 179) By Sam Richards, Totnes, Devon. Written in 1977.

This was originally written for the satirical production 'And To Crown It All' put on by the Peoples' Stage at the end of 1977.

The Great Unpaid (p. 180) From *The Revolt of the Field,* Arthur Clayden, Hodder & Stoughton, 1874.

This song, and a number of others, were composed by one Mr Howard Evans of London. Arthur Clayden says: '(they) have been published in a penny book, and are used very extensively at the outdoor meetings', referring to the meetings of the farmworkers in their fight for unionization.

The Honest Ploughman (p. 182) Sung by Tom Sprachlan, Hambridge, Somerset. Collected by Cecil Sharp, 1903.

This song was, conceivably, one of the most often printed agricultural protest songs of the 19th century — and there were a vast number. The early 19th century saw the final stages of old-style agriculture, and the songs of the period are marked by bitterness and a tendency to look back to better times '90 years ago' as this song says. The complaint at the end that aged labourers are treated with indifference was justified, although it also signifies the indifference towards everything that the past symbolized.

Drinking (p. 183) Sung by Beckett Whitehead, Delph, Oldham, Lancashire. Collected by Ewan MacColl, 1947.

This extremely rare gem has been roughly dated by Ewan MacColl to the 1840s, sufficiently soon after the clearances to make the references in the song immediate to its contemporary audience. The name Peabody in the last verse refers to an American multi-millionaire, George Peabody, who spent some of his fortune on building flats and almshouses in London. A broadside in the Kidson collection, Mitchell library, Glasgow, tells us the song was written and composed by Mr H. Dale, also by George Lingforth. No other details are given, not even the publisher. The printed version has five verses.

Early One Evening (p. 184) By Miles Wootton. Written in 1974.

Who's Who? (p. 185) Written by John Brunner, South Petherton, Somerset, 1965.

John Wesley (p. 186) Collected by Bob Patten, Lynton, Devon, 1970s.

Bob Patten's singer, who wished to remain anonymous, comments: 'It depended for its humour on a sort of sly anti-climax in each verse and no doubt reflected the traditional farmer's animus to the growth of Methodism in these parts'. We can't pretend to understand all the satire of the song, although its cumulative effect in performance is to make Wesley look highly ridiculous. The tune is often used in Cornwall for 'The Old Grey Duck' and 'The Seven Joys of Mary'.

The Lofthouse Colliery Disaster (p. 187) By Sam Richards, Totnes, Devon. Written in 1973.

In March 1973 seven miners lost their lives after working too close to the disused workings of a mine that had been closed over a century earlier. Water and rubble rushed in, making rescue operations almost impossible. There was strong feeling in some quarters that ignorance of the old workings could have been avoided by use of available maps in Doncaster Library.

Oh Dear What'll Become Of Us? (p. 188) From *The Agricultural Lockout of 1874*, Frederick Clifford, published by William Blackwood & Sons, 1875.

Another piece typical of the large number of songs of agricultural agitation from the 1870s.

Canteen Tea (p. 190) By Allan Lavercombe, Torquay. Written in 1975.

AUTHORITY

The essence of many ballads is conflict and conflict implies reaction to some kind of authority — magical, religious, social, legal or customary.

Some of the most ancient stories in oral literature concern gods and immortals locked in combat for supremacy and ultimate authority. In later narratives the protagonists are more down to earth, the mystical background being exchanged for the familiar environment of human society. In medieval outlaw ballads conflict lies in rebellion against the harsh inequalities of an intricately stratified social system. Yet the epic magic of old can be glimpsed in the exploits of these larger-than-life heroes such as Robin Hood, who use their wit, daring and strength in their never-ending campaign to right wrongs.

It is not fanciful to see the highwaymen and poachers of later ballads as descendents of these medieval heroes. Although often deserters, prisoners and thieves, and a far cry from the outlaws of the greenwood, they still win the songmaker's sympathy. When it comes to conflict with authority, the best of our folk songs are compassionate, even about 'The Prentice Boy' who is portrayed as a murderer probably unable to help himself, caught by convention and, most likely, poverty. The unfolding of his crime is drama of the most gripping and horrifying kind.

This section also includes that arch-defier of authority, a favourite of countless children wherever his striped booth is set up — Mr Punch rebels against all kinds of authority, and yet we still shout for him when the crocodile creeps up behind.

VAN DIEMEN'S LAND

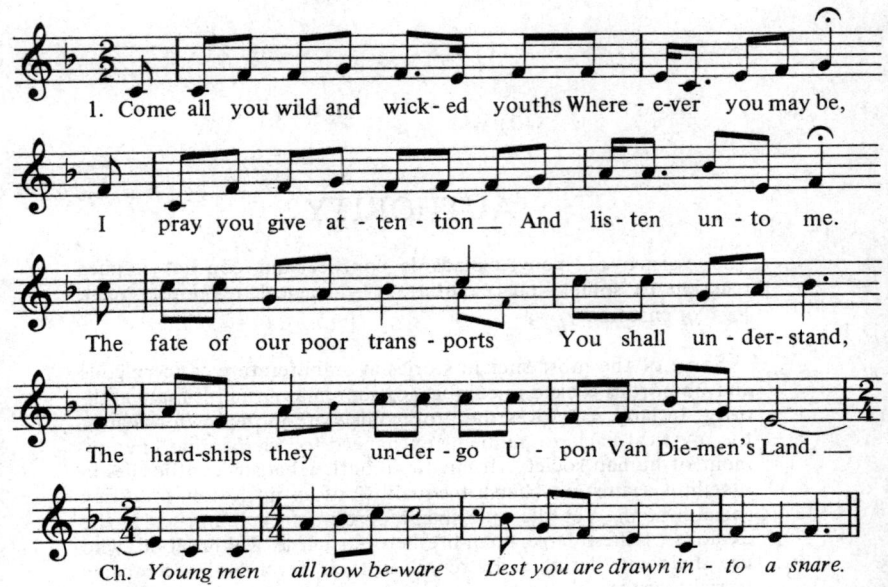

1. Come all you wild and wick-ed youths Where-ev-er you may be,
I pray you give at-ten-tion— And lis-ten un-to me.
The fate of our poor trans-ports You shall un-der-stand,
The hard-ships they un-der-go U-pon Van Die-men's Land.—
Ch. *Young men all now be-ware Lest you are drawn in-to a snare.*

2 I and five more went out one night
  To Squire Dunhill's park,
 To see if we could get some game
  But the night it proved too dark.
 And to our sad misfortune
  They hemmed us in with speed,
 And sent us off to Warwick Gaol
  Which caused our hearts to bleed.

3 And at the March assizes
  At the bar we did appear.
 Like Job we stood with patience
  To hear our sentence there.
 We being old offenders
  It made our case more hard.
 Our sentence was for fourteen years
  And I got sent on board.

4 The ship that bore us from the land
  Speedwell was by name.
 For about six months and upwards
  We ploughed the raging main.
 No land nor harbour could we see
  Believe me it is no lie,
 Beneath us one black water,
  Above us one blue sky.

5   I often looked behind me
      To see my native shore.
That cottage of contentment
      That I should see no more,
Nor yet my poor old father,
      He tore his old grey hair,
Likewise my aged mother,
      In her womb she did me bear.

6   On the fifteenth of September
      Was where we made the land,
At four-o-clock next morning,
      All chained hand to hand.
To see my fellow sufferers,
      I'm sure I can't tell how,
Some were chained to a harrow
      And others to a plough.

7   No shoes nor stockings had they on
      No hats had they to wear.
Leather breeches and linen drawers,
      Their feet and heads were bare.
They drove about in two and two
      Like horses in a team.
The driver he stood over them
      With his malacca cane.

8   As we marched into Sydney Town
      Without no more delay,
A gentleman he bought me
      His book-keeper to be.
I took the occupation.
      My master loved me well.
My joys were out of measure
      I'm sure no tongue could tell.

9   He had a female servant,
      Rosanna was by name.
For fourteen years a convict
      From Wolverhampton came.
We often told our tales of love
      While we were blest at home
But now the rattling of our chains
      In a foreign land to roam.

ROBIN HOOD AND THE OLD BEGGAR MAN

(Robin Hood Rescuing Three Squires)

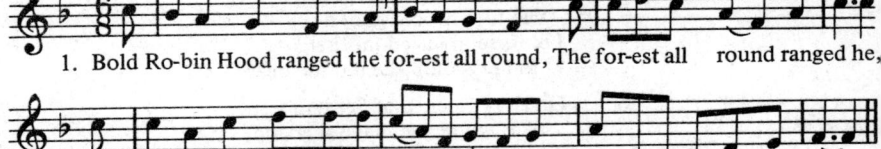

1. Bold Ro-bin Hood ranged the for-est all round, The for-est all round ranged he, And there he did meet with a gay_ la-dy,_Come wee-ping a-long the high-way.

2.   O why do you weep my gay lady
   Either for gold or fee,
   Or are you weeping for your maidenhead,
   It is gone many years from thee?

3.   I'm not a-weeping for gold said she
   And I'm not a-weeping for fee
   And I'm not a-weeping for my maidenhead,
   It's been gone many years from me.

4.   Then why do you weep my gay lady,
   I pray thee come tell unto me?
   Why I do weep for my three sons
   For they're all condemned to die.

5.   What church have they robbed said bold Robin Hood
   Or what parish priest have they slain,
   What maid have they forced against her own will,
   Or with other men's wives have they lain?

6.   No church have they robbed the lady replied,
   Nor no parish priest have they slain,
   No maid have they forced against her own will,
   Nor with other men's wives have they lain.

7.   Then what have they done said bold Robin Hood,
   I pray thee come tell unto me?
   They have killed sixteen of the king's fallow deer
   And they're all condemned to die.

8.   O what will you give me in gold he cried
   Or what will you give me in fee,
   If I will go to Nottingham town
   Get your three sons freedom this day?

9   O I will give you all of my gold
    And part of all my fee
    If you will go to Nottingham town
    And get my sons freedom I pray.

10 Bold Robin he marched the forest along
    As hard as he could hie
    Until he met with an old beggarman
    And he kept drawing so nigh.

11 What news what news my old beggarman
    What news come tell unto me?
    There's weeping and wailing in Nottingham town
    For the loss of the squires all three.

12 Change clothing change clothing my old beggarman
    Pray change your clothing with me.
    Here's fifteen bright shillings I'll give you to boot
    If you will change clothing with me.

13 Bold Robin Hood went to fair Nottingham
    To Nottingham town went he
    And there he did meet with the master sheriff
    And likewise the squires all three.

14 One favour one favour says bold Robin Hood,
    One favour I beg on my knee.
    That is for these three squires sake
    Their hangman I might be.

15 Soon granted says the master sheriff,
    Soon granted unto thee.
    And you shall have their gay clothing
    And all their white money.

16 O I will have none of their gay clothing,
    Nor none of their white money,
    But I'll have three blasts of my bugle horn
    As their souls into heaven may flee.

17 He gave three blasts with his bugle horn,
    He blew both loud and shrill,
    And eight score and ten of bold Robin Hood's men
    Came tripping all down the green hill.

18   Whose men are all these said the master sheriff,
      I pray thee come tell unto me?
      Why they are all mine and none of them thine,
      They are coming for the squires all three.

19   Take them along says the master sheriff,
      Take them along with thee.
      There's not another in Nottingham town
      Can borrow three more of me.

20   Bold Robin he marched the forest along
      As hard as he could go
      With his eight score and ten of bold Robin Hood's men
      And his three squires all in a row.

BOTANY BAY

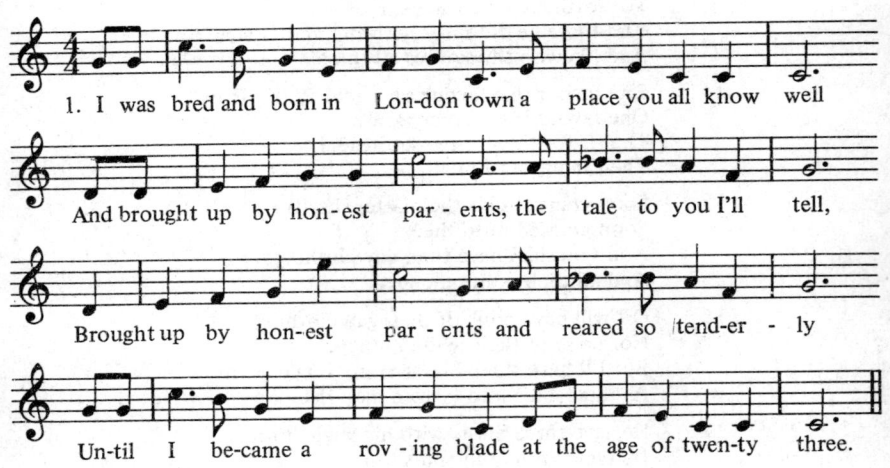

1. I was bred and born in London town a place you all know well
And brought up by honest parents, the tale to you I'll tell,
Brought up by honest parents and reared so tenderly
Until I became a roving blade at the age of twenty three.

2   My character soon was taken
      And I was sent to gaol.
    My friends and parents did their best
      To get me out on bail.
    But the jury found me guilty
      And the judge to me did say
    I sentence you to twenty years
      In a place called Botany Bay.

3   My poor old father stood at the bar
         His head was bowed with care.
      Likewise my poor old mother
         Who tore out her grey hair.
      My son, my son what have you done,
         I heard my mother say,
      They've sentenced you to twenty years
         In a place called Botany Bay.

4   They put me aboard a sailing ship
         One cold December morn
      And I never will forget the time
         We passed around Cape Horn.
      The captain as he passed me by
         These words to me did say,
      You'll rue the transportation, me lad,
         Now you're bound for Botany Bay.

5   There is a lass in London town,
         A place I know quite well,
      And when I gain my freedom
         With her I'm going to dwell,
      And when I gain my freedom
         I'll marry her one day.
      No more I'll be a roving blade
         And adieu to New South Wales.

6   Now you that have your liberty
         Pray keep it if you can
      And don't go midnight rambling
         Or break the laws of man.
      For if you do you're sure to rue
         And the judge to you will say,
      I sentence you to twenty years
         In a place called Botany Bay.

POACHER'S SONG

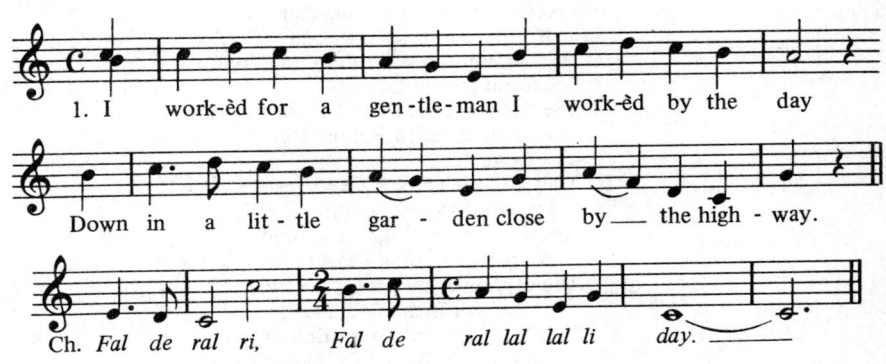

1. I work-èd for a gen-tle-man I work-èd by the day
Down in a lit-tle gar-den close by — the high-way.
Ch. Fal de ral ri, Fal de ral lal lal li day. ——

2   I saw something dancing, I thought it was a hare.
    Why don't you go and catch it, and catch it in a snare?

3   I got up the next morning a-seeking for my prey.
    A keeper sat in an arbour-bush close by the highway.

4   He hopped me off to prison, I suffered more and more.
    For six long months or better my bed was made of straw.

5   I had a very large family at home and all my neighbours say.
    They only had one half-peck loaf for eight long summers' day.

TEA-LEAF SONG

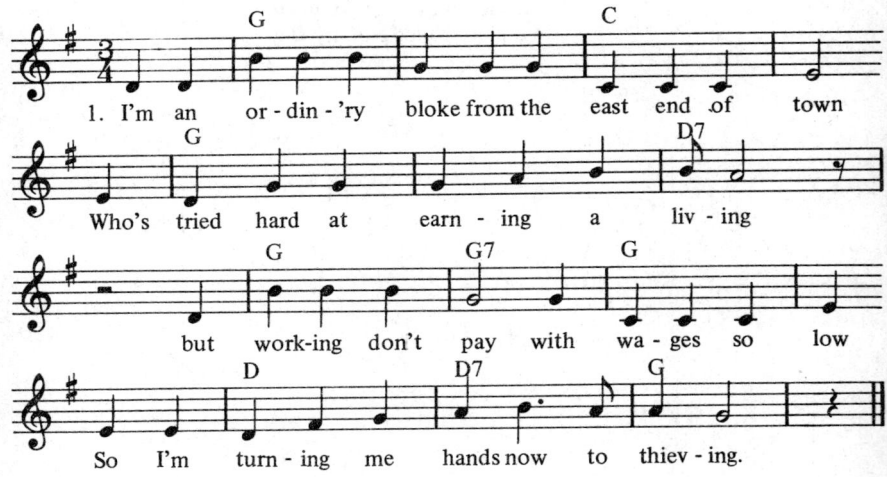

1. I'm an or-din-'ry bloke from the east end of town
Who's tried hard at earn-ing a liv-ing
but work-ing don't pay with wa-ges so low
So I'm turn-ing me hands now to thiev-ing.

2   When you folks are asleep, that's when I'm at me work,
    Down the docks with me mates in a motor,
    Keep an eye out for cops and security men
    While I jump up there quick and off-load her.

3   If it's lighters or watches or fags that you want
    Well, why don't you come round and see me?
    The gear that I've got is the best you can get
    And it's cheaper from me than from any.

4   But don't try and find out where my gear comes from,
    Don't go snooping or else you'll be sorry,
    If you ask how I get it, well, all I can say
    It fell off the back of a lorry.

5   I've never been pulled by the filth in me life.
    That must be because I'm so clever.
    And if they don't nick me, you know what I'll do?
    I'll carry on thieving for ever.

THE BORSTAL BOY

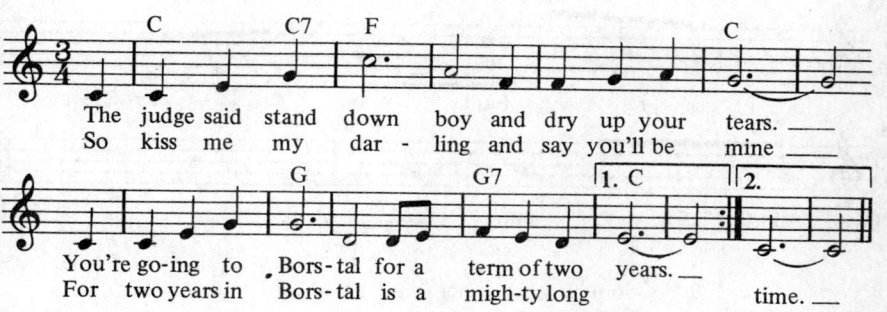

The judge said stand down boy and dry up your tears. _____
So kiss me my dar - ling and say you'll be mine _____

You're go-ing to Bors-tal for a term of two years. ___
For two years in Bors-tal is a migh-ty long time. ___

2   At six in the morning you'll hear the gaol-bell.
    Along comes the warder and unlocks your cell.
    Says: Roll up your blankets and empty your slops
    And off to the workhouse till early next day.

3   I counted the moonbeams I've counted the stars,
    Counted ten thousand through my borstal bars.
    There are bars on the windows and bolts on the door,
    Screwy came in — kicked him around the floor.

4   Now I've done one year now, only one year to do.
    I lost my remission for jumping a screw.
    He took me to the guv'nor and did all he could
    To get me down chokey but it did me no good.

5 If I were the gaoler and the gaoler were me
   I'd get up one morning and set myself free.
   But I'm not the gaoler and the gaoler's not me
   So I'll keep on waiting for my liberty.

   (Sung to the second half of the tune)

6 Now I've done two years now, only one week to do,
   They opened the gate boy and I'm back on the screw.

BOLD ARCHER

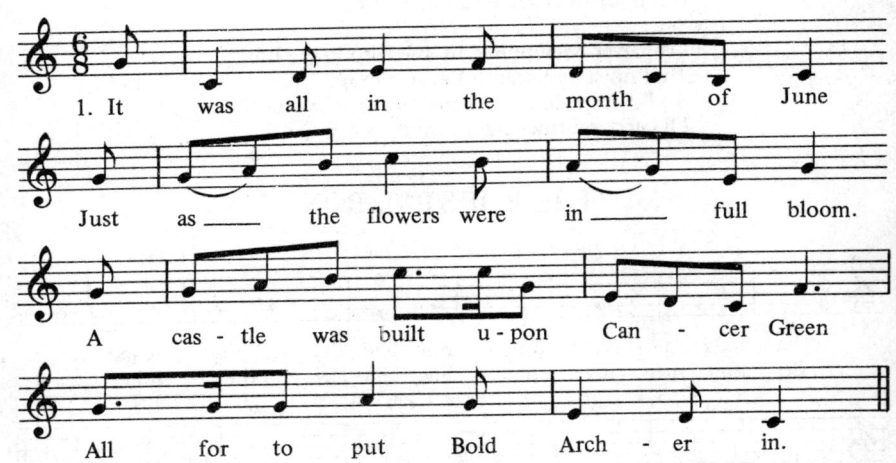

1. It was all in the month of June
Just as ___ the flowers were in ___ full bloom.
A cas - tle was built u - pon Can - cer Green
All for to put Bold Arch - er in.

2 So now our brother in prison do lay
   Condemned to die is he.
   If I had eleven such brothers as me
   So soon the poor prisoner I'd set free.

3 Eleven said Richard is little enough
   Full forty there must be.
   The chains and the bars will have to be broke
   Before Bold Archer we can set free.

4 Now ten to stand by our horses heads,
   Ten for to guard us round about,
   Ten for to stand by the castle door
   And ten for to bring Bold Archer out,

5 So Dick he broke locks and Dick he broke bars,
   Dick he broke everything he could see.
   He took Bold Archer under his arm
   And carried him out most manfully.

6   They mounted their horses, away they did ride,
Bold Archer he mounted so merry and free.
They rode till they came to the far water-side,
There they dismounted so manfully.

7   Bold Dickie, bold Dickie, Bold Archer he says,
Take my love to my wife and my children three,
My horse he is lame and I cannot swim
So condemned this day I shall be.

8   Bold Dickie then set him up behind,
Who but they so daringly,
They swam till they came to the other side,
There they dismounted so manfully.

9   Oh look back, look back Bold Archer he cried,
Look back, look back, cried he,
Here comes the High Sheriff all on his dundee
With a hundred men in his company.

10   Oh come back, come back now cried the High Sheriff,
Come back, come back cried he,
If you don't return my irons to me
Bold Archer a prisoner still must be.

11   No nay, no nay that never can be,
No that can never be,
For the irons will do our horses to shoe
And the smith he now rides in our company.

12   And there they ordered the music to play,
It played so sweet and joyfully
And the very best dancer amongst them all
Was Bold Archer who they set free.

THE HEARTY POACHER

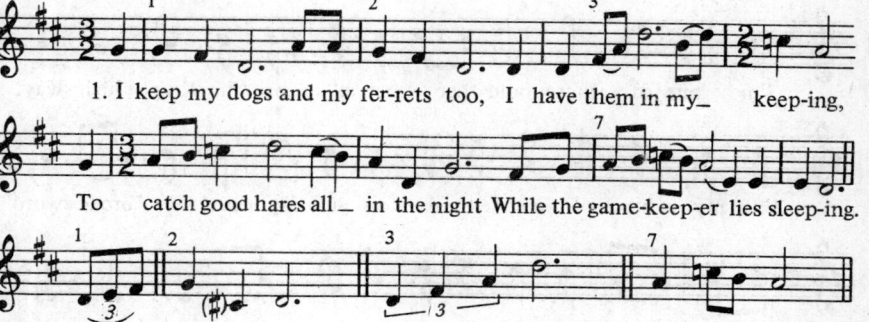

1. I keep my dogs and my fer-rets too, I have them in my_ keep-ing,

To catch good hares all _ in the night While the game-keep-er lies sleep-ing.

2   My dogs and I went out one night
      To view our habitation,
      When up jumped a hare and away she ran
      Straight into my plantation.

3   She kicked she squealed she hollered out 'aunt'
      Till something stopped her running.
      I says poor puss I pray lie still
      For your uncle is just a-coming.

4   Then I picked her up and cracked her neck
      And into my pocket I put her
      Says I to my dogs let us be going
      For fear we shall meet some looker.

5   We hadn't been gone scarce half a field,
      Scarce half a field or further
      Before up jumped another and away she run
      My dogs and she cried murder.

6   I took them to a neighbour's house.
      I asked them what they'd give me.
      They says they'd give me a crown a brace
      If I could catch them fifty.

7   I went into a public house.
      I sat till I got quite mellow.
      I spend a crown and another put down.
      I says I'm a hearty good fellow.

CAPTAIN GRANT

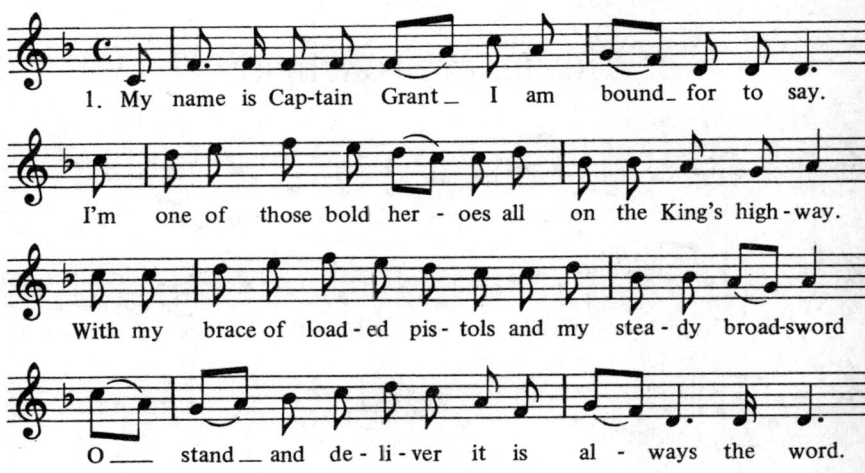

1. My name is Cap-tain Grant _ I am bound _ for to say.

I'm one of those bold her - oes all on the King's high - way.

With my brace of load - ed pis - tols and my stea - dy broad-sword

O _ stand _ and de - li - ver it is al - ways the word.

2 To do a dirty action I always did scorn.
In robbing of the rich I thought it was no harm.
With the gold and the jewels I always did secure
One half I kept myself and the other gave the poor.

3 If I meets with a traveller that's hungry and dry
I'll take him to some ale-house and his wants I will supply.
With good ale, wine and brandy boys till I spend all my store.
When my money is all gone I'll boldly rob for more.

4 To Edinburgh gaol they marched me along
And there I did remain till my trial it did come on.
For shooting at the King I was then condemned to die
But I never had no hand in that same robbery.

5 Out of Edinburgh gaol then I made my way out
And those that did oppose me I put them to the rout.
With my bars and iron bolts I knocked the sentry down
And I made my escape out of Edinburgh town.

6 Out of Edinburgh gaol then I made my way good
And I took up my lodgings in the centre of a wood,
Until some wicked woman she did me betray
And she had me surrounded as sleeping I did lay.

7 I flew to my arms but my powder being wet
And to my sad misfortune I found that I was beat
And to my sad misfortune I gave myself up
To that noted hero called Natty take-up.

8 To Edinburgh gaol then they marched me again
And there I did remain in sorrow, grief and pain.
God bless my wife and family and may they never want
And the Lord have mercy on my soul, cries bold Captain Grant.

ROBIN HOOD AND THE PEDLAR

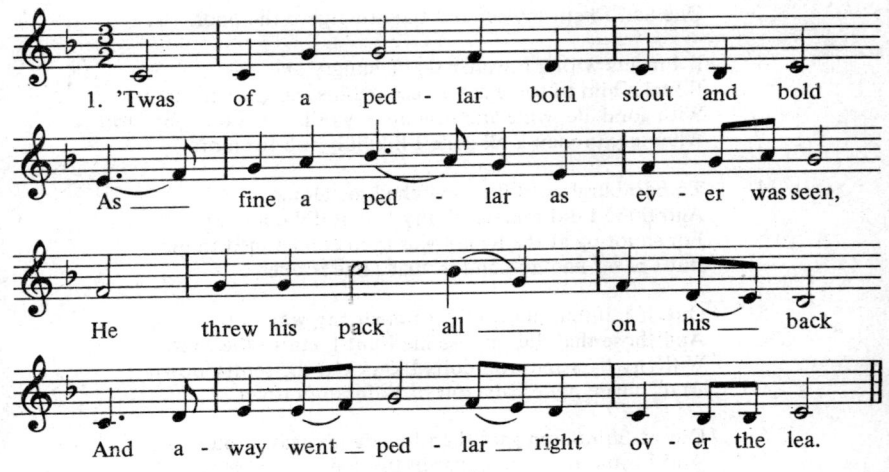

1. 'Twas of a ped - lar both stout and bold
As __ fine a ped - lar as ev - er was seen,
He threw his pack all __ on his __ back
And a - way went __ ped - lar __ right ov - er the lea.

2   The first he met two troublesome men,
Two troublesome men he there met him.
What have you on your pack cried Robin Hood
What have you on your pack come tell to me?

3   I've several sorts of the gay green silks
Silken bow-strings by one two three.
There's not a man in fair Nottingham
That can take one half of this pack from me.

4   Then Little John drew out his sword.
The pedlar by his pack did stand.
They heaved about till they both did sweat.
He now cries, Pedlar pray hold your hand.

5   Bold Robin Hood was standing by
To see them fight so heartily.
Says, Surely a man of a smaller skill
Could whop the pedlar and likewise you?

6   Go you try master says Little John,
Go you try master do all you can,
Go you try master without delay
For the pedlar this night has well whopped me.

7   What is your name cries bold Robin Hood,
What is your name come tell to me?
My name to you I'll never tell
Till both your names you tell to me.

8   For one of us is bold Robin Hood
The other is Little John so free,.
So now it lays in my goodwill
Will you tell me your name or no?

9   I'm Gamble Gold from the merry green woods,
I'm Gamble Gold from over the Dee.
For killing a man in my father's land
From my native country I was forced to flee.

10   If you're Gamble Gold from the merry green woods,
If you're Gamble Gold from over the Dee
It's you and I are two sisters sons
And here are cousins as ever can be.

11   So they sheathed their swords without delay,
Into the tavern they went straightway,
Into the tavern they all did dine,
Where they cracked their bottles and drinked their wine.

TAUNTON GAOL

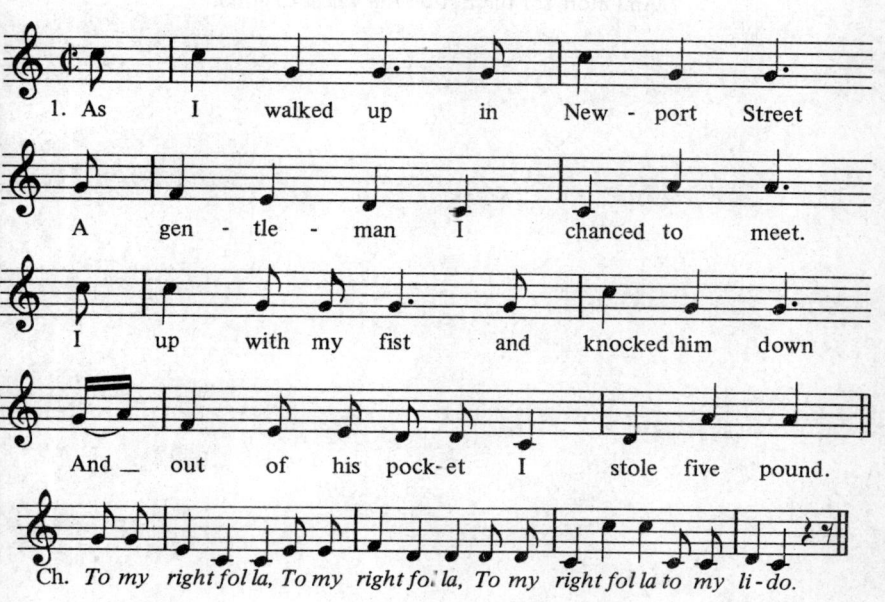

1. As I walked up in New - port Street
A gen - tle - man I chanced to meet.
I up with my fist and knocked him down
And — out of his pock-et I stole five pound.
Ch. *To my right fol la, To my right fol la, To my right fol la to my li-do.*

2   The policemen they surrounded me
And to the station house took me.
They kept me there a very long time
Till eight o-clock in the morning.

3   They took me up before Mr Hook
And in his black book he did look,
Said: Now young man look in my face
And see the marks of your disgrace.

4   I boldly answer-ed my name
And I answered: Will, sir,
If your name be Will it shall be Will.
You shall have six months on the treading-mill.

5   At eight o'clock the bells did ring
And to church we marched on.
If any one of you looked behind
There's more for the rest on the wheel to grind.

6   At twelve o'clock the bells did ring
And now the gates is open again.
If anyone asks you how you do
Say, Very bad off and starving too.

7   Now six months is gone and past,
And poor old Will's returned at last,
Leaving Taunton Gaol behind,
And more for the rest on the wheel to grind.

AUSTRALIA

1. Come all ye young fel-lows where so - e'er you may be,
Come lis - ten a - while to my sto - ry.
When I was a young man, my age sev - en - teen,
I ought ha' been serv - ing Vic - tor - ia our Queen,
But those hard-heart - ed judg-es O how cru-el they've been
To send us poor lads to Aus - tra - lia.

2   I fell in with a damsel, she was handsome and gay,
I neglected my work more and more every day,
And to keep her like a lady I went on the highway
And for that I was sent to Australia.

3   Now the judges they stand with their whips in their hand.
They drive us like horses to plough up the land.
You should see us young fellows working in that gaol-yard.
How hard is our fate in Australia.

4   Australia, Australia, I would ne'er see no more,
Worn out with fever, cast down to death's door,
But should I live to see, say seven years more,
I would then say adieu to Australia.

(The melody for verses 2, 3 and 4 begins at * .)

THERE GOES A MAN

1. There goes a man just gone a - long.

He's gone to the pri - son that is built so strong.

He's gone to the pri - son that is built so strong

And so bold - ly they leads — him a - long.

Ch. *Whack fol lol, lid - dle lol le day*

Whack fol le dol lol lid - dle lol le day.

2   And when they came to the prison door
How they began to laugh and stare,
How they began to laugh and stare,
The prisoners all round him, I declare.

3   The very next day the turnkeys say,
Oh come young man, you come this way,
Oh come young man, you come this way
For I will iron you down this day.

4   Now the irons they are on,
They are so heavy and so strong,
They are so heavy and so strong
That I can scarcely move along.

5   Now Salisbury Assizes is drawing near,
Oh come my lads begin to cheer,
Oh come my lads begin to cheer
And wipe away all weeping tears.

6   Now Salisbury Assizes is over and past
And I'm condemned for to die at last,
And I'm condemned for to die at last
All in some dark and lonesome place.

7   And when I come to the gallows tree
Jack Ketch will be there waiting for me.
He'll take my watch and money too
And this wide world I'll bid adieu.

THE DESERTER

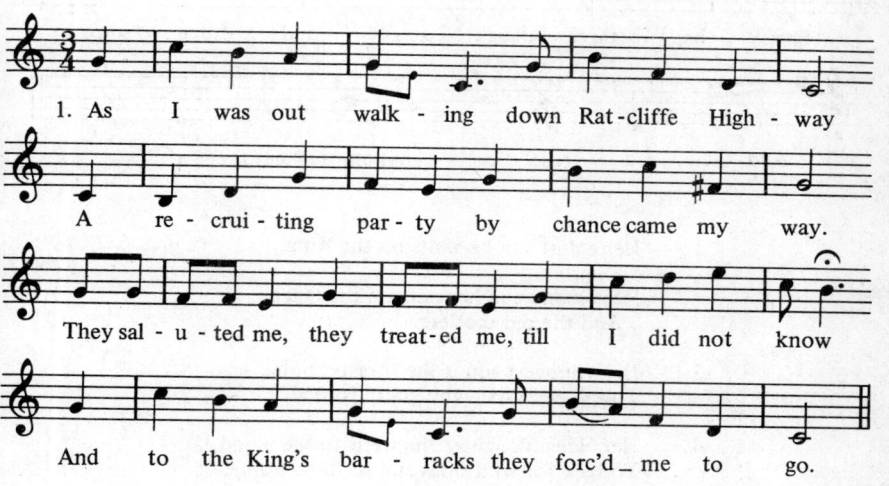

1. As I was out walk - ing down Rat-cliffe High - way
A re - crui - ting par - ty by chance came my way.
They sal - u - ted me, they treat-ed me, till I did not know
And to the King's bar - racks they forc'd _ me to go.

2   But I soon deserted and thought myself free
But my cruel companions they informed on me.
I was quickly sought after and brought back with speed,
Handcuffed and guarded, heavy irons on me.

3   Court martial, court martial, court martial I got,
The sentence passed on me all for to be shot.
May the Good Lord have mercy on this sad cruelty
And now the King's duty lies heavy on me.

4   Then up drove Prince Albert in his carriage and six.
Go fetch me that young man whose coffin is fixed.
Shake off those heavy irons and let him go free.
He'll make a good soldier for his King and country.

BABYLON

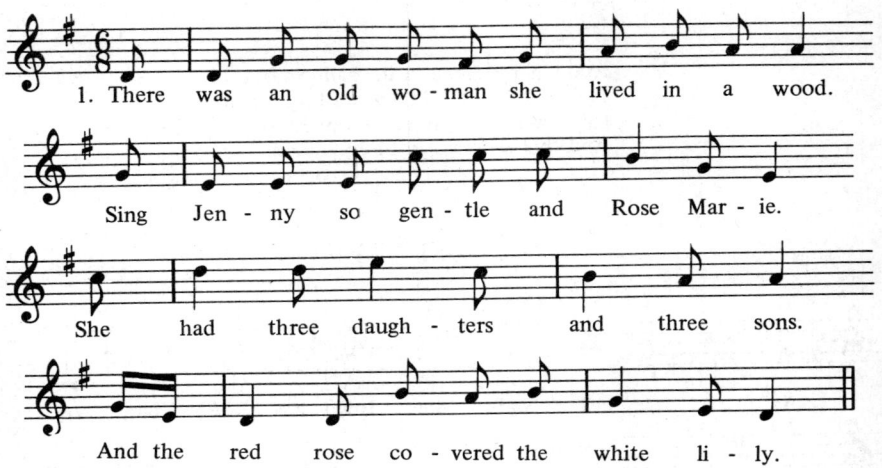

1. There was an old wo-man she lived in a wood.

Sing Jen-ny so gen-tle and Rose Mar-ie.

She had three daugh-ters and three sons.

And the red rose co-vered the white li-ly.

2   Her eldest son he waits on the King.
      Sing Jenny etc.
    Her second son he waits on the Queen.
      And the red rose etc.

3   Her youngest son is the forester bold
    To kill everyone who goes his road.

4   Her eldest daughter she went to the wood
    To seek for wild sloes and so to go home.

5   She had not long been therein
    When there came up a tall young man.

6   My pretty brown girl will you be my wife
    Or would you rather lose your life?

7   Indeed kind sir if I must have my choice
    I would much rather lose my life.

8   He pulled out a penknife both long and sharp
    And plunged it through her gentle heart.

9   He pulled her through a brake of briar
    And bade her lie there till morn should retire.

10   The second daughter she went to the wood
    To seek for her sister and so to go home.

11 She had not long been therein
    When there came up a tall young man.

12 My pretty brown girl will you be my wife
    Or would you rather lose your life?

13 Indeed kind sir if I must have my choice,
    I would much rather lose my life.

14 He pulled out his penknife both long and sharp
    And plunged it through her gentle heart.

15 He pulled her through a brake of briar
    And bade her lie there till morn should retire.

16 The youngest daughter she went to the wood
    To seek for her sisters and so to go home.

17 She had not long been therein
    When there came up a tall young man.

18 My pretty brown girl, will you be my wife
    Or would you rather lose your life?

19 Indeed kind sir if I must have my choice
    I would much rather lose my life.

20 But if I had my three brothers here
    I would not have my life to fear.

21 My pretty brown girl come sit on my knee
    And tell me who your three brothers be.

22 My eldest brother he waits on the King.
    My second brother he waits on the Queen.

23 My youngest brother's a forester bold
    To stop everyone who goes his road.

24 He pulled out his penknife both long and sharp
    And plunged it through his own black heart.

MR FOX

Out-side Mis-ter Fox's gar-den, Three maids play-ing with a gol-den ball,

Jen-ny threw it up and Su-san caught it, Ma-ry bounced it ov-er the wall.

The wall is high, Mis-ter Fox has a lit-tle red eye.

2   In she ran to fetch it back again.
     The garden gate stood open wide.
     Suddenly it was shut and bolted.
     Mr Fox was just inside.
     The wall is high,
     His smile is cruel and his eyes are sly.

3   He said I'll keep your ball Miss Mary.
     I shall have it and here you'll stay.
     You'll keep my house and be my servant
     And never go out for a year and a day.
     The wall is high,
     The long grass shivers and the tall trees sigh.

4   Spring and summer passed like shadows.
     She watched the green leaves fade and fall.
     She walked alone in the empty garden
     And Mr Fox said nothing at all.
     The wall is high,
     Never a soul comes near or by.

5   Three strange things he did forbid her,
Never you touch my iron box,
Never go near the thirteenth bedroom
Nor near the bed said Mr Fox.
The wall is high,
Don't you dare to ask me why.

6   Mary she rose-up one morning.
She saw an iron box on a shelf.
But of all the rooms at Mr Fox's
Bedrooms there were only twelve.
The wall is high,
Mary don't you peep or pry.

7   One day Mr Fox went walking,
In that box she found a key.
It fitted a door she'd never unfastened
And when she opened it what did she see?
The wall is high,
The door said stop and the key said fly.

8   In Mr Fox's thirteenth bedroom
A naked sword hung on the wall.
In a silver bowl on the bed's black counterpane
Mary saw her golden ball.
The wall is high,
The bed said come and the sword said die.

9   In she ran to get her ball again
To snatch it off the great black bed.
Out crept Mr Fox and leaped at her
His teeth flashed white and his eyes burned red.
The wall is high. . . .

PUNCH AND JUDY

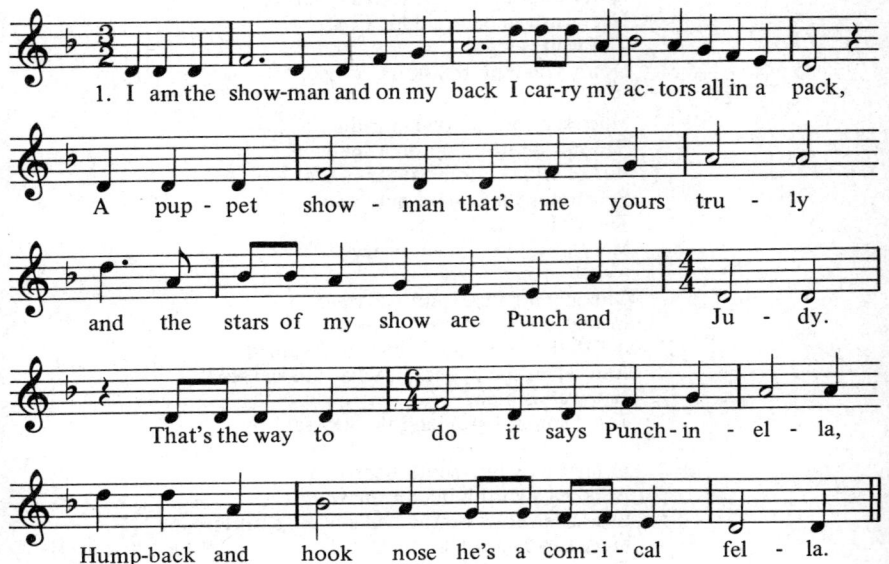

1. I am the show-man and on my back I car-ry my ac-tors all in a pack,
A pup-pet show-man that's me yours tru-ly
and the stars of my show are Punch and Ju - dy.
That's the way to do it says Punch-in - el - la,
Hump-back and hook nose he's a com-i-cal fel - la.

2 And the first comes up is old Punch hisself.
Ladies and gents, he says, here's your good health.
He carries a big stick wherever he goes,
It's thick and strong and as long as his nose.
That's the way to do it, says Punchinella,
Long stick and big nose, symbolic old fella.

3 Next comes up Judy Punch's old lady,
Says, I'm off out now Punch so mind the baby.
No I won't, says Punch, yes you will, says Judy,
Cop 'old of your kid my lad none of your old moody.
That's the way to do it, says Punchinella,
Cocksure but henpecked he's a pathetic old fella.

4 The kid keeps howling old Punch he thumps it.
It cries he calms it down, into bed he dumps it.
It bawls, he belts it, it bites his finger.
Punch up and bungs it through the bloomin' winder.
That's the way to do it, says Punchinella,
That'll teach the bleedin' brat to yell and beller.

5 Here's Mrs Judy, now, she's back again
Not knowin' Punch has done their nipper in.
She goes, where's baby Punch? Gorn, gorn to sleep, he says.
Don't you know where your own son is? You make me weep, she says.
That's the way to do it, says Punchinella,
I threw it out the winder, he has to tell her.

6   She cries her heart out, where's me little son gone?
Says Punch, there's plenty more where that one come from.
With a stick she bangs and beats him something lovely.
He gets it, clubs her, kills her kicks her ugly.
That's the way to do it, says Punchinella,
Why keep a wife you hate if you can kill her?

7   Up jumps a copper all dressed in blue,
Says: Mr Punch I am arresting you.
I got a warrant to take you for what you've done.
And I've got a warrant, says Punch, to knock you down.
That's the way to do it, says Punchinella,
Knocking him arse over head right down in the cellar.

8   The law soon catches him again and in a while
Before Judge Blackcap he's standing trial.
Killed wife and child, he says, you guilty wretch,
Take Punch away and hang him Mr Ketch.
That's the way to do it, says Punchinella,
Hang 'em all but don't hang me he cries in terror.

9   See this 'ere noose, says Jack, poke your head through.
Old Punch lets on he don't know what to do.
In here Mr Ketch, or perhaps in there?
Hang on, says the hangman, I'll show you where.
That's the way to do it, says Punchinella,
Stringing up the hangman, he's a swinging old fella.

10   Jack Ketch is dead says Punch, hooray I'm free.
Don't care if the Devil himself should come and call on me.
Jack Ketch is dead, he cries, Old Punch'll do 'em all.
Up pops Old Nick 'isself tails horns and hooves and all.
That's the way to do it, says Punchinella,
Leave orf me I'm your best friend, we're birds of a feather.

11   The Devil darts at Punch but he ain't having it.
Nick gets 'isself a stick and Punch keeps grabbing it.
He lands a mighty swipe on Satan's nut an'
The Devil's out for the count as dead as mutton.
That's the way to do it, says Punchinella,
He's beat the Devil, heroic old fella.

12   So now the show is done, the dolls need mending
But Punch and Punch's play are never ending.
Inside each one of us there's a Punch and Judy,
In you and you sir, you ma'am and in me yours truly.
That's the way to do it, says Punchinella,
The Punch and Judy game goes on for ever.

KING KONG

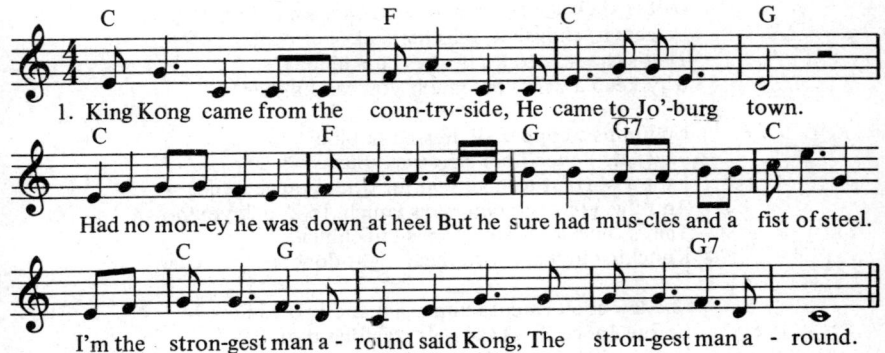

1. King Kong came from the coun-try-side, He came to Jo'-burg town.
Had no mon-ey he was down at heel But he sure had mus-cles and a fist of steel.
I'm the stron-gest man a-round said Kong, The stron-gest man a-round.

2   I'll be the top man I'll be champ,
       Be a boxing man.
       Get up in that canvas ring,
       Make them punches whistle and sing,
       Got death in both my hands said Kong,
       Death in both my hands.

3   They came from far and near to fight
       But King Kong laid 'em low.
       All the townships loved King Kong.
       He couldn't do a darn thing wrong.
       All the little kids said 'Hello, King Kong',
       The little kids said 'Hello'.

4   King Kong he's a one man show,
       Fighting on his mind,
       Running in the morning sun,
       Boots of steel just swinging along,
       And the people all run behind King Kong,
       The people all run behind.

5   Some say he was a bragging man,
       Pushing folks around,
       But he'd fought everyone there was to fight
       And they wouldn't let him in the ring with a white
       For they knew he'd knock 'em down King Kong,
       They knew he'd knock 'em down.

6   My name's King Kong I'm a big black man,
Lightning follows me round,
Heavy as lead, light as a cloud,
By myself I'm a one man crowd.
But I'm king without a crown King Kong,
King without a crown.

7   King Kong soon began to lose heart,
A fighter without a fight.
Next time he got into the ring
A fly got up and belted him
And he went out like a light King Kong,
He went out like a light.

8   Next time anyone heard of Kong
He was standing at his trial.
Got himself in a big gang-fight
Killed his girl at a dance that night.
He never made no denial King Kong,
He never made no denial.

9   Judge he said just swing me high
Hang me till I'm dead.
But the judge looked up and told him no
For fifteen years to jail you'll go,
So he killed himself instead King Kong,
Just killed himself instead.

10   He should have been the king of the world
But the rules wouldn't let him win.
When he died the word went round
From Jo'burg down to Simonstown,
Look what they done to him King Kong,
Look what they done to him.

NOTES

Van Diemen's Land (p. 194) Sung by Walter Pardon, Knapton, Norfolk. Collected by Sam Richards and Tish Stubbs, 1977.
   A full and superb version of a classic transportation ballad.

Robin Hood and the Old Beggar Man (p. 196) Sung by Mrs Cole. Collected by George Gardiner. Some collation made with a Catnach broadside from the Kidson collection.
   The singer gave this song the above title but it is generally known as 'Robin Hood Rescuing Three Squires'. It is not an uncommon Robin Hood ballad in England; it circulated on broadside as well as remaining in oral circulation.

Botany Bay (p. 198) Sung by James Lyons, Batley, Yorkshire. Collected by A. E. Green, 1966. In the archives of the Institute of Dialect and Folk Life Studies, Leeds University.

Poacher's Song (p. 200) Sung by Mrs Joiner, Chiswell Green, Hertfordshire. Collected by Lucy Broadwood, 1914. JFSS vol. 5, p. 197.
   In a few short verses this simple but graphic song displays the vicious circle in which a poacher was caught. Lucy Broadwood adds this note: 'In Herts, the keepers still make seats with bended boughs, to use whilst watching in the woods. . . . Mrs. Joiner says she means such an "arbour-bush" and not "ambush" as might be supposed.'

Tea-Leaf Song (p. 200) Written by Colin Meadows c. 1971.
   Tea-leaf is cockney rhyming slang for thief.

The Borstal Boy (p. 201) Sung by an ex-Borstal boy. Collected by Peter Nalder in Coventry, May 1968.
   This parody was generally known amongst Borstal boys at this time. It was learned by the singer from a man in Hindley who knew more verses and put some of the verses to it himself. The song was officially frowned upon in prison because of the use of the forbidden term 'screws' (warders).

Bold Archer (p. 202) Sung by Harry Cox, Catfield, Norfolk. Collected by Bob Thompson, November 1970.
   This ballad, essentially a tale of Scots clan in-fighting, seems to have found a foothold in the south of England and North-East America, as well as its native land. It is remarkable that a version should have been obtained from Harry Cox, a classic singer then in his 80s, who had been providing collectors with songs since the 1920s when he sang for E. J. Moeran.

The Hearty Poacher (p. 203) Sung by Shepherd Hayden, Bampton, Oxfordshire. Collected by Cecil Sharp in 1909.
   This sly song is still popular, especially with gypsies who often include much of their own cant in the verses. Shepherd Hayden, who seems to have been a melodic character, varied his melody structurally and we give some of Sharp's alternative phrases. His tune is one of the most attractive to be found for this song.

Captain Grant (p. 204) Sung by Charles Benfield, Bould. Collected by Cecil Sharp, September 1909.
   Captain Grant, the highwayman, is known by this one ballad. Few sets have turned up in oral tradition, this song from Sharp's collection being one of the most complete. Broadside versions abound.

Robin Hood and the Pedlar (p. 206) Sung by Job Francis, Shipley, Somerset. Collected by Cecil Sharp, 1908. JFSS vol. 5, no. 18.
   Bronson has remarked of this melody, 'It is very near perfection in its modal kind'. Robin Hood ballads have not lasted well. Child included over 30 in *The English and Scottish Popular Ballads* but they are a rarity today – less so in North America. 'Robin Hood and the Pedlar' is an exception. A handful of sets have come down to us, mostly to fine tunes.

Taunton Gaol (p. 207) Sung by Tom Sprachlan, Hambridge, Somerset. Collected by Cecil Sharp, 1903.

Australia (p. 209) Sung by Bob Hart, Snape, Suffolk. Collected by Rod and Danny Stradling, late 1960s.

This song has appeared in recent years only, and always in East Anglia. It seems to be clearly modelled on another equally rare song 'Virginny' which Gardiner collected in Hampshire in 1907.

There Goes a Man (p. 210) Sung by George Blake, Southampton. Collected by George Gardiner, 1906. Previously published under the title 'Gaol Song' in *The Foggy Dew* (ed. F. Purslow), EFDS Publications Ltd, London, 1974.

We do not know this song from elsewhere. Its rugged classic-style verses suggest an interesting origin outside the normal round of broadside publishers.

The Deserter (p. 211) Sung by Walter Pardon, Knapton, Norfolk. Collected by Sam Richards and Tish Stubbs, 1977.

Sometimes printed as the 'New Deserter' on broadsides, and called 'Ratcliffe Highway' by some country singers, this song is well known. Walter Pardon's melody with its insistence on the tritone interval is an interesting variation on a whole class of melodies used for this song.

Babylon (p. 212) From E. Shekleton, Bristol.

Considering that no other English version has come to light, this austere classic ballad must be regarded as something of a find. Unfortunately, we know only that it was found in a miscellaneous file in the Vaughan Williams library, Cecil Sharp House, London, and appears to have been sent by E. Shekleton of Redland High School for Girls, Bristol. There is no date but we are told that she learned it from her nurse. It is a very complete set.

Mr Fox (p. 214) Written by John Pole, London, 1964.

In our folk revival there seems to be an obsession with antiquarian folk legends versified into song, and it must be said that much of it is poor stuff. This remake of a well-known tale from John Pole, a poet of formidable talent, is one of the few successful efforts in this genre.

Punch and Judy (p. 216) Written by John Pole, London, 1970.

The composer is himself a Punch and Judy man.

King Kong (p. 218) Written by Sam Richards, Totnes, Devon, 1977.

This song was written for a programme of song and poetry about South Africa, *Amandla,* which was put together by the People's Stage, Torquay. It tells a true story, which was also told a few years back in a successful musical. The idiom is an approximation of township jazz, the urban black South African folk music which reached the proportions of a craze in the 1960s.

GLOSSARY

We Poor Labouring Men
cutters: reaping or mowing machines
shares: crossbars of a harrow

The Bermondsey Boys
Old Kent Road: famous road in East London
Woodbines: cheap make of cigarette

The Soldier on the Battlefield
gads: large long chisels
blaw: blow

The Factory Doll
winders: mill hands employed to wind weft, yarn, etc., usually a girl of 13-16 years.
reeler: one who transfers thread from the spool to the reel, usually a woman of 18-30 years.
bad ends: thread of yarn, silk, etc., a single piece of cloth. Broken threads.
brat: working clothes
togs: clothes
clogs: heavy wooden working shoes

From Sweet Dundee
ring-tails: pennants

The Months of the Year
breeching: strong leather strap passing round the posterior of a horse and enabling him to push backwards

The Big Hewer and the Little Marra
grit: great
marra: work mate

The Clayton Analine Song
napthas/paras/pap: see note to song
vitrol: an acid

The Sheffield Grinders' Song
grinder: one who grinds cutlery

They're Closing Down the Pit I've Always Worked In
Brockwell: one of the richest coal seams in the Durham coal field
ramble: mud or shale which, since it is black as coal, becomes a hewer's problem when it appears in a seam
siddle: a face 'on the siddle' is a face broken by a fault
owerman: overman, foreman
bait: food
busty: well-known seam of coal
clarts: bits of mud

Hopping Down in Kent
pole-puller: man employed to pull the poles out of the ground and lay them down for the pickers

When That I Was Weary
billets: thick pieces of wood cut to a suitable length for fuel

Jackie's Building Site
hard core: rubble
JCB: large machine for digging holes
ready mix: ready-made concrete

Callerforney
hinny: term of endearment
splint: coal with a splinty fracture
duck: darling
choke-damp: noxious gas

'Ware Out Mother
'ware: beware

A Handy Ship
belay: stop — that's enough

Dance to Thee Daddy
codlin: small or young codfish

We Be
board: work surface
wrasslin': wrestling
cackin': cackling
soggin': could be like sloggin', or foot-sloggin' — walking heavily, wearily.
twank et: to give a slap
wish't and thurl: cursed and miserable
tiddley: pressure
puttin' on: blaming on
piskies: pixies, little folk

The Game of Football
spalpeen: disagreeable, contemptible person

The Forty Pound Car
gans: goes
marra: coal miner's work mate
poppely-eyed: wide-eyed, eyes popping
grit: great
gannin': going
lip: argument
bool: throw
AA: Automobile Association

Shepton Beauchamp Wassail Song 2
maypoling: slightly obscure: the may-pole has nothing to do with the wassailing custom; other versions of the song have 'maplin' which is also obscure, but perhaps both are derived from maple.
apell: the singer thought it meant a donkey; in other versions 'filpail' is the name of a cow.

The Leg of the Mallard
toe-nippins: claws
pillagee-o: the singer said it meant belly.

Bless This House
light or dark: light ale or brown

All Through the Ale
jag: (in context) I don't give a damn

The Farmer in Leicester
chambers: pistols

The Little Back Parlour
Ratcliffe High bobbies: the policemen on Ratcliffe Highway — a notorious road in East London
luby: stupid fellow, usually lubby
thick sticks: possibly big forearms
pickwick: trade name for a cheap cigar

bonneted: crushed a man's hat over his eyes
snout: nose

Hecketty Pecketty
my eye: nonsense

Joan to Jan
bee butt: beehive

Timothy Briggs the Barber
dot and go on: sound of a person walking with a wooden leg

The Owd Chap Come Ower T' Bank
clogs: rough wooden shoes
girt: great
clout: cloth used for wrapping puddings

Cock-A-Doodle-Doo
judy: (in this context) girl friend

The Buxom Dairy Maid
tapering pipe: musical instrument, like a whistle, but tapered at the end

Do Ye Know My Father?
gans: goes

Jingle Bells
Batman/Robin/Kojak/Kermit: TV characters widely known in 1970s

Guy Fawkes Song
pennorth: pennyworth

Paul Jones
buckskin: nickname for American troops during the Revolutionary war — hence a native American

The Bold Richard
quarters: cry of clemency or mercy

Admiral Nelson
match tubs: gunpowder tubs

George Keary
stag frigate: ship sent out as an observer; spy ship

cutter: (in this context) fast ship employed to look out for smugglers

The Trico Strike
cowboys: non-union lorry drivers

See It Come Down
Meals on Wheels: social service provided for the old or infirm whereby a van takes round cooked meals

The Chartist Song
gree: argeement

The Honest Ploughman
blood-horses: thoroughbreds

Who's Who
Babus: Hindus

Canteen Tea
bromide: chemical substance with the reputed property of reducing sexual urge

Tea-Leaf Song
tea-leaf: Cockney rhyming slang for thief
gear: goods
pulled: arrested
filth: police
nick: arrest

Borstal Boy
screws/screwey: prison warders
chokey: solitary confinement

The Hearty Poacher
'aunt': noise a hare makes
looker: onlooker

There Goes A Man
Jack Ketch: traditional name for a hangman, named after a real character

Punch and Judy
cop 'old: take hold roughly
moody: moods

INDEX